COACHING FOOTBALL SUCCESSFULLY

Allan Trimble

Head Coach
Jenks High School

Human Kinetics

Library of Congress Cataloging-in-Publication Data

Trimble, Allan, 1963-
    Coaching football successfully / Allan Trimble.
        p. cm.
    Includes index.
    ISBN 0-7360-5544-4 (soft cover)
    1. Football–Coaching. I. Title.
    GV954.4.T65 2005
    796.332'07'7–dc22   2005004441

ISBN: 0-7360-5544-4

Developmental Editor: Cynthia McEntire
Assistant Editor: Scott Hawkins
Copyeditor: Annette Pierce
Proofreader: Jim Burns
Indexer: Dan Connolly
Graphic Designer: Nancy Rasmus
Graphic Artist: Kim McFarland
Photo Manager: Dan Wendt
Cover Designer: Keith Blomberg
Photographer (cover): © Mary Sharp Photography
Photographer (interior): © Mary Sharp Photography unless otherwise noted.
Art Manager and Illustrator: Kareema McLendon
Printer: Versa Press

We thank Jenks High School in Jenks, Oklahoma, for assistance in providing the location for the photo shoot for this book.

Human Kinetics books are available at special discounts for bulk purchase. Special editions or book excerpts can also be created to specification. For details, contact the Special Sales Manager at Human Kinetics.

Printed in the United States of America   10 9 8 7 6 5 4 3 2 1

Human Kinetics
Web site: www.HumanKinetics.com

United States: Human Kinetics
P.O. Box 5076
Champaign, IL 61825-5076
800-747-4457
e-mail: humank@hkusa.com

Canada: Human Kinetics
475 Devonshire Road Unit 100
Windsor, ON N8Y 2L5
800-465-7301 (in Canada only)
e-mail: orders@hkcanada.com

Europe: Human Kinetics
107 Bradford Road
Stanningley
Leeds LS28 6AT, United Kingdom
+44 (0) 113 255 5665
e-mail: hk@hkeurope.com

Australia: Human Kinetics
57A Price Avenue
Lower Mitcham, South Australia 5062
08 8277 1555
e-mail: liaw@hkaustralia.com

New Zealand: Human Kinetics
Division of Sports Distributors NZ Ltd.
P.O. Box 300 226 Albany
North Shore City
Auckland
0064 9 448 1207
e-mail: blairc@hknewz.com

To Courtney, my wonderful wife of 14 years,
and our two daughters, Tylar Rose and Tori Allan.
No matter what the final score of the ball game is,
you are always my biggest fans.
Thanks for your unconditional love and support.
I love you guys and thank God every day that you are in my life.

CONTENTS

Part III Instruction

Part IV Performance

FOREWORD

Over my first six years at the University of Oklahoma, nearly half of the 15 All-Americans from our program hailed from Oklahoma, a state of just three and one-half million people. That says two things about our state. First, football is important to the people here. Second, the high school coaching in the state is nothing short of outstanding. Combining the two, I am convinced that a large portion of Oklahoma's interest in football can be traced to the quality of the high school experience.

Allan Trimble stands as a testimony to Oklahoma and football. His teams at Jenks High School routinely rank among not only the best teams in the state, but the best in the nation. The teams at Jenks achieve that notoriety because they are coached to perform at the highest level. The outcome on the field is simply a result of the preparation.

Of course, sound preparation is anything but simple. Coach Trimble understands that success, particularly on the high school level, requires the maximization of time. That's why this book is of such great value. All of us are looking for the streamlined and most direct path to the top. We constantly seek the methodology that will help our players and programs reach optimum performance in the shortest period of time. In these pages, you will find proven principles minus any wasted motion. Coach Trimble has adopted and devised strategies that will work now.

There is no shortcut to winning football, but there are pathways that lead more quickly to a positive outcome. Coach Trimble, armed with a record to support his methodology, has included those here. I would encourage any coach to give the content very close examination.

Bob Stoops
University of Oklahoma

ACKNOWLEDGMENTS

Coaching football successfully can only be accomplished by the combined efforts of dedicated people. No single person can be successful in the great sport of football without solid people to share the journey with.

For me to recognize everyone who has had a positive impact on my success as a person, a coach, a husband, and a father would take another entire book, but I do want to take a moment to acknowledge and thank those very special people who have made an unselfish effort to help me during my journey.

Thanks to superintendent Dr. Kirby Lehman, principal Mike Means, athletic director Tommy Burns, and school board members Mark Sharp, Billie Mills, Ben Maples, Mike Baab, and T.C. Blair, who all found a reason to justify hiring a young, inexperienced coach to operate their football program at Jenks High School. I don't know what they saw or why they put themselves at risk back in 1996, but I appreciate the opportunity they extended me. It's been a wonderful and fulfilling journey.

To Tag Gross and Matt Hennesy, my first two coordinators, thanks for developing and establishing a first-class championship atmosphere and leaving your mark on the proud Trojan football tradition.

To all the coaches who have dedicated their lives to the success of our football program: Antwain Jimmerson, Eric Fox, Toby Tillman, Wes McCalip, Darren Melton, David Tenison, Kevin Johnston, J.J. Tappana, Brad Calip, Steve Patterson, Ryan Meyer, Steve Heldebrand, Tom Arrington, Tim Beacham, Keith Riggs, Chris Opitz, Doug Buckmaster, Herb Rhea, John Kincade, John Timmons, Darrell McBride, Scott Rossman, Loren Montgomery, Jay Wilkinson, Scott Kempenich, and Randy Lewis. I applaud each of you and your effort and dedication to excellence.

To Larry Cariker who encouraged me to be a coach and taught me what being a coach is really all about. I appreciate you Larry; you are a great Christian example to everyone who knows you.

To Ray Hall and John Scott, who gave me my first coaching job at Owasso. I appreciate the opportunity to be a part of the greatest profession in the world.

Thanks to Ted Miller and Cynthia McEntire of Human Kinetics for all the support, encouragement, and professionalism in the preparation and publication of this book. I value this great opportunity.

To my Mom and Dad and little sister Kim for your support through this entire journey of being a coach. Thank you for teaching me to keep my priorities in order and letting me know when I need to work on them. I love you all.

INTRODUCTION

In one of my initial interviews before I was named head football coach at Jenks High School, I was asked by one of the committee members to define success as it related to my coaching philosophy. Fortunately for me, I had spent three years with one of the finest coaches I have ever known when I was rookie assistant girls' track coach at Owasso High School.

When Larry Cariker asked me to help him build a girls' track program at Owasso High School, I had just landed a 6A football assistant position as my first job out of college, and I must say, I was way above coaching girls' athletics, especially a girls' track program that was literally at its lowest hour—low numbers, low expectations, almost no budget. The program was literally withering on the vine. After all, I was a "big time" varsity football assistant and really shouldn't risk my tough, linebacker mentality to go coach a bunch of girls in the spring. I told Larry I would think about it, but in my mind I knew I really didn't want to coach a girls' team.

Spring rolled around and I still hadn't committed to Larry, so I went to the first team meeting to tell him I was going to stay in off-season football with my players and see if I could help them get better. Coach Cariker had already started the meeting when I arrived so I just stood in the back and listened to what he had to say. He began the talk with a story of a small young shepherd boy named David who took on a giant warrior (nearly 9 feet tall) named Goliath in a real death match. He talked about how none of David's countrymen, not even the best of the best soldiers, would challenge Goliath and his army. They were either lazy, scared, intimidated, or didn't care enough about their freedom to rise to meet the challenge of the Philistine giant. After all, if Goliath won the death match David's people would be enslaved and continue to live a hard life.

Coach Cariker explained how David could have approached the situation. David could have looked at Goliath and said, "He is so enormous and so well trained that I don't have a chance. After all, I only have a slingshot and a couple of small stones. Goliath has a sword that I can't even lift and giant pieces of armor to protect him. I could never defeat him in a million battles." None of David's countrymen would have blamed him, he would have continued to be accepted by his peers, and nothing would have changed.

Coach Cariker brought the story to a close by explaining how David really handled the situation. David knew that his faith in God would overcome anything this world could put up against him. David stood in front of Goliath with his slingshot and stones and said to himself, "This guy is so big, I can't miss him!" Then with one aggressive, confident toss of a stone—and God's help—David brought down the giant Goliath, preserved his countrymen's freedom for another day, and etched his way into history as one of the world's best leaders.

The dozen or so girls in that meeting, as well as a rookie football coach, learned a lot that day. Coach Cariker taught us that we were all in charge of our attitudes and we could choose how we would approach each day. Challenges can either be so big we can't overcome them or so big we can't miss—it's our choice. Thank goodness we chose the second part of the story that day. Owasso girls' track became a top 10 track program from that day forward. It was the greatest coaching and learning experience I have ever had. I learned how to work with people and how to approach life with God as the light of my path and to constantly maintain my attitude.

Back to the initial interview question on defining success. Success comes in many shapes and sizes. One must be careful to recognize it in its many forms as often as possible. Many programs judge success by wins and losses alone, and not by the limitless number of positives that occur each day within successful organizations.

Success is helping a young man who has no family develop character and integrity and giving him a chance to perform in society. Success is teaching a young coach how to manage his family time with his work time and become a better leader for his family. Success is teaching a group of young men how powerful they can be if they believe and trust in a worthy cause. Success is teaching people how to respond to hardship and setbacks with a positive, David-like attitude. Success is seeing young men and coaches win with humility and be thankful for their abilities and accomplishments. Success is having a player call you long after he's graduated to thank you for teaching him to take the high road in life or to tell you he was getting married or having a new son. Success is watching your players sit down on the edge of a sick child's hospital bed to brighten her day. Success is watching a player sign a national letter of intent, guaranteeing him a college education. Success is helping a young coach develop the attitude and skills to become a successful head coach. Success is helping someone choose a positive attitude toward life.

Success comes in many shapes and sizes. In this book, I'll discuss various philosophies, methods, and techniques I've used to accomplish success. Football is the greatest environment ever created to develop and achieve success.

When I was hired as head track and field coach at Jenks High School in 1995, the assistant superintendent, Dr. Sterling Ming, gave me a set of audiotapes of the bestselling book *The 7 Habits of Highly Effective People* by Dr. Stephen R. Covey. I was commuting about 25 miles to work each morning and took the opportunity to listen to Dr. Covey's ideas about basing your life on principles. After a few minutes of listening, I knew I was onto something big.

Covey explained how all of us have many, many maps in our heads, maps that can be divided into two basic categories: maps of the way things are—realities—and maps of the way things should be—values. We interpret everything we experience through these mental maps. We seldom question their accuracy; we're usually even unaware that we have them. We simply assume that the way we see things is the way they really are or the way they should be. Our attitudes and behaviors grow out of those assumptions.

How we perceive things is the source of the way we think and the way we act. The concepts in Dr. Covey's book have been a big influence on my coaching career, especially when developing the championship attitude and expectations within our football program here at Jenks.

A principle-based life is one of control, contentment, and destiny at all levels—personal, professional, and spiritual. I am very fortunate to work at a high school that believes our football program is as much a part of the curriculum as math, science, or English. Our superintendent and school board believe athletes learn valuable life lessons from football and support our football program just like every other student program in our district.

The life lessons learned from the sport of football are valuable and endless—developing character; working as a team; making a commitment; winning with humility and class; maintaining a positive attitude when dealing with setbacks; showing a strong work ethic, integrity, and responsibility; and being a quality role model. These qualities are invaluable in the development of quality young people.

These qualities are also vital when developing championship football programs. I'll share many of the concepts, principles, philosophies, and methods of developing these qualities in people, including players, coaches, and other members of your organization. When every member of your team develops a high level of integrity and trust, you have a strong chance to be successful. Just like David, choose to have a great attitude and you can't miss.

Coaching young men is truly a blessing and a responsibility that one must not take lightly or for granted. The principles and values that can be instilled in young men through the tools of football are endless and exciting. As I constantly remind each team, "Life is a journey." Focus on it one day at a time. When an airline pilot programs the coordinates of the destination into the autopilot, he establishes the goal for the flight. Once the autopilot takes over control of the plane, the plane is technically off-course 90 percent of the time as the autopilot makes course adjustments several times each second during the trip. A coach's task is much the same.

Developing and maintaining a football program requires charting the best possible route with a clear destination (goals) in mind, then constantly striving to find the best way to achieve them while constantly making adjustments based on our principles and priorities. Focus on—and enjoy—the journey.

KEY TO DIAGRAMS

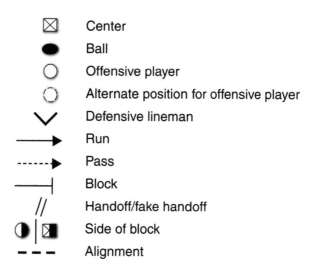

⊠	Center
●	Ball
○	Offensive player
◌	Alternate position for offensive player
∨	Defensive lineman
→	Run
----▶	Pass
⊢	Block
//	Handoff/fake handoff
◐ | ◪	Side of block
- - -	Alignment

Position abbreviations

FB	Fullback
QB	Quarterback
LT/RT	Left/right tackle
LG/RG	Left/right guard
Z	Flanker
TE	Tight end
TB	Tailback
WR	Wide receiver
T	Tackle
CB	Cornerback
LB	Linebacker
FS	Free safety
$	Strong safety
E	End
N	Nose tackle

PART I FOUNDATION

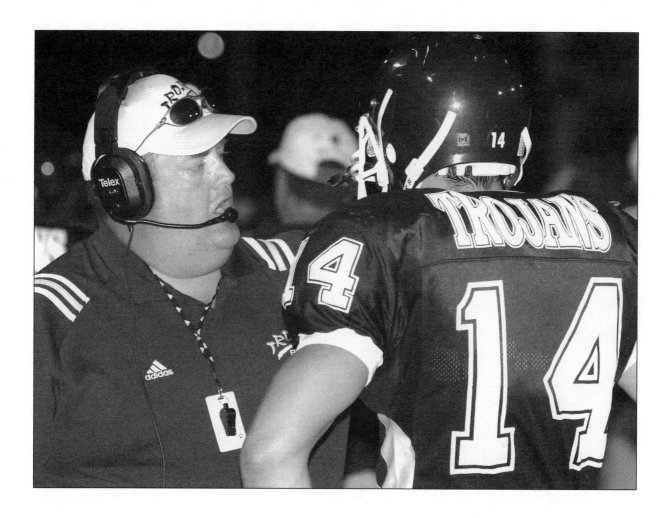

CHAPTER 1
DEVELOPING A COACHING PHILOSOPHY

I remember as a young child singing the timeless vacation Bible school song "The Wise Man Built His House Upon the Rock." It wasn't until I was older that I realized the importance of building not only my house but also my life, family, and organization on a stable foundation. My foundation is my faith in God. The contentment, stability, and confidence that come from knowing there is one who truly loves me and is genuinely interested in my life are without question my rock. In this first chapter I address many of the principles and priorities that make up a rock-solid foundation.

The ultimate goal of my coaching career has been to teach young men, players, and coaches the value of living life with Godly principles and priorities as their guide. Winning is a by-product of keeping our priorities in order and living life to the fullest with our internal value system leading the way. Maintaining priorities and keeping them in the right order are an all-day, everyday job but one that is paramount for success in all areas of life. (The Xs and Os are the easiest part of

the process when a coach is surrounded by principle-based players and assistants.)

In the football program at Jenks High School, we begin with four priorities—faith, family, academics, and football—which are essential for each person and our overall program if we are to reach our highest potential not only in football but also in all areas of life.

The first priority is *faith*. The apostle Matthew said, "Now faith is being sure of what we hope for and certain of what we do not see." Faith affects our lives in many ways, all of them positive. Faith led Noah to spend nearly 100 years of his life building a boat and saving his family, and he did it in a time believed by many scholars when the Earth was watered by dew and not rain. Noah faced daily ridicule and setbacks but was relentless and labored daily to complete the ark because of his faith in God. Ultimately, his faith saved Noah and his family.

A personal faith in God can be a great source of strength for a coach and for players. In addition, having faith in your coaches and teammates makes your football team a powerful unit capable of accomplishing great things. The by-products of a strong faith are boldness and confidence. The belief in each member of your organization to do the right thing at the right time to the best of his ability is a core principle that cannot be compromised if you are going to be successful in your endeavor. Each of us as coaches, players, trainers, and managers must walk across the white line on game day and be sure of what we hope for and be certain of what we do not see. Simply stated, I believe beyond a shadow of a doubt in what my organization stands for.

I have never hit my players over the head with a Bible or forced religion on them because personal faith is developed by each person's personality and relationship with God. However, at Jenks we do place our players in a position to grow spiritually. Harold Phillips is a local pastor and has graciously volunteered to organize and manage our own Fellowship of Christian Athletes (FCA) program within our football organization. Harold arranges for a pregame FCA speaker to present a motivational speech with biblical principles to the players before each game. These FCA meetings allow a time of reflection and focus before the ball game. I believe these FCA meetings have benefited our players' performance in addition to their spirituality. Harold also leads a weekly coaches' Bible study on Thursday mornings in our war room. The study is open to all of the coaches at Jenks High School and has helped bring our coaches closer together and helped us maintain our priorities.

People who make their faith their number one priority have the firm foundation on which to embark on any worthy task. People searching for something to lean on can be less dependable and effective in an organization.

The second priority is *family*. Young men who have great family relationships shine like the sun. They have the support of the people who are the most important and influential to them. Young men who lack that family structure and support often suffer from its absence in a variety of ways.

We constantly strive and encourage our players and coaches to work hard to develop positive relationships with their families. Spending time with those you love is a healing salve for the problems and setbacks that life may sometimes bring.

Simply holding my daughters on my lap in my recliner erases the pain and stress of a hard day or tough loss. They don't know or care if the Trojans won or lost; they just enjoy spending time with their dad.

Within the framework of our football booster club, we have established a moms' club to help meet the needs of our players who do not have a firm family structure at home. I want our football program to be an extension of family. After all, we spend so much time and effort working here at the stadium that we are a kind of family anyway. Our moms' club provides a variety of services for our players, including weekly locker room decorations with personal messages on the players' lockers. If a certain player doesn't have a mother to decorate his locker, another mother adopts him. The mothers also provide pre- and postgame meals for the players. If a young man doesn't eat well at home, he will eat well at the stadium or on the road with the team. To some, meals don't sound very important. To those who don't know where their next meal is coming from, meals are very important. Our moms' club is also a support group for the moms. The senior moms advise and groom the moms of the underclassmen to keep the tradition of the moms' club alive and growing. There is nothing more powerful than a group of motivated mothers. They love their boys, and they love their football, so I encourage every coach to utilize this valuable resource when developing your football family.

Being a responsible member of a family is a rewarding position. Being a part of young men's lives, especially those who need family support, is one of the highlights of being a coach.

The third priority is *academics*. Approximately 1 out of 17,000 high school football players will sign an NCAA Division I scholarship. NFL teams carry only 45 players on their rosters. The odds are against receiving a free education or making a living playing football.

Our program has been fortunate to produce dozens of Division I players, and we currently have four active players in the NFL. Even so, we stress to our players that great effort in the classroom puts them in control of their future. A great education empowers young men and gives them attractive choices in life if football doesn't work out. On the flip side, players who fail their classes will be ineligible to experience the benefits of being a member of the football team. Hard work in the classroom is just as important as great effort on the football field.

Many people are shocked when I tell them that *football* is the fourth priority in our program at Jenks. The order of priorities is simple to justify but difficult to maintain. We sometimes focus so much on winning and performing on the field that we forget the key elements that lead to great performance.

We place great value in nurturing strong faith, family support, and an education that will serve as the base for the future. If the coaching staff and young men in a program have their priorities in order, focusing on football is easy. Therefore even for practical reasons, football should come fourth, not first, on the priority list.

Once the first three priorities are in order, the way is paved to teach the fourth priority: football. Football is a technical game requiring sound instruction and a lot of intense physical training. Much of this book explains various positions, techniques, and methods of teaching football. Keep in mind, though, that teaching football also involves developing players and coaches in the areas of teamwork, self-discipline, unselfishness, humility, and attitude, all of which are vital to the success of an organization. Football includes a range of physical and mental concepts.

The philosophies created for the football program and the coaches on the staff are developed with these four priorities in mind. As we create team, coach, offensive, defensive, and special team philosophies, these four priorities remain the foundation.

Coach's Keys

1. Remember your priorities and seek to keep them in order: faith, family, academics, and football. Football is easy when your priorities are correct.

2. Remember your vision, purpose, and mission. Teaching football must be a passion and must come from the heart.

3. It is easier to match your philosophy to your players than to match players to your philosophy.

TEAM

All of us can do it together, but none of us can do it alone. From the first day of summer workouts through fall camp and on throughout the season, we preach that the team comes first. Coaches and players are constantly reminded of the importance of working together for a common purpose. Teamwork works; a team with members who truly believe in each other is more powerful than athletic ability or a great playbook alone.

Several team-building activities are held throughout the summer, including a senior retreat at which we gather around a campfire to discuss expectations and goals for the upcoming season. I invite famous alumni to talk to the players; they reflect on their own experiences as members of championship teams and discuss what it takes to be in position to continue the great tradition of championship football at Jenks. Players walk away from this retreat fired up and ready to meet the challenge of making a group of young men into a team.

Throughout the season I allow a different position coach to address the team at the Thursday night team dinner. Each coach presents a positive message about what we can do to continue to grow as a team as we accomplish great things together. Players enjoy hearing from the assistant coaches and gain even more respect for them when they hear how much the success of the organization means to them.

Working together toward a common goal—that's the power of team.

The power of team and the importance of every player's understanding of his role within the organization are stressed constantly. I search for examples of teamwork during practice and games and praise players and coaches for their contributions to the team's success. Having everyone in an organization pulling on the same end of the rope is vital. If everyone's not on the same page, we won't win consistently, no matter how much talent takes the field on game day.

Here is a great example of teamwork. It was a crucial district game during the 2000 season. We were blessed with two great tailbacks, Bobby Klinck (who was the starting strong safety) and Kejuan Jones (who was the starting tailback), both of whom signed to play with the University of Oklahoma that year. The opponent kicked off to Kejuan, and

he made a tremendous run, avoiding nearly everyone on the coverage team and breaking many tackles en route to an 85-yard return down to the 6-yard line. Kejuan gave great effort and was very winded after the return, so I put Bobby in to run the first offensive play. As usual, he made a tremendous cut at the line of scrimmage and scored a crucial touchdown for our team while Kejuan was on the sideline catching his breath. Kejuan's mother was upset and later asked me why I was stealing her son's glory by taking him out of the game on the goal line. I replied, "Our team is not here for your son's glory. Your son is here to bring glory to our team, and he did by putting us in position to score a touchdown. Bobby was fresh, and that's what we needed to get the ball in the end zone." Kejuan was cranked up when Bobby scored the touchdown and was even more excited for the success of our team. His mother, on the other hand, was worried about her son and his statistics, which is okay from a mother's perspective but not from a coach's perspective. I knew when those two guys made room for each other in the backfield, no one could stop us.

Creating a Vision, Purpose, and Mission

Three of the components of developing a firm philosophy are vision, purpose, and mission. All three are closely related; in fact, they are parts of each other, but they are also individual components that have special meaning in the grand scope of a program.

Vision is simply how you see your organization, or the mental picture generated from your program. When you break down and research your program, what picture do you see? Team purpose is linked to vision and puts the vision into action. The relentless pursuit of excellence is our program's defining statement. We will work tirelessly and constantly strive to be excellent at what we do. With confidence in our priorities, we will not waver in the pursuit of being the best we can be. The mission statement puts a personal touch on vision and purpose. The mission statement gives vision and purpose internal value and creates passion for the job ahead. Knowing that your mission is part of you gives you confidence and assurance that you are pursuing your calling in life.

At Jenks, we want to mentor young men to achieve their highest potential in all areas of their lives. Our vision for the program is this: The Jenks Trojan football program will be respected as the very best high school program in the nation in helping young men achieve their highest potential. I want young men to leave our program better people than they were when they joined the team.

Many coaches are surprised when I present the vision of our program at clinics and seminars. They expect me to knock them over with a vision of robotic muscle heads who can function only on the football field. I believe in educating the whole athlete in all areas of life.

When developing a vision for your program, look deep into your heart at your core principles and values. If you write down a vision that sounds good but you don't believe in it or can't relate to it, the vision will be useless. If your vision is one of heartfelt belief and is part of you, it will empower you and your program because all decisions and thoughts will be developed with this vision in mind.

All actions, decisions, and planning are based on the purpose of the program. At Jenks, our purpose is "The relentless pursuit of excellence in high school football." Although only nine words, our purpose statement is the lighthouse of our program. It keeps us on course and brings our program's compass back on track when we stray.

We are careful not to confuse excellence with perfection. Excellence and perfection are miles apart. A team striving for excellence has hope and faith that they will accomplish great things; their goals are achievable. A team striving for perfection will eventually find frustration and dead ends. No organization is perfect or ever will be perfect. Make sure that goals are accomplished along the journey.

Our program operates with our purpose constantly in mind. Actions and decisions are made with our purpose as the flagship. Operating under this format diminishes trivial issues that can take away from truly important, program-developing actions. Purpose places everyone on the same page and helps everyone involved with the program make decisions based on a common worthy cause. Are our actions building our program or tearing it down?

A mission statement is a compilation of personal core values and principles. It expresses what you are all about. It meshes your conscience with what you truly believe. Once you are comfortable with why you are who you are and do what you do, you can accomplish amazing things and maintain a positive, fulfilling attitude about life.

Before each season begins I meet with my staff in a relaxed setting, and we discuss our personal mission, that internal fire that drives us to be football coaches. Every person is a unique being, and every member of my staff has a different reason for working with young people, but that drive and mission are essential for fulfillment and satisfaction. We close the meeting with thoughts about our staff mission statement. Each year the exact wording of the mission statement varies a little, but always it states the principles and ideas that we live by.

An individual mission statement developed by each member of the staff is empowering. It allows each member of the staff equal footing and a feeling of ownership in the football program. Our common mission statement creates a bond that will not be broken easily.

Our recent staff mission statement was *excellence through teamwork*. From this general statement, we developed four key areas to work on to achieve our mission:

1. Build confidence, self-esteem, and a feeling of contribution within each person in our program.
2. Encourage open and honest communication from all team members.
3. Respect the dignity and diversity of each person on the team.
4. Commit to team unity through strong leadership principles and trust in each other.

The mission statement is very simple in scope, but it's our way of life. It's not superficial. It is who we are and what we believe.

My mission in life is to influence people in a positive way. I constantly strive to improve ways of motivating and assisting players, coaches, and others around me. I feel that

Our purpose—the relentless pursuit of excellence in high school football—is stressed in the practice room and demonstrated on the field.

this type of work is my calling in life. I receive a great deal of praise and accolades from the media and people in my profession, but I would trade all of it to see a young man from the inner city overcome his environmental adversity, graduate from high school, and go on to become a successful citizen.

Remember, mission statements evolve, they change, and they grow. Take great pride and care when developing your mission. Once you find what you love to do, you never have to go to work again.

Building a Program Philosophy

With our mission statement in mind, we develop a program philosophy. This shared philosophy is vital for program unity and growth.

Underlying and supporting any sound philosophy is a set of key principles—essentials for taking the philosophy from the paper to the field. We've identified the following principles as prerequisites to implementing our program's philosophy successfully.

- *Show commitment.* It's easy to recognize the coaches and players who are committed to the program. They are the beacons of your program, and they stand out. Surrounding yourself with committed people is a cornerstone for program success.
- *Have integrity.* We will always maintain and preserve integrity in our program. We will always play and coach within the rules and confines of the game. Integrity, when instilled in young men, will make them leaders.
- *Be unselfish.* In today's world of professional sports and professional egos, unselfishness is a challenging trait to instill in young men. We will find players who are willing to do things the Jenks way and who will always put the team ahead of themselves.
- *Exercise discipline.* We place a high value on discipline in our program. Doing the

little things right is important in the heat of battle. We constantly develop and demand discipline in our program. Young people enjoy being a part of a structured program.

- *Engage in purposeful work.* As I stated earlier, all actions in our program are performed with our purpose in mind. We don't have time for poor attitudes, sloppy work habits, or trivial items that take away from our purpose.
- *Be models of good conduct.* Our coaches will be positive role models for our players, and our players will be positive role models for their peers. If our priorities are truly in order, we'll be great examples for those around us.
- *Display intensity and enthusiasm.* Enthusiasm is contagious and powerful. It spreads from coach to coach, from player to player, and from coach to player. We believe in enthusiasm, and we script and schedule enthusiasm into every meeting and practice. Football is an intense game played by intense players. We coach it the same way.
- *Be honest.* Coaches will always be honest with players and let them know exactly where they stand and what we expect of them. Honesty in communication builds trust in players and lets them know you want them to succeed and improve.
- *Execute fundamentals.* We win by eliminating bad play and mistakes. We are fundamentally sound in all we do. We work a new play in, not put a new play in. There are so many great football plays, but your team must be able to perform them at a very high level to be successful.
- *Develop players.* We want players to leave us better people than when they arrived. Our program educates the whole person and prepares him for life after football. There is no better classroom than the football field. The sport of football parallels life. Those who have the work ethic and attitude will succeed, and those who don't won't succeed.

- *Have a positive attitude.* Attitude, like enthusiasm, is contagious. We are all in control of our attitudes and constantly strive to approach every task with a great attitude. We want members of our program to have a "can do" outlook, a willingness to give their best effort for the benefit of the team at all times.

- *Be persistent.* We will compete and never give up as long as there is time on the clock. This approach teaches a great life lesson to players. No matter what the obstacle or the situation, never, never, never quit.

- *Voice solutions, not complaints.* Our team purpose places staff on level ground in regards to making decisions and acting on behalf of the program. If a staff member complains, the solution to the problem better be the next thing he says. We are all in this project together, and want to do things the best way, not necessarily my way.

Establishing a Practice Philosophy

We constantly emphasize controlled effort and intensity in practice. We are aware of the importance of remaining injury free, but we also believe in practicing at a very high level of intensity. We constantly emphasize effort and control in gamelike practice sessions.

Demand outstanding performance in practice. I am big on "run it again" practices. All of my coaches carry a practice script during practice and check off the plays we need to see again because of poor performance. The team understands the importance of performing well in practice.

Practice under pressure. We find many ways to put pressure on our team during workouts. It is important to improve a team's mental toughness and concentration level. We put our quarterback in check situations, we script snap count variance, and we make our defense adjust on the run—any situation

In practice, put players in pressure situations.

to put additional pressure on players and coaches in order to prepare for game-night situations.

Give all players a chance to be successful. It is crucial for each player to feel like he has a chance to contribute to the cause. I encourage coaches to find places and situations for kids to help the team. Emphasize what the athlete does well and take advantage of it. This will help give each player a sense of ownership of and belonging to the team.

Prepare your athletes. Football teaches valuable life lessons. It teaches us more about life than any other endeavor or any class we might take. Be aware of your responsibility to teach and prepare young men. This preparation includes not only the physical preparation through strength and conditioning workouts and football practice but also the mental preparation including the development of attitude, toughness, teamwork, and unselfishness. Developing these winning characteristics is just as vital as physical training when preparing your personnel.

COACHES

One of my favorite Bible verses comes from II Timothy 4:2: "Be prepared in season and out of season. Correct, rebuke, and encourage— with great patience and careful instruction." This defines the approach you should take not only as a football coach but also as the leader of any organization. "Be prepared" speaks for itself. Don't take anything for granted; don't wing it. Do your homework so that nothing sneaks up on you. However, if something does sneak up on you, you will know how to react to it if you are prepared. The verse also lets us know that we should be good teachers who are patient, constantly correcting and encouraging our students even to the point of being stern with them to achieve the outcome we expect. I don't read anything about being negative, impatient, or hasty, only patient and careful. With these thoughts in mind, let's discuss my philosophy of coaching football.

Along with the overall program philosophy, it's essential to develop your own core approach to coaching football. Your personal coaching philosophy will dictate how you handle both off-the-field and on-the-field responsibilities and decisions.

I can think of no other profession I would rather be a part of. People may think that the adrenaline of the big game on Friday or the championship seasons make my job great, and I do enjoy both situations. However, the relationships with players and coaches are what make coaching football a great profession. The idea that I am actually helping a young man develop into a great citizen is very fulfilling. Football is my calling. If a person coaches for any other reason, he will never be complete in his profession.

There is never a dull moment when coaching young men. Each season is full of new and different challenges and players. The notion that you, as a coach, can bring together a hundred different players and coaches for one common cause is exciting, challenging, and fulfilling. What a great job!

Whatever your professional coaching philosophy may be, make sure it is true to who you are as a person. Players can read a phony faster than anyone. Coaching young people must come from the heart and be part of your personality. Coaching must be a part of your value system. It must be your mission if you are going to be successful. If your heart is not in it, the team will notice and take the same approach.

The first element of my personal coaching philosophy is that team comes first. Team development is everything in football. I would rather have a great team than great athletes any day. I always base my decisions on what is best for the team. I will always put the team ahead of the individual.

The second element of my coaching philosophy is to keep my players' interests at heart. It doesn't matter what you are selling if the players aren't buying. Unless every member of your team is pulling on the same end of the rope, your chances of success are limited. My thought process always includes what is best for my players. They don't care how much you know until they know how much you care. Be sincere and genuine with

The Power of Team

The power of team is tremendous. For example, my 1997 squad was 14–0 and for the most part was not threatened during the campaign to win a second consecutive state championship. The defense that year still retains the nickname "Legion of Doom" for their outstanding accomplishments. The 1997 team was an amazingly talented squad that played at a high level of intensity.

The big problem came in 1998. We had 20 new starters, few with the ability or confidence that the Legion of Doom had possessed. Our squad lost the season opener 28 to 24 to a 5A school from Tulsa, and the crowd was brutal after the loss. Then in the third week, we lost 55 to 45 to our arch rival, and the community and school instantly became worried that the string of championships would end with these no-name young players.

That night in the locker room, a couple of seniors presented the pure definition of football. They let all of us know that the Legion of Doom, which included Rocky Calmus (Tennessee Titans) and Sean Mahan (Tampa Bay Buccaneers) were no longer playing for Jenks High School, and our only chance for success was to come together as never before. The team's success must be paramount, and personal agendas must be put aside. This was a strong message, but the most important part about the message was the fact that it came from our players.

We won 10 consecutive games and avenged our third-week loss to our arch rival, Union, in the state championship game by winning 41 to 28. Those seniors that night pressed home the point of the tremendous potential in team.

your young men. They are the lifeblood of your football program.

I encourage players and coaches to relentlessly pursue victory. The one constant in our program is effort. Players are reminded constantly that no matter how much God-given ability they are blessed with, or how little, they can always give their best effort. Effort is a constant and an area in which we give no slack to players or coaches. The most important part of a successful organization is to find people who will give their best effort for a noble cause.

In any successful organization, program development and growth are important. If all thoughts and efforts are used in the now without making time and effort for younger players, the future of the program could be in jeopardy. As Dr. Stephen Covey, author of *The 7 Habits of Highly Effective People*, says, "Begin with the end in mind." Be aware of the impact today's decisions will have on future teams.

OFFENSE

The first step of our offensive philosophy is a relentless, physical running game. The word *relentless* in our philosophy means to never give up and always give your best effort. Relentless to victory—this statement is printed on our program manual, and we live by it. We outwork our opponents. We always give our best effort. It's a constant in our program.

Rather than limit ourselves by saying that we are an I-team or a veer team, we take a different approach in our system. We have a relentless, physical running game, a running game that will bloody your nose, one in which the offensive lineman can fire off the line and hit people. We want to run the ball well enough that teams must gear up to stop us or face losing control of the game. Letting our players and coaches know that we want a physical running game opens up the door for creativity and flexibility. If we have a great I-back, we'll run some I. If we have a great running quarterback, we'll run him. It's the same if we have a great fullback or flanker. Limiting our players and coaches to being an I-team would drastically reduce our chances of success.

An effective running game allows us to have big-play capability in the passing game. When the defense commits to stopping the running game, we take advantage of their aggressiveness and throw the ball over their heads with play-action passes. We also take advantage of defensive aggressiveness by running reverses and misdirection running plays. We do not limit ourselves to certain plays or formations, but instead empower ourselves with a vision of offense.

We take pride in doing what we do well. At a championship level, talent is usually about the same on both teams. The team that is able to execute its system is the one with the best chance to win. Execution is the key to success.

We take care of the football and emphasize ball control. Every weekend you can read about teams who threw the football more than 400 yards and lost the game. You never read about teams that run the ball 400 yards and lose. Ball control is huge in the game of football and can be accomplished in many ways. Running the ball and play-action passing are great ways to keep the ball away from the opponent and to win ball games.

DEFENSE

In keeping with our offensive philosophy, our defensive philosophy is empowering as well. We commit to stopping the run. If an opponent can consistently run the ball against our defense, we will lose control of the ball game and risk defeat. We make every attempt defensively to stop the best part of our opponent's running game, thus making our opponent beat us with something they are not used to executing.

Stemming from our philosophy of controlling the running game comes our pressure philosophy in the passing game. If in fact we take our opponents out of their comfort zone in the running game, we then must control the passing game. We prefer to put pressure on the quarterback in several ways. Certainly pass rush is important, but we also disguise our secondary coverages and blitzes to disrupt passing execution as well as rerouting receivers with linebackers and secondary players. At times we need to play defense

On defense, our first priority is to stuff the run.

and make the offense outexecute us, but we prefer to force the issue most of the time and maintain control of our opponent's offensive tempo.

Create turnovers. We teach it, and we preach it. We script it in our practices and create a mentality in our defensive unit that we must force turnovers. Turnover margin is huge in the game of football. If your team comes out on top in turnovers, the odds are in your favor to win the ball game.

We never want to give the offense success because of a mental breakdown. If our players are unsure, they will not be aggressive. We constantly stress and teach the importance of understanding responsibilities and being able to line up and play with confidence and aggression. If there are questions or doubts, we use automatics to line up the defensive unit in a sound system that we can play with confidence. If we see something we can't line up to, our defensive captains have the power to call time-out to prevent a big offensive play.

One of the most important approaches we take defensively is to make the offense execute to be successful against us. We make them earn everything. We were in a championship game against a big rival that had an All-American receiver who, because of his size and speed, gave us tremendous matchup problems. No one on our team could cover him one on one, and our opponent did a great job of isolating him for just that reason. It was a tight ball game, but we had the lead toward the end of the game. They were threatening on offense, and we had to make a play on fourth down to win the ball game. We called a pressure, and our veteran cornerback went out and manned up on the All-American. I knew in my heart where they were going with the ball. I just prayed that our pressure would disrupt their timing enough that our corner could make a play. The play was a double move, and we got beat, got beat badly. But the veteran had been there before. He dropped his head and burst with all the speed he had to regain position on the play. He realized he was going to give up a game-winning touchdown if he gave up the catch. Our corner dived and tackled the receiver as the ball came down for the easy score. The ball was incomplete, but penalty flags were everywhere. The crowd moaned and groaned because of the penalty, but I was elated that our veteran had prevented the score and our defense had another chance to win the game. It was a tremendous heads-up play and one that won the game for us three plays later when we sacked their quarterback and time expired. Make your opponent earn everything.

SPECIAL TEAMS

We take an aggressive and progressive approach to special teams play. Special teams are a system just like offense or defense, and we allot the same amount of preparation and emphasis to special teams as we do to offense and defense. We execute special teams plays at a high level and force our opponents to prepare well or risk losing this phase of the game. We take pride in scouting opponents and using special teams to their fullest potential.

We set the tone by utilizing speed and physical play. We emphasize speed and aggression on special teams, no matter which phase. We want to be the aggressor and establish a toughness mentality. We pressure every punt or kick and hit return teams hard. We are relentless in our effort and intensity in every situation.

Special teams that execute at a high level will consistently help shift the momentum in favor of your team. Winning the field-position battle, blocking a kick or punt, or scoring a special teams touchdown can deflate an opponent and boost your squad's momentum.

Select players who use good judgment and execute their specialty. Just because a player is a great athlete doesn't necessarily mean he will be a great special teams player. Special teams players must use great judgment along with great effort and execution. Nothing can cost your squad momentum faster than foolish plays in special teams. It is imperative to find and develop players who can play with great intensity, ability, and still use good judgment.

CHAPTER 2 COMMUNICATING AND MOTIVATING

Communication and motivation are 365-day-a-year jobs. Both actions are closely related, and it is extremely difficult to be successful at one without being successful at the other. Solid communication skills without positive motivation tactics are of little benefit to an organization and vice versa. Positive motivation without an effective medium to carry it is also ineffective. Communication and motivation are both one-on-one propositions. You can set goals for the team, but you must communicate with and motivate individuals. As the head coach you must spend time with your players and coaches in order to motivate them.

Each person is unique and responds differently than the person sitting next to him. Motivation is important in getting someone to accept the team concept and his role in it, which are necessary for your organization to be successful. Not every player will be first team, but the team must come first. This chapter covers the vital keys to communicating with and motivating those in your organization.

COMMUNICATION

Think about how many hours per day you spend communicating. Most of us read, write, talk, and listen for many hours each day. Communication is the heartbeat of any successful organization. Those who do it the most effectively reap the greatest rewards. To be a great teacher and coach you must create solid, positive lines of communication with players, staff, support personnel, parents, officials, faculty members, alumni, and members of the media.

Every person communicates in his or her own way. What may work well for one person, won't work at all for another. However, some constants in effective communication hold true for everyone. Effective communicators are great listeners and observers. They try to understand the person they are attempting to communicate with and go to great measures to gather information before responding. Great communicators respect the thoughts and feelings of those they are communicating with even when they are not in agreement.

They display *empathy.* Do your best to see the world from someone else's perspective before responding.

This may sound crazy, but sometime when you have time on your hands, cover your ears and simply watch two people talk to each other. Pay careful attention to their body language and their facial expressions. You will be surprised by just how much is communicated through body language alone.

In a football environment, the correct body language can be vital. Imagine that it's a crucial time in the ball game and you're staring into the eyes of your defense before they take the field on a critical fourth-down play that could win the game. Does the team see a gleam of confidence and strength in your face, or do they see lines of concern and worry? Are your fists clenched and your teeth grinding in triumph and strength or in frustration and lack of confidence?

Body language is the glue that holds verbal communication together. Sometimes I can motivate a player with my competitor's glare, the one my wife says is the look of a person fighting for his life. Players can see that the head coach is into the intensity of the ball game and they feed off the look. Unfortunately, they feed off the head coach's frustration as well. Be mindful of the extreme power of body language.

People may doubt what you say, but they will never doubt what you do. Actions speak louder than words. As coaches, we must model our philosophy and approach. We can't expect players and staff to just do what we say if we are not willing to set the example. Because communication is not always oral, we must constantly be aware of our example to others.

Coaches should constantly strive to communicate character, ethical conduct, and the importance of walking the walk every day. Players' actions and words send a message to their school, their community, and their state. Players should be aware of how important it is to set a high standard of character for all young athletes who look up to them, and they should know that their actions are a direct representation of their football program wherever they may be.

Coach's Keys: Communicating

1. Be a great listener and try to understand the situation before you respond.
2. Be an empathetic listener.
3. People may doubt what you say, but they will never doubt what you do.
4. Practice your communication skills and become a great communicator.
5. Use the media to paint a positive picture of your program, school, and community.
6. Keep comments to the media team oriented. No matter how much you want to talk about referees or an opponent, if you don't have anything positive to say, say nothing at all.

Communicating With Players

Players don't care how much you know until they know how much you care. I include this statement in my coach's manual each year, and I believe in this statement completely.

When conducting off-season interviews with players, the staff and I do everything we can to let them know of our sincere concern for them both on and off the football field. We communicate four priorities to each player—faith, family, school, and football. We want each player to know that he is our most prized possession and we are interested in his success in all areas of life. As mentors, teachers, and coaches, our mission should be to educate the whole person, not just the part that plays football. Maintaining the proper priorities has been the key to our success on the football field even though football is the fourth-ranked priority. The other coaches and I constantly communicate our philosophy and the characteristics we expect of a championship-caliber player. The worst thing a coach can do to a player is to be less than truthful with him. Be open and honest with players and let them know exactly where they stand. It's the most important thing you can do to help them become better players and citizens.

Through hard work and dedication, each player has earned the right to be a member of your squad, and he should be shown the respect he deserves even if he is not a front-line player. It is vital to communicate to each player how important he is to the squad, especially mid- to low-level players. If you show more respect to the All-American than you do to the average, solid player, team cohesiveness will suffer. Respect should be constantly communicated from the top to the bottom of the program.

Building Coach–Player Relationships

Build close, solid relationships with your players. Treat each player as an integral part of a championship team, no matter what his abilities or grade level may be. Set the same standards and expectations for every member of the team. There is a great chance that someday that young, inexperienced player will, in fact, be an important part of your program.

Be fair with all players, although not necessarily the same with all players. The days of drawing the line in the sand are over. I run a disciplined program, but the "my way or the highway" days are over at Jenks. Be fair in all situations, remembering to always put the team first and the player second. Young people are diverse, so adapt and modify your approach to each athlete. After all, the ultimate goal is to get the most out of each player in a team setting.

Adapt to the special needs of each player to ensure that he is reaching his maximum potential on the field and off. We are fortunate

Make each player feel that he is a respected, important member of the team.

at Jenks to have developed an excellent support network for our athletes. Randy Lewis, my assistant coach in charge of community service and academic performance and my liaison to the faculty, researches each player for special needs. Many of our players have special learning needs that directly affect their abilities on the playing field and in the classroom. Because coaching is teaching, it is imperative to understand the best teaching methods and environment for each player.

Enlisting the Support of Team Leaders

At Jenks the entire team votes for captains each fall and each class votes for two representatives to serve on the team council. I meet with the team council weekly to discuss a variety of issues. Some are vital to team success, and some are as simple as what color game socks the team wants to wear. As head coach I make the final decisions, but it's important to let players have their say and for them to understand that I am interested in their concerns.

During these council meetings I also discuss leadership expectations and techniques with team leaders. I expect the captains of the team to lead by example in attitude and effort. Having just a few core players who are consistently good leaders makes a huge impact on a squad. I discuss leadership both on and off the field. Players need to be dedicated to activities that will benefit the team at all times. If our core group of men decides not to participate in drinking or other detrimental activities, the rest of the team will almost always follow suit. When the team's leaders understand their responsibilities, the team can develop into a very powerful unit that will be hard to tear apart when times get tough.

Communicating During Practice and Games

I prefer a positive, upbeat practice environment. We build excitement and enthusiasm into every practice. I'm a big effort guy, which includes both mental and physical effort during practice and game preparation.

Practice tempo is important, and we try not to be too wordy between plays. Coaches who talk too much can disrupt the player's concentration during a drill. Let the athlete know what he did well and what he can improve or change and then move on.

Don't delay practice because of inefficient and ineffective communication skills. Make every play in practice a learning experience. Evaluate each player's effort and assignment on every play and grade the rest of the areas on film after practice. Run repetitions on the field with short precise communication between plays and then communicate more thoroughly after practice during film sessions.

Our offensive, defensive, and special teams systems allow rapid, precise adjustments during a game. Football games evolve and change rapidly, and the teams who effectively make adjustments the most quickly have the best chance of success. Each position coach is aware of his respective game plan.

All coaches wear headsets so that they can communicate with the coordinator constantly. If the opponent throws something unexpected at us, we can make adjustments between each series of plays or sometimes during the series through a series of hand signals from the sideline. The headset communication system we use allows us to talk just like we're sitting around the coaches meeting room table. Each coach can hear the others and talk with the others. The only downside to this type of system is coaches who sometimes get caught up in the game and can't quit talking. Mike cancel buttons are great inventions.

Communicating With Staff

The men I hire are self-starters who are driven to be the best they can be at their profession. My coaching philosophy empowers assistant coaches to take ownership of the program. When coaches take ownership of the program, they give their all to see the program succeed. They exhibit great loyalty. I encourage assistant coaches to make decisions just as if they owned the place. I let them coach. The only

The football environment can be intense, possibly leading to confrontations between coaches. Keeping the lines of communication open and empowering assistant coaches helps to prevent bad feelings from simmering.

boundaries are our priorities; their decisions must fit our mission. I am very approachable and open minded when communicating with assistants. I take great pride in being empathic to each of them. When making decisions, I constantly refer to three questions: What's best for the program? What's best for the team? What's best for the person involved?

I'm not a big meeting guy. I meet with coaches to discuss issues that are important to the success of the program. But most of the time, we work on our specific responsibilities. However, I do meet with each coach individually at the conclusion of each season to discuss a variety of things. We discuss each assistant's performance and the expectations I have of him. We talk about career and personal goals and make a plan to help each coach reach those goals.

Coaching football can be a very intense job, and the football environment, whether game or practice, can be one of high emotion and pressure. This type of environment can lead to heated confrontations between coaches and players as well as between coaches themselves. We are all guilty of getting caught up in the emotion of a situation and flying off the handle from time to time. When this happens, it's important to make things right as soon as possible. My coaches and I never let players leave the practice field feeling that they have been personally put down or disrespected. If a coach gets after a young man and the situation goes a little too far, it's the responsibility of not only the coach involved but of all the coaches to make sure the player understands the problem and what we will do to fix the situation.

The same thing goes for other coaches when they don't see eye to eye. I make every effort to handle coaching problems behind closed doors to avoid the risk of the assistant losing the team's respect. If some of the emotion spills out in front of the players, it is my responsibility to make the situation right by publicly recognizing the mistake and rebuilding any part of the bridge that may have been torn down.

Communicating With Game Officials

Football officials are honest men who try their best to control football games within the rules and confines established for the sport. They want the players to settle the score. They do not want to be noticed by anyone at the ball game.

However, football officials are also human and make mistakes just like coaches and players do, mistakes that can lead to disagreements during the heat of battle. I've learned over the years to work with the officials and understand that mistakes will be made.

In my career as a head coach, I have received two unsportsmanlike penalties and a letter of reprimand. All three events occurred when I felt that the rules were not being enforced correctly or I thought an official had made a call to make up for a previous mistake.

If you and the official interpret the rules differently, that's one thing. But if you use poor judgment and respond to the official inappropriately, that's something else. Your approach as the head coach is critical. If you let your emotions get the best of you, you will lose focus on what's important—coaching the ball game. If you, the head coach, lose your focus, what will that do for your assistant coaches and players? Will they lose their focus because you are spending more time confronting officials than you are coaching your team?

I am the only coach from our team who communicates with officials. I want my assistant coaches completely focused on the tasks at hand. I also want players to stay focused on their job. Players have plenty of responsibilities to take care of and none of them has anything to do with officiating. As coaches we need to teach players the rules of football and

When communicating with officials, keep your focus on coaching the game. Don't let your emotions take you out of the game.

to study film to make sure players understand how officiating crews call certain areas of the game. Football officials go to school and seminars to keep their techniques current. It's our job as coaches to make sure our players and assistants are fully aware of how the game will be called.

Communicating With Parents

When communicating with parents, empathy comes up. As coaches we must keep in mind that we are working with a parent's most prized possession. Parents may have a completely different perspective on their children than we do as coaches.

Maintaining an appropriate coach–player relationship is an important component of effective parental communication. If the player completely understands where he stands and where he fits in the program, he can sometimes eliminate or reduce parental concerns. Again, being honest and upfront with a player lets him know that you have his best interests in mind. Sometimes the player forgets that the most important factor is the team and the advancement of the overall program and as the head coach all your decisions are ultimately made with the team's best interest in mind.

I give each parent a copy of the football program manual at the beginning of each season. The manual outlines every area of the football program, from team policy to how to pack a travel bag for a road trip. It's the same book that each player receives. This manual puts everyone on the same page and answers a lot of frequently asked questions about the program. Here is our list of 15 points parents need to understand about our program:

1. We strive to treat our players like they are our sons.
2. We coach hard, loudly, and aggressively. You are welcome to observe, but beware.
3. Football is a loud, tough, disciplined, and emotional game. We coach it the same way.
4. We believe, stress, and teach our priorities.
5. We require your child's undivided attention when we are teaching him.
6. The team always comes first. We have no stars.
7. We may require your child to be more disciplined than you do.
8. We don't play kids to make them happy. Athletes are played because they have great attitude, they do the things that are required plus more, they add the most value to the team, they understand their roles on the team, their number one goal is to make the team better, and they do the job better than someone else.
9. A parent's influence or position makes no difference.
10. A player is put in the best college-potential position only if it's best for our team.
11. Evaluation of your child happens 24 hours a day, seven days a week.
12. Players who do not work out with the team in the summer start at the bottom of the depth chart.
13. Publicity is used to promote our team, school, and community.
14. Schedule meetings with me in advance. Remember our philosophy when evaluating a situation—the team comes first. My door is always open and so is my mind; please have the same attitude. I always meet with the player before I meet with the parent.
15. Being simple and boring but winning is better than being complex and exciting but losing.

Parent meetings are vital for building the communication bridge necessary to build a football program. Organize a program manual containing your philosophy and your team's policies and distribute it to parents before the season begins. Positive communication is good communication and will reduce the number of parental issues during the season.

Communicating With Faculty and Administration

I communicate clearly in my monthly newsletter and through our school e-mail system that our coaching staff is always available to support our administrators and faculty members in any way. We want to be positive, active members of the educational team. In certain situations, a coach's influence on a student may help resolve a situation for a teacher. Our willingness to be involved can reap benefits for our program.

If possible, we try to assign a member of the coaching staff to each department at the school to communicate information about the football program and to support the faculty in dealing with our athletes. Having the faculty know that you are there to assist them is priceless for your football program.

Communicating With Media Personnel

I want our football program to be an ambassador for our school and community. With success and popularity comes the opportunity to face members of the media and present the football program in a positive light. As the head coach you must be prepared to communicate with the media. Be aware of the message you want to convey regarding your team, school, and community. When used properly, the media can create positive, program-building opportunities for your football program. When used improperly, the media can tear down your football program.

It is important to communicate positive, team-related information when chatting with the members of the media. Take the opportunity to communicate classroom successes your student-athletes have achieved throughout the year as well as extracurricular activities they may participate in. The media is a great avenue for recognizing other organizations and painting a positive picture of your academic institution. The band, pep club, fans, community, parents, booster club, administration, and school board are always supportive of successful programs, so recognize them publicly as often as possible to show your respect and appreciation for those who value your program. Using the football program to benefit and build other worthy programs at your school leads to positive growth of the program's overall value to the school and community.

Preseason is the favorite time for everyone associated with football, but especially the members of the media. It's a time of projections and predictions and, honestly, none of them mean anything except for maybe selling a few extra papers or magazines. At best, the polls are educated guesses based on returning lettermen, strength of schedule, and school tradition.

I want my program recognized in the preseason media reports, but I would rather not have to sit through all the preseason hype. I would rather play the games and find out who the best team really is. Preseason predictions are not reality, so here are my suggestions for talking about your team before they actually play a game. Be honest about your evaluation of your squad without giving away weaknesses or strengths. Be team oriented. Do not use the media to hype an individual player or your team; this tactic could backfire by giving opponents locker room material as motivation. I speak often about potential and tradition and leaving the door open for our team to improve and be competitive in the league. I strongly discourage comparing teams from different years and usually tell the media to decide whether this team is as good as some of the other ones, citing different players and different opponents as reasons for not being able to accurately compare two of our teams.

Pregame comments to the media also should be thought out. I believe we will win every game we play if we execute at a high level. When the media asks me what I believe the outcome of a game will be, I have one answer: "If we play well, we have a great chance to win the game. Our opponent is an excellent team, and we'll have to go out and execute at a very high level to have a chance to beat them." I'm straight up with the media

Use the media to promote a positive view of your football program.

and let them know exactly how I feel. I am always excited before big games, and I let the media know how excited our team is to have the opportunity to play another first-rate football team. I usually pay sincere compliments to our opponent and their star players when they are deserved, and that usually concludes the pregame interview.

All of our games are televised and on the radio, and I am often asked to make comments at halftime regarding the first-half play. The only things I'm thinking about are what adjustments we need to make and how I will address my coaching staff and team, none of which need to be broadcast on television or radio. When asked to make halftime comments, I take a minute to reflect on some of the positive team-oriented situations that occurred during the first half and try to elaborate on the positive as much as possible. The media always ask what we need to do differently or better, and I'll be honest and make a few general comments then head to the locker room

as fast as possible. Halftime interviews are a necessary evil, but one that I could certainly do without. Be cautious and remember to relax and speak in a positive, confident tone even though there are a thousand other things on your mind.

Postgame is a very sensitive time because of all the emotions following a well-fought game. Whether we have won a close ball game or lost, the emotional intensity of the game is still in my system for several minutes. Being mindful of this, I try to address the team first no matter what the outcome of the game was. If we were victorious, I want to celebrate with them. If we lost, I need to be there for them. This time with the team allows me to cool off and regain control of my emotions and senses. It also gives me time to gather my thoughts for the postgame media barrage.

After the game, I take the same approach to the media that I always do. I'm honest in my assessment and try to be as straightforward as possible without taking away from my philosophy of putting the team first. I compliment players who had great performances, but I'm also quick to credit all areas of the team to make sure no one feels slighted or mistreated. Postgame is another opportunity to credit all the friends of the program in a positive environment. Be cautious after a big loss not to make excuses or throw verbal punches at your opponent or the referees. There is no reason to talk about anything but your program after a tough defeat. I prefer to give credit where credit is due and credit the opponent with a strong performance when they deserve it. Negative comments about your opponent or the officials will open the door to a lot of things and none of them will be positive for your program.

Postgame Breakdown

During our state championship game against Union in 2000, more penalties were called than in any game I have ever played or coached. Even though we dominated the game and won handily, I could not overcome the intense emotion and animosity I felt for the game officials. From my perspective, our players had played well and hard, but their emotion and confidence had been taken away by overcontrolling officials.

In the postgame interview, I tried to restrain myself when answering the questions posed about the officials, but finally broke down and made honest, yet derogatory, remarks about the officiating crew. Two days later I received a letter of reprimand from the state association regarding my comments. Once the words leave your mouth, you can never get them back.

MOTIVATION

It is scary to think the greatest scouting report ever created and the most well-constructed game plan are completely worthless if players aren't willing to step across the line and play with motivation and passion. Players who believe in the importance of personal sacrifice for the benefit of the team and who develop love and respect for their teammates will win in the ultimate arena of competition. Here are some of the motivational techniques and tactics I have incorporated over the years.

Motivation starts with the head coach. It is imperative for the head coach to establish the standard of excellence for his program through his example. If you want coaches and players to be motivated at a high level, then as head coach you should be the beacon of commitment, leadership, and motivation. You will get out of your program exactly what you put into it. How could you expect coaches and players to be motivated if you are not motivated? Expecting a great deal from yourself as head coach will allow you to expect a great deal from those around you.

The head coach should constantly exude composure and confidence. During tough times everyone on the team will look to the head coach for answers and guidance. If you want your organization focused and composed, then you must be the ultimate leader by example.

You cannot motivate a player if you do not see him and spend time with him. As the head coach, make sure that you are there for your staff and players. As we discussed at the beginning of the chapter, motivation is a one-on-one proposition. You can set goals for the team, but you must motivate individuals.

Live by your priorities. Consistency is established when everyone in the program bases their decisions and actions on the program's priorities. When everyone in your program is striving for the same worthy cause, they will bond in a special way and develop into a motivated squad with common goals and ideals. Surround yourself with players and coaches who want to live by these principles and priorities. When a group of people pull on the same end of the rope, motivation will grow and so will production and unity. However, if someone is pulling on the opposite end of the rope because his priorities are out of order or out of balance, it will be difficult for him to develop into a motivated football player or coach.

Player and staff motivation begins with the head coach. Be confident and focused. Lead by example.

Be thoroughly organized and prepared. Organization develops confidence and boldness; being unprepared and disorganized leads to dissension and sluggishness. Structure and the ability to develop structure for your program are great motivating tools. Many coaches and players learn and work at a much more productive level in a structured environment, and most successful head coaches are great organizers. It is much safer and easier to begin the season too structured than to begin the season too loose and then try to get organized. You can always loosen up when the organization learns what you expect of them and they become more self-sufficient.

Work hard in a focused direction. I am always looking for better, more efficient ways to do things, but it is very important to remember that there is no substitute for hard work. When everyone in your organiza-

tion rolls up his sleeves and puts on his work boots, a bond develops. The members of your program are working for a common cause. Players and coaches understand that they are important to the project and the success of the organization depends on their effort and improvement. Hard work and diligence are great motivational tools. Establish clear-cut expectations and goals and work hard each day to accomplish them.

Build close, sincere relationships with players. Sincere concern and love are great motivators. If your players believe that you have their best interests in mind, they will respect you and do everything in their power not to let you or the program down. If they feel like you are using them to win games or for personal gain, the bonding and mutual respect will not develop, and your team will be in danger of crumbling under the least bit of pressure or during hard times.

Coach's Keys: Motivating

1. Motivation begins with the head coach. Be the beacon of light for your program.
2. Build close personal relationships with players. Let them know how much you love and care for them.
3. Make the hard work enjoyable.
4. Develop lofty personal and team goals and evaluate them often.
5. Develop a sense of ownership in your program by listening to your players and coaches.
6. Be well organized and use structure to create an efficient and productive learning environment.
7. Avoid complacency by focusing on performance and not just victory.
8. Make effort a constant in your program.
9. Always be positive and find reasons to praise players.

Establish lofty, well-defined goals and evaluate them often. Develop a great plan and work hard to achieve it. I encourage coaches to establish daily goals to accomplish with their players. We also establish lofty, team-oriented goals. A goal can be something simple, such as improving a stance or developing eye–hand coordination, as long as it will improve the team and have an outcome that can be evaluated. These goals are like a carrot in front of a rabbit and a rabbit in front of a dog. They are simple in scope, but powerful motivators when used correctly. Once a skill or play is learned and perfected, we develop another carrot. An individual will never give up or quit unless he feels he cannot be successful. All individuals must feel that they will eventually achieve their goals or they will quit.

Each off-season, we meet individually with each player. Together we develop personal goals that include body weight, strength, conditioning, faith development, family development, and academic performance. We touch on all four priorities and make sure the athlete understands why we prioritize them the way we do. We clearly explain what we hope each player can accomplish and put the players and the coaches on the same page. These personal meetings further reinforce the value we have for players and enhance the player's feeling of value and ownership to the program. It's a huge part of developing the close, personal relationships you need with players.

I try very hard to point team goals in the direction of performance and not victory. After all, if your team plays its best and still doesn't score enough points to win the game, have they been unsuccessful? Team goals motivate the whole program. Each season our team goals include having no off-the-field altercations or distractions that are detrimental to the team. In other words, put the team ahead of yourself and make something special out of this group of people. Again, keep priorities in the proper order. By allowing players to develop and commit to these goals, you have made great motivational strides for the team.

The tradition of excellence at Jenks that we have been blessed to be a part of has led us to make winning the state championship one of our annual team goals. We used to include conference and district championships as well; however, during three separate seasons we were unable to win our conference but played well during the playoffs and won the championship. Now we simply want to win the last game of the season because if we accomplish that goal, we know we will have accomplished our biggest team goal.

Make hard work and preparation enjoyable. Because I am aware of the dangers of letting practices become boring, my coaches and I constantly look for ways to implement enthusiasm and fun in the practice schedule. Our purpose is much too important not to take advantage of great practice sessions. Coaches need to remind players of the importance of developing their skills to the highest level and how beneficial each member of the squad is to the team. The satisfaction in knowing that you have improved as a player and as a team makes working hard enjoyable and fulfilling. Be aware of your team's practice personality.

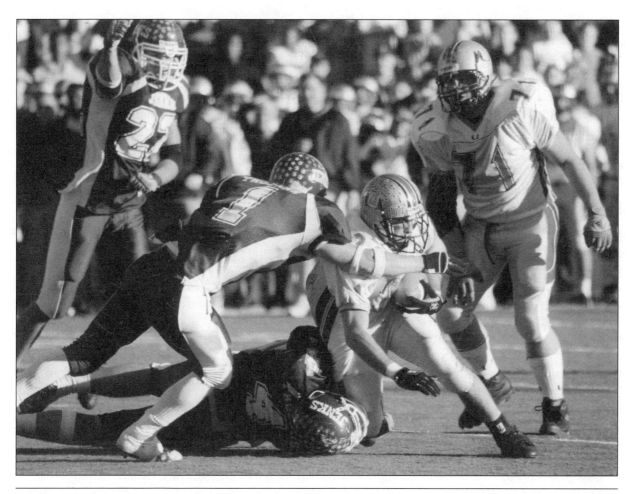

Helmet stickers reward players for meeting on-the-field, and off-the-field, goals.

Are they upbeat and enthused or burnt out and mentally tired?

Praise your players and be positive. When developing and motivating players and teams, it is important to praise them when they do something well. We are all professionals at pointing out mistakes. But if we are not careful, we focus too much on the negative and ignore the positive. When times are tough or when a young team is developing, find any good action, pat your players on the back, and tell them you are happy with their performance. Something as simple as making a good block or tackle can merit a big "atta boy!" I constantly remind players that winning and losing do not define them as people. Effort and attitude are far more important than the scoreboard, and there will be times when our best simply isn't good enough to win the game. We give out several player-of-

the-week awards at our weekly team dinners to make sure we recognize great effort and attitudes.

During the season we distribute helmet stickers for reaching offensive, defensive, and special teams goals during the game each week. They are great motivational tools because players look forward to weekly evaluations and sticker distribution. I also give out helmet stickers for good grades. We monitor class progress through weekly grade checks throughout the season and give stickers to players who have As and Bs. It's a small but effective way to motivate players in the classroom.

We partnered with a local pizza restaurant to give out a free pizza buffet to the players of the game each week. It's amazing what players will try to accomplish for a trip to the all-you-can-eat pizza place.

During off-season training periods, athletes are awarded T-shirts for lifting performance based on three testing dates. The three players who show the greatest improvement by position are awarded a dominator T-shirt. We also proudly post the improvement results of every team member on the bulletin board. Motivation during the off-season is vital.

Victory is nice, but performance is the key. When things are going well and your team is playing at a high level and winning games, it is easy to think that because you are winning you are playing well. I know this sounds crazy, but we constantly remind our great teams that winning doesn't necessarily mean they are playing their best. It is frustrating and disappointing to wait until you have been beaten to realize that you could have been making improvements. Winning can make players and coaches satisfied and complacent, so remember to distinguish between winning and performance. Performance evaluation can be a great motivator.

Make great effort a constant. We emphasize great effort in all areas of our program. We preach it, teach it, and practice it. We spend a great deal of time in the off-season, preseason, and early season coaching and evaluating effort. We post a performance index each week on the team board that shows each player's effort for each play of the game. This score does not include alignment, technique, or production, it just evaluates whether or not the athlete gave championship effort. This has become a great motivating tool because each player strives to maintain the highest index he possibly can.

Make sure players and coaches understand that it is "our" team, not "my" team. Listen to your players and assistant coaches. I understand that as head coach I am responsible for all aspects of the program, but developing a sense of ownership among players and coaches is a vital motivational tool. Paint a picture for everyone that we are all in this together and that your number one priority is the success of everyone involved in the program. If you listen to the team and the coaches, they will understand the significant role they play in the success of the organization.

CHAPTER 3

BUILDING AND MAINTAINING A PROGRAM

In the first two chapters we covered some of the most important factors in building a football program. Building a program on a firm foundation based on maintaining the four priorities is a must. Establishing a vision, purpose, and mission statement to ignite your passion for your profession is vital when embarking on a project as broad in scope as building and maintaining a football program.

The difficulty in presenting a separate chapter on building a football program is the diversity of conditions and factors that affect program development. Every school, community, school administration, athlete, assistant coach, and budget is different, and the thoughts about, plans for, and methods of building a program are unique to each environment. Things that work at Jenks may not fit the needs of another program and vice versa. In this chapter I discuss the most important areas of program building and some of the ideas and techniques I have applied in the building process at Jenks.

When I got the job at Jenks, the program was in great condition except for the rubble

left behind from the firestorm that occurred when the previous head coach was removed. Assistant coaches were in limbo, the community was on pins and needles, and the players were concerned about the coaching change. With a solid background in the philosophy of education, I knew my main objectives at Jenks were to mend the fences that had been torn down with the administration and to convince parents, faculty, administration, community, and players that a rookie coach could pilot the ship by winning their trust and confidence. With these objectives in mind, the other coaches and I put together a plan and rolled up our sleeves and went to work. Eight years and seven state championships later our sleeves are still rolled up and we are still building the tradition known as Jenks Trojan football. Jenks football teams won a lot of games before I showed up, and they will win a lot of games after I am long gone. I'm just honored that God has blessed me with being a small part of such a great tradition. I'll share with you some important components for laying out the blueprints of a successful program.

The desire to build a successful organization must surround your football program from top to bottom or the likelihood of building a consistent program will be small. I am blessed to be served by a school board that establishes lofty expectations for all academic and athletic programs. Their decisions are student driven: They want all kids to be successful in whatever they choose to do and are willing to support programs as much as the budget will allow.

The school board also understands the advantage of having a successful football program within the community. A successful football program raises the spirit and expectations of everyone in the school and community and unites an already proud institution. At Jenks, the community support is phenomenal, and not just for football.

A school-bond proposal has never failed to pass when voted on during or after a successful football season. The financial rewards of having a successful football program are very important today when government funding for schools has been reduced in some states. The revenue generated from our football program supports other sports and other programs including Fellowship of Christian Athletes (FCA) and Special Olympics. The list of positive things that result from a successful football program could probably be another chapter in this book. Having a school board and administration that realize the positives and support the program is vital when building a program. If the expectations and support are not present, the odds of building a successful program are slim.

While talking about expectations, beware of institutions with unrealistic expectations. Expectations must be consistent with the talent and other related resources available. The school board and administration must understand that certain schools have a talent level that wouldn't allow Paul "Bear" Bryant to be successful. Make sure your school board and administrators have realistic expectations that consider your talent level, your opponent's talent level, and other factors that may affect the program-building process.

Coach's Keys

1. Make sure the expectations of your institution are high but realistic.

2. Be creative in developing ways to attract players to your program. You need good numbers to ensure program growth and improvement.

3. Have a highly structured off-season workout program for all ages.

4. Organize a booster club and use it to acquire the special things your players and program need. Surround yourself with great people who will be ambassadors for your program.

5. Develop your coaching staff and put them in position to be great teachers. A united staff is a powerful resource.

6. Create a winning environment by finding small successes and bringing them to light with praise. Preach and teach teamwork, effort, and unity.

7. Build a tradition by developing a high level of consistency through teamwork and effort.

PLAYER DEVELOPMENT AND PARTICIPATION

For the most part, you have to play the hand you're dealt when it comes to players in your system. You cannot go out and recruit players, so you must do a great job getting potential athletes interested in playing football in your system, and you must develop the skills that players already possess.

I am active in our youth football program and try to be as visible as possible to young Jenks Trojans. We organize coaching clinics for youth coaches to introduce them to our systems of offense and defense and to let them know that they are a crucial part of our football program's development. At one time or another, 90 percent of our seniors at Jenks played youth football in our system. I fully understand the importance of player development at a young age.

We also organize several player camps for youth football organizations. We make sure to have plenty of our most popular varsity players work the camps so that the young boys are exposed to their heroes and role models. For many young players, camp is a life-changing experience and they want to grow up and be just like their favorite Jenks Trojan player.

I also select our most popular players and schedule student body meetings at all of our intermediate and middle schools to encourage participation in our program. I present all of the summer camp opportunities and allow our varsity players to talk about the program and let the potential players understand how special it is to be a Jenks Trojan.

My philosophy has always been to promote participation more than competition throughout a young football player's career. Walking away from a fourth-grade football season with a great love for the game of football is priceless. Walking away from the same game distraught or frustrated can turn a young man away from the sport forever. We try to maintain the most positive environment possible for youth players, easing them into the competitive phase during seventh and eighth grade. By the time they are freshmen, they are ready to compete and win.

Our numbers have increased so much at the eighth- and ninth-grade levels that we split each school from one team into two equal teams to increase player participation. The talent level and number of players allowed us to field two equally competitive teams, and we went from 30 players to nearly 60 players getting on the field. This strategy enhanced our individual class sizes greatly and kept several players in the program longer.

Make sure you have the numbers and talent to field competitive teams. Lack of competitiveness can lead to negative attitudes and outcomes because players won't believe they can win. I allow the eighth- and ninth-grade coaches to simply practice their players for a couple of weeks and then draft their two teams just like in the NFL. This allows the coaches who are the most familiar with the players to put them in the best position to be successful.

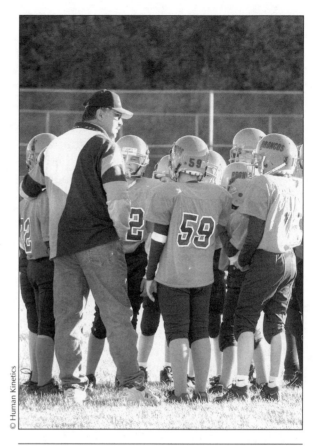

© Human Kinetics

Youth football programs should focus on participation rather than competition. Involvement in youth football provides opportunities for you to advertise your program to the young men who may one day make up your roster.

At the sophomore and junior varsity level, get your players on the field against high-quality competition. We have both a sophomore and a junior varsity schedule to ensure that our younger, developing players get the enjoyment and competition they need to keep working hard and improving. Their practice duties usually involve going up against older, better players, so any chance we have to put them on the field against players in jerseys of another color, we do it.

When dividing the sophomore and junior varsity roster, pay careful attention to placing kids within their proper talent levels so that they have a chance to compete and improve. It does no one any good to stack a junior varsity team against a lesser sophomore team and smash them. Match up players and place them in the proper competitive environment.

Another aspect of participation and development you must consider is building depth on your team. It takes a conscientious effort to evaluate and prepare younger players to be game ready when the opportunity arises. Find ways to get second-level players valuable game reps from time to time; they are one sprained ankle or academic mishap away from playing for you. Getting that taste of playing time can spur a player's career and development. Plan carefully and be ready to substitute developmental players into game situations that will develop their skills and their confidence for the future when you will need them.

In my eight seasons as head coach, we have graduated as few as 24 seniors to as many as 32. Attrition is a part of competitive sports. When players realize the amount of dedication and work it takes to be a varsity player, some are simply not willing to make a commitment that big. As coaches, we should do everything in our power to dangle the carrot in front of the rabbit and give players hope and encouragement to stick it out. The ability to work hard and dedicate yourself to a team project is a valuable life lesson we teach young men and one that will greatly assist them in their adult lives.

Physical development is also crucial to program growth and success. Because we must play the hand we are dealt and can't recruit players to fit our system, we must develop them. Our strength and speed development program is available to all players in grades 1 through 12 during the off-season and throughout the summer. Younger players are simply taught the techniques and fundamentals of running and lifting; their intensity and skill level increases from year to year. By the time players are in ninth grade, they are able to do the same workouts that varsity players do.

Players develop physically at different rates, so be patient and encourage them to be diligent and stick it out. Many times I've seen athletes stick it out long enough to become the most consistent team players on the field because playing means a lot to them and they have sacrificed to get on the field.

A Late Bloomer

Andrew Spankuch is a great example of a late bloomer. As a sophomore, he was so clumsy and nonathletic that we had to protect him in practice because he could not protect himself during full-contact drills. He simply was awful—no balance, feet, or ability of any kind.

Andrew was an intelligent kid who was respectful and appreciative of the opportunity to be in the program, but he became frustrated and discouraged when the reality of his lack of ability hit him. One afternoon he came into my office to quit the team and pursue his academic career. For a minute, I thought about telling him he was making the right decision and wishing him luck and sending him on his way, but after mentally reviewing my philosophy and purpose I asked Andrew to stay with us and be our manager and filmer. I knew he was trustworthy and a hard worker and wanted to be a Trojan very badly; he was just being realistic about his ability.

Andrew agreed and did a great job with his filming and managing responsibilities. After the season ended, Andrew came into my office and wanted to give football another chance. I welcomed him back after discussing the areas he had to work on to have a chance to get on the field in the fall. Andrew went to work and made great strides during the off-season. Genetics kicked in; he gained about 30 pounds and grew about 4 inches. He was still a little clumsy, but certainly much improved. Unfortunately, Andrew blew out his knee in a full-contact practice early in the season and missed his second season of football.

Even though he was very disappointed, he continued his rehabilitation and weight training every day and was bound and determined to win a spot in his final season as a Trojan. Another two inches and another 30 pounds and Andrew Spankuch had developed into a young man and a big football player at nearly 6 feet, 4 inches tall and 240 pounds. Andrew won the starting job at left guard and was voted offensive lineman of the year at our state championship banquet. He signed his letter of intent and now attends Southeastern State University and plays center. Andrew is a perfect example of never giving up and keeping an eye on the prize.

The physical benefits of off-season training are obvious, especially for athletes who are willing to spend all four years working out with us. Those skinny little eighth and ninth graders eventually become big, strong, confident seniors.

Equally important to the physical development of athletes is their mental development. Players who dedicate themselves to the weight training and running regimen throughout the off-season and summer gain a sense of pride from working with their teammates. Giving up free time and summer time to train for football is the best team-building tool I have found. Going through the tough times together with their coaches is a time of bonding, a way to collect chips that can be cashed in during the fall when the going gets tough. Have a well organized off-season training program.

COMMUNITY SUPPORT

If they are for you, they are not against you. I take this idea seriously when striving for success. Gain support for your program by becoming an integral part of your school and community.

Establish a football booster club under the parameters of making the football program better and forming an organization for the promotion of the football program in all areas of the community. The booster club is made up of people from all walks of life who work and live in the community. What better way to promote and build a program than with people who work hard to make the program better on a daily basis? They are the ambassadors of your program.

Our booster club provides extras that make a big difference in the attitude and approach of players and coaches. Team dinners and specialized equipment, you name it, and we

Strong community support is a vital part of any successful football program.

can get it if it will help our program improve and will benefit our kids.

As the head coach, be sure to build a strong working relationship between the booster club and the athletic department. Some projects will be large enough to need both athletic and booster club money. The athletic department should always provide the basic necessities for a program, while the booster club should strive to provide items over and above the norm that will make players feel special.

COACH DEVELOPMENT

It's not my program, it's our program. Surround yourself with coaches who have the same principle-based philosophy and expectation level you require of yourself. Attitude and work ethic give you a chance to excel in coaching because knowledge of the game and teaching methods can be learned.

Let coaches know what you expect of them, and they will improve. Now that I am the head coach, I coach coaches and encourage them to lead with their personalities and use their own strengths when teaching. I have never tied my coaches' hands. However, I do expect our philosophies and principles to be the same. Unity leads to strength and loyalty, which are vital to program development. A unified staff is a powerful teaching unit. Players witness a living example of teamwork and unity and follow right along.

You will learn a lot about each staff member after the first day of practice. Are they organized, assertive, and upbeat? Find specific areas that coaches can improve and teach them how to improve. Are their teaching methods producing the results you want? If not, offer other ideas and methods and reevaluate. Unfortunately, some coaches will not make the grade, and you will have to dismiss them. This is the worst part of my job as head coach. However as with all decisions I make, I do what is best for the program. No one wants to fire someone, but sometimes removing a coach is simply what is best for the program, and you must make the change.

WINNING ENVIRONMENT

Teaching players how to win is what coaching is all about. Begin by teaching teamwork. Practice teamwork, teach teamwork, talk about teamwork, and show players how playing as a team with everyone executing their individual roles makes the team better than any one player can be. Search practice and game film and find examples of players making great plays. Praise them in front of the team, give awards, and brag about them. Even the smallest hints of teamwork should be brought to the front and reported. Players will begin to take pride in the team and start molding themselves into a unit.

Take every opportunity to sell your coaches to the players and sell your offensive and defensive systems and special teams plays. Players will come to believe in your system and the coaches who teach them. Their confidence and faith in the overall system will grow and so will their efforts to build the team. Pat your players and coaches on the back when they do something well. With praise comes confidence and loyalty, and with confidence and loyalty come commitment, and with commitment comes great effort.

Effort is the heartbeat of any successful program. Everyone can give his best effort no matter how much or how little ability he has. Start with a simple pursuit drill that lasts only five seconds and work up. Place your players in position to give their all-out best effort for five seconds. This may take a day or a week or a month, but no matter how long it takes, do not waver from your demand of their best effort. Once the team can go hard for a five-second interval, add another interval or two and start building their mental toughness by demanding great effort through every exercise and drill. Coach it and demand it. Without effort, your team will never succeed at a high level.

At the University of Nebraska, every member of the varsity defensive unit received a black jersey to signify the hard work and pride of the defensive unit. When the players

A winning environment begins with teamwork. Practice it, teach it, and make your players believe in it.

put on their jerseys, they knew they were part of something much bigger than themselves. They played with all their hearts to ensure the success of their team. I encourage our coaches to give nicknames and special shirts for different teams within the program. For the past few years, our defense has adopted the name the Wolf Pack, and each member wears a special T-shirt to signify his pride and pursuit of excellence.

With the help of the booster club, I started another tradition to award seniors their jerseys at the football banquet each winter. It's a small gift, but is significant. The players who choose to stick with our football program and make it better get to take their jerseys with them. It means a lot to the players and helps them remember the dedication, pride, and hard work it takes to be a Jenks Trojan.

One thing I can say about our program at Jenks is that when a team plays us, they are in for a battle. We may not win every contest, but our opponents will have to play very, very well to beat us. This is part of a great tradition, the idea that when you play our team you will have to play your best or lose. The consistency that comes from executing a system that every player, coach, and fan believes in is like having a 12th man on the field. Every time we take the field we believe that we will win the game no matter who the opponent is. This is the definition of tradition. It takes years of building and winning to reach this position, but with continued focus and direction you can achieve a proud tradition.

PART II ORGANIZATION

CHAPTER 4

PREPARING FOR THE SEASON

A well-conceived, well-organized plan is just as important as offensive and defensive playbooks. This chapter addresses many areas requiring written plans for structuring and organizing a football program. Well-structured planning and organization allows you and your coaching staff to focus on the important tasks of coaching football while taking away last-minute crises that can disable the most well-thought-out game plan.

In this chapter we discuss strategy and management ideas related to equipment; medical and rehabilitation staff and services; physical conditioning and preparation; scheduling; travel; staff planning of roles, responsibilities, and expectations; and personnel planning, placement, and recruitment.

EQUIPMENT

Player safety and health must be a major concern in your program because you have a limited number of top-notch players to help the program succeed. Injuries are a part of football, but you cannot afford to take short-

cuts when it comes to protecting players with the best equipment available.

At Jenks, we build into our annual equipment budget enough money to provide our top-30 athletes the best equipment available. Your resources may allow for more or less top-rate equipment. The rest of the squad is equipped with the same type of equipment, but it is a year older. We do not want to lose a player to a preventable situation.

Helmets and shoulder pads are the two most expensive items and the two most important pieces of equipment you can supply players. Most quality helmets range from $120 to $170 each, depending on the additions you install. Shoulder pads have a broader price range, but upper-end pads cost $150 and up to $250 for custom-color, air-management systems. Budget about $350 per varsity player for new helmets and shoulder pads. Remember, these are the two most important pieces of safety equipment you can provide players, so avoid shortcuts in these areas.

I keep on hand a lot of high-quality practice clothes and game clothes at all times. We have a woman who sews and maintains our repairable jerseys and pants throughout the season to ensure that we get the most mileage possible out of our clothing. Practice jerseys and pants are relatively inexpensive, so we try to purchase enough practice clothes each year to replace clothing that is worn out. The best time to buy new clothing is immediately after the playoff season; manufacturer discounts are highest from December through January. We generally try to use game uniforms for two full seasons if possible. Artificial grass surfaces seem to allow uniforms to last longer. Game uniforms vary greatly in price and quality, but my experience has been that you get what you pay for. Budget approximately $120 per player for new game pants and jerseys. Remember, the broad price range in game uniforms allows you to be flexible from year to year and spend as your budget allows. We generally spend a little more money on our game gear, and in my opinion this practice has been well worth the money.

Game and practice shoes are important equipment, especially on artificial field surfaces and during games in wet weather. I want players to have the best shoes for the conditions they play in. Nothing is more paralyzing and frustrating than letting a preventable shoe problem hinder a player's performance. Because we practice on artificial turf, we encourage players to have practice cleats, usually an inexpensive rubber, molded cleat. This type of shoe is easy on the feet and provides above-average performance but is not overly sticky and is somewhat forgiving in the injury department. Players are equipped with three types of game shoes to counter various weather conditions and field composition. Shoes for wet turf and dry turf are included for artificial fields, and shoes with aggressive screw-in cleats in a variety of lengths to match field conditions are usually the choice for natural grass. Because each player's feet and needs are unique, we try to be as flexible as possible and allow players to choose and wear the shoes they are most comfortable in. We are fortunate to have a deal with a major shoe company that has numerous shoe styles that work well for us. Each fall their repre-

sentative and our equipment manager size all players. Players try many styles and choose the ones that will allow them to perform their best in the upcoming season. Practice shoes are relatively inexpensive, but game cleats range from $60 to $120 depending on the features and styles.

Soft equipment such as footballs, chin straps, thigh and knee pads, belts, shoestrings, and hardware such as helmet snaps, face masks, rib pads, and eye shields are all important, but are relatively inexpensive compared to the helmets, shoulder pads, and shoes. Make sure you have a complete inventory of these small, but important, pieces of equipment so that players will never lose game reps because of equipment replacement issues.

You know approximately how many players will suit out for practice, so calculate your equipment budget accordingly. Have your equipment manager or assistant coach take inventory of the equipment in stock that is of acceptable quality and discard the rest. Once you have enough equipment for each player, your annual equipment budget should remain fairly consistent. During years in which you need to make major purchases, such as new game uniforms and a new blocking sled, that go well above your annual budget, look to your boosters and other fund-raising techniques to reduce the burden on your athletic department. If your institution and community are interested in building and maintaining a championship program, they will find a way to finance it.

Blocking and tackling dummies, sleds, quarterback nets, and other specialized equipment are all important for teaching players various football techniques, but most are very expensive. One option is to find a great welder and craftsman at your school who can build exactly what you need for a fraction of the cost. Custom-built equipment made by someone who is a loyal fan is the best equipment you can buy. The other specialized equipment you need must be researched carefully and put out for bid to reduce the cost as much as possible.

Coach's Keys

1. Don't take shortcuts on helmets or shoulder pads. They are the most important pieces of equipment you can buy. Buy clothes in the winter to get the best prices. Make sure you have the right shoes for the conditions.

2. Clearly define the roles, responsibilities, and expectations of every member of your staff. Use a duty sheet, have staff members volunteer for the areas they want, then assign the rest. Planning and organizing start with the head coach.

3. Focus on the journey. Schedule competitively. Remember, mentally and physically healthy teams have a chance to win; mentally and physically injured teams don't. Always keep your team's best interests in mind.

4. A great off-season conditioning program will make the greatest impact on your team. Great conditioning prevents injuries and builds pride and unity that can be used during the season.

5. Track each player's academic progress and NCAA qualifications and make plans for each player to be recruitable. The final decision when choosing a school must come from the player, but be there for him when he needs your assistance.

MEDICAL AND REHABILITATION SERVICES

Even the greatest conditioning program and the finest equipment cannot overcome the violence and wear and tear of the game of football. Injuries are inevitable, so plan on them. The key is a well-planned, coordinated system that includes prevention, maintenance, and rehabilitation of injuries that range from a bad blister to major joint surgery, fractures, and concussions.

All members of our coaching staff are required to take a course in care and prevention of athletic injuries. We are blessed with the greatest training and medical staff anywhere, but a firm foundation in injury care and prevention is important for all members of your staff who deal directly with players. Coaches and staff members are able to make better decisions when they are educated about injuries and how to care for and prevent them.

Other ideas to consider while discussing medical and rehabilitation services are having a defibrillator on hand at all practices and games and having members of your staff certified in CPR. None of us think a heart problem will happen on our watch, but every week a defibrillator or properly applied CPR saves the life of a player or coach. I strongly encourage including a defibrillator in your medical supply kit at all times.

We are fortunate at Jenks to have a sports medicine budget separate from our football budget. Whether or not your sports medicine supplies come from a separate budget or from your football budget, do not take shortcuts and compromise the care and treatment of players. Have your sports medicine staff maintain an accurate inventory of medical supplies and keep supplies replenished and up to date. Include plenty of tape, support wraps, ice bags, bandages, and gauze pads along with blister ointment, antibiotic ointment, and a good warm-up rub such as Flexall or Icy Hot. The use of heat and ice to assist circulation and healing are vital for players, so make sure you have hot and cold tubs and ways to apply hot and cold treatments. Other supplies to consider are good scissors, tape cutters, and emergency face mask removal tools. Care and prevention of injuries are vital to your program's success, so do not take shortcuts in this area.

The sports medicine staff is the lifeline of any football program. The bottom line is getting players back on their feet and back on the field as soon as possible. A capable sports medicine staff allows you and your assistants to coach football and make injury substitutions based on professional medical advice and not gut feelings. In today's world, record keeping and keeping the athlete's best interest in mind are important and even further validate the necessity of having a solid sports medicine staff.

Another important factor in developing and planning your sports medicine staff is to remember that the head trainer and sports medicine staff are members of your coaching team just like your assistant coaches are. The thoughts and ideas of the sports medicine staff must be in harmony with your program's mission and purpose, or team dynamics can be affected.

Handling practice and game emergencies is another responsibility of the sports medicine staff. We have a team of trainers and assistant trainers on hand at every practice session to not only maintain the general care of our players but also to ensure immediate care of severe injuries.

Central States Orthopedics has sponsored our football program for several years. Their organization has made a tremendous difference in the success of our program with their exceptional care of our players over the years. Their group assigns a team of orthopedic specialists to every game, both at home and on the road. Their expertise and sincerity toward our program have helped hundreds of players recover from injuries of all kinds. Be diligent and locate an orthopedic group that will go the extra mile with your program; this will provide your program and players a very valuable service.

Injuries in football are inevitable. Be prepared with a strong sports medicine staff equipped to handle everything from blisters to more serious injuries such as fractures and concussions.

Another area of medicine that has benefited our program is our acquisition of a team chiropractor. Dr. Paul Harris has dedicated his time to our football program for many seasons and has made a positive impact on the treatment and maintenance of our players. Certainly there are injuries that must receive medical attention, but realignment and chiropractic treatment can provide immediate improvement in athletic performance for many football-related injuries. If you have a good chiropractor who is willing to assist your football program, bring him on staff to assist the sports medicine team with injury management.

The ability of the coaching staff, sports medicine staff, chiropractors, and team doctors to work together is a powerful tool that will ensure that your football players reach and maintain their potential. Schedule a preseason meeting with all parties and reinforce the staff mission and purpose to ensure that everyone agrees on procedures for injury care and prevention.

Our school and state association require all athletes to receive a thorough physical examination by a medical doctor before participating in football. Our head trainer arranges a date late in the summer for this exam. We assemble a group of orthopedic surgeons, family doctors, and nurses to accomplish this task at the same site on the same day with every player on our roster.

Players should be screened thoroughly by doctors who specialize in athletic injuries. I want the peace of mind of knowing that players are healthy and ready for the rigorous demands of the upcoming season. Orthopedic doctors check all joints and skeletal components for problems and report to our training staff situations that must be addressed. Doctors check vision, hearing, respiration, pulse, and blood pressure and look for potential problems. If questions arise during the screening process, the player is immediately referred to a specialist for further evaluation or treatment. At the conclusion of the physical exams, the head trainer compiles a list of players who need attention and the areas of concern and then formulates a maintenance or rehabilitation plan for each athlete.

What better way to prevent, maintain, and rehabilitate players than to have a complete physical exam for every player before fall camp ever begins? Modern sports medicine has come far, and its ability to assist players is vital to the success of a program; make sure you have a thorough evaluation of every player and a maintenance and rehabilitation plan before the season begins. It provides the peace of mind every coach needs before pushing players to their limit each day in the summer heat.

I also recommend the same physical examination and evaluation for all coaches and staff members. Coaching football is a mentally and physically demanding profession that can consume even the most focused man, leading to several health problems if care is not taken to prevent them. As the saying goes, if you have five days to cut down a big tree, spend four days sharpening your ax. Maintaining your mental and physical health is vital to your family and your profession, so have your own plan for maintenance and rehabilitation.

PLAYER STRENGTH AND CONDITIONING

Players are expected to report to fall camp in midseason condition, so we implement a year-round athletic enhancement program for players. If we have to sacrifice football practice time to make up for poor conditioning, we will not be a very good football team, and the percentage of injuries related to poor conditioning will dramatically increase. Poor conditioning makes cowards out of the most talented players, while great conditioning makes warriors out of players of any ability.

To accomplish this high level of conditioning, the athletic enhancement program is a year-round training regimen divided into several phases. The off-season phase begins immediately after the playoffs and continues until spring drills. The off-season phase addresses the general strength and conditioning needs of the team as well as the individual needs of each player. Linemen may be too big or too little; linebackers may need more agility, explosion, or size. Whatever the postseason evaluation determines, we attempt to address it in the off-season.

The spring football phase is still goal driven with an exception made for the intense on-field spring practice schedule. The spring ball phase features moderate aerobic activity and is four weeks long with 20 workouts over the four-week period. In this phase, the focus is on maintaining muscular strength and endurance. The number of heavy weight room workouts is reduced to ensure that athletes can perform at a high level on the practice field. At the end of the spring football phase, athletes are evaluated again. Results for the bench press, squat, power clean, vertical leap, pro agility test, and 40-yard dash are recorded and compared to off-season data to ensure that athletes are improving.

Preseason training or summer training is the most intense phase of the program. We want players not only improving their conditioning but also their speed, agility, flexibility, and strength. Strength, conditioning, and speed workouts are run four days a week during this phase. Coaches must make sure that athletes adhere to strict nutrition, hydration, and resting guidelines to gain the maximum benefit of the preseason workouts. Preseason training ends approximately one week before fall practices to allow players to mentally and physically regroup for the beginning of the season.

The first phase of preseason training is the hypertrophy phase (table 4.1). This phase features minimal aerobic activity and is six weeks long with four workouts per week. The objective of this training phase is to increase muscular strength, endurance, and development. Muscles, ligaments, and tendons are conditioned through different resistance exercises. Each workout begins with agility drills that provide a dynamic warm-up followed by passive stretches. The amount of weight used for the strength exercises is low to moderate, and 8 to 12 repetitions of each exercise are completed.

The second phase of preseason training is the strength phase (table 4.2). This phase features moderate aerobic activity and is four weeks long with four workouts per week. The main objective is to increase muscular strength through various resistance exercises. Submaximal weight is used for exercises and three to five repetitions are executed. Stretch bands are used to create eccentric overload and work a full range of motion. Sprints, sled drags, and plyometric exercises are added to increase the athlete's power output.

The third phase of preseason training is the power phase (table 4.3). This phase features moderate aerobic activity and is four weeks long with four workouts per week. The objective of this phase is to increase the speed and force of muscle contractions in order to increase power. This phase is centered around core (total-body) movements that are football specific. Moderate intensity is used for weight exercises, and five to eight repetitions are completed. Stability balls, balance disks, medicine balls, and weeble boards are used to condition core stability and balance.

The in-season training phase begins immediately after the first week of fall camp. Athletes are allowed to adjust to the intensity and preliminary soreness of fall drills before beginning the in-season training phase. During in-season training, all linemen and power players lift weights three days a week, and all skill players lift weights two days a week. Conditioning drills are accomplished each Monday, while speed development and enhancement drills are completed on Wednesdays after practice. Just like the other phases, in-season training is constantly monitored and adjusted to ensure that players are performing at their highest level.

Our conditioning program makes an enormous impact on the team's performance for several reasons. First, player injuries have been drastically reduced since we implemented a year-round athletic enhancement program. Second, players develop a great deal of pride and unity by sacrificing their effort and time to ensure that the team succeeds. Finally, the team is always as conditioned, strong, and fast as the teams we play, which lets players and coaches know that we always have a chance to succeed.

Table 4.1 Hypertrophy Phase of Summer Training

	Monday			
	Set 1	**Set 2**	**Set 3**	**Set 4**
Bench press	10 reps at 40% 1RM*	10 reps at 70% 1RM	8 reps at 75% 1RM	8 reps at 75% 1RM
Hang clean	6 reps at 40% 1RM*	6 reps at 65% 1RM	6 reps at 70% 1RM	6 reps at 75% 1RM
Military press	10 reps at 30% 1RM	8 reps at 40% 1RM	8 reps at 45% 1RM	8 reps at 50% 1RM
Pull-down	12 reps	12 reps	12 reps	
French press	12 reps	12 reps	12 reps	
Front and side raise	12 reps	12 reps		
	12 reps	12 reps		
Face pull	12 reps	12 reps	12 reps	

	Tuesday			
	Set 1	**Set 2**	**Set 3**	**Set 4**
Squat	10 reps at 40% 1RM*	10 reps at 70% 1RM	8 reps at 75% 1RM	8 reps at 75% 1RM
G/H raise	10 reps	10 reps	10 reps	
One-leg squat	8 reps each leg	8 reps each leg	8 reps each leg	
Hypers	12 reps	12 reps	12 reps	
Calf raise	15 reps	15 reps	15 reps	
Lateral duck walk	10 reps	10 reps		
	10 reps	10 reps		
	10 reps	10 reps		
	10 reps	10 reps		
Rollout on ball	6-10 reps	6-10 reps	6-10 reps	

	Thursday			
	Set 1	**Set 2**	**Set 3**	**Set 4**
Incline press	10 reps at 30% 1RM*	6 reps at 60% 1RM	6 reps at 60% 1RM	6 reps at 60% 1RM
Hang snatch	4 reps*	4 reps	4 reps	4 reps
Seated dumbbell military press	10 reps	10 reps		
Bent-over dumb-bell row	16 reps	16 reps	16 reps	
Medicine ball push-up	10 reps or more	10 reps or more	10 reps or more	
Upright row	10 reps	10 reps	10 reps	
Plyo-line push-up	9 reps	9 reps	9 reps	

	Friday			
	Set 1	**Set 2**	**Set 3**	**Set 4**
Front squat	6 reps at 30% 1RM*	6 reps at 50% 1RM	6 reps at 50% 1RM	6 reps at 50% 1RM
Lunge	10 reps each leg	10 reps each leg		
RDL	10 reps (slow)	10 reps (slow)	10 reps (slow)	
Hypers	12 reps	12 reps	12 reps	
Hamstring curl with band	12 reps	12 reps	12 reps	
Overhead squat	5 reps	5 reps	5 reps	
Tuck-in on ball	10 reps	10 reps	10 reps	

* Warm-up exercise.

Table 4.2 Strength Phase of Summer Training

Monday

	Set 1	Set 2	Set 3	Set 4	Set 5
Bench press	8 reps at 45% 1RM*	5 reps at 60% 1RM (bands)	4 reps at 65% 1RM (bands)	3 reps at 70% 1RM (bands)	3 reps at 70% 1RM
Hang clean	6 reps at 45% 1RM*	4 reps at 75% 1RM	4 reps at 80% 1RM	3 reps at 85% 1RM	3 reps at 90% 1RM
Military press	6 reps at 40% 1RM	6 reps at 40% 1RM	5 reps at 50% 1RM	5 reps at 50% 1RM	
Chin-up	10 reps	10 reps	10 reps		
Floor press	10 reps	10 reps	8 reps	8 reps	
Medicine ball push-up	12 reps	12 reps	12 reps		

Tuesday

	Set 1	Set 2	Set 3	Set 4	Set 5
Squat	8 reps at 45% 1RM*	5 reps at 60% 1RM (chains)	4 reps at 65% 1RM (chains)	3 reps at 70% 1RM (chains)	3 reps at 75% 1RM
Legs squats on disk	10 reps	10 reps	8 reps		
Hypers	12 reps	12 reps	12 reps		
G/H raises	8 reps	8 reps	8 reps		
Single-leg calf raise	12 reps	12 reps	12 reps		
Lateral duck walk	40 reps	40 reps			
Rollout on ball	12 reps	12 reps	12 reps		

Thursday

	Set 1	Set 2	Set 3	Set 4
Incline press	8 reps at 40% 1RM*	5 reps at 45% 1RM (chains)	5 reps at 45% 1RM (chains)	4 reps at 50% 1RM (chains)
Hang snatch	4 reps	4 reps	4 reps	4 reps
Dumbbell military press	12 reps	10 reps (add weight)	8 reps (add weight)	
Front and side raise	8 reps 8 reps	8 reps 8 reps	8 reps	8 reps
French press	10 reps	10 reps	8 reps (add 10 lbs)	8 reps (add 10 lbs)
Curl	10 reps	10 reps	8 reps	8 reps

Friday

	Set 1	Set 2	Set 3	Set 4
Front squat	6 reps at 35% 1RM*	5 reps at 55% 1RM	4 reps at 65% 1RM	3 reps at personal best
RDL	10 reps	8 reps	6 reps	4 reps
Calf raise	15 reps	15 reps		
Lunge	8 reps	8 reps	8 reps	
Hypers	12 reps	12 reps	12 reps	
Hamstring curl with bands	12 reps	12 reps	12 reps	
Leg extension	12 reps	12 reps	12 reps	

* Warm-up exercise.

Table 4.3 Power Phase of Summer Training

Monday					
	Set 1	**Set 2**	**Set 3**	**Set 4**	**Set 5**
Squat	10 reps at 40% 1RM*	8 reps at 55% 1RM*	8 reps at 70% 1RM	6 reps at 75% 1RM	5 reps at 80% 1RM
Single-leg squat on disk	8 reps each leg	8 reps each leg	8 reps each leg		
G/H raise	8 reps	8 reps	8 reps		
Calf raise	15 reps	15 reps	15 reps		
Side lunge with medicine ball	8 reps each side	8 reps each side	8 reps each side		
Hip pull with band	10 reps	10 reps	10 reps		

Tuesday					
	Set 1	**Set 2**	**Set 3**	**Set 4**	**Set 5**
Bench press	10 reps at 40% 1RM*	8 reps at 55% 1RM*	8 reps at 70% 1RM	6 reps at 75% 1RM	5 reps at 80% 1RM
Hang clean	6 reps at 40% 1RM*	6 reps at 55% 1RM*	6 reps at 65% 1RM	5 reps at 70% 1RM	5 reps at 75% 1RM
Military press (chains)	10 reps at 30% 1RM*	6 reps (chains)	6 reps (chains)	6 reps (chains)	
Pull-up	12 reps	12 reps	12 reps		
Dip	15 reps	15 reps	15 reps		
Plyo-line push-up	9 reps	9 reps	9 reps		

Thursday					
	Set 1	**Set 2**	**Set 3**	**Set 4**	**Set 5**
Front squat (chains)	6 reps at 30% 1RM*	6 reps at 40% 1RM*	5 reps at 45% (chains)	5 reps at 50% (chains)	5 reps at 50% (chains)
RDL	10 reps	8 reps (add 20 lbs)	8 reps (same weight as set 2)	6 reps (add 20 lbs)	
Single-leg calf raise	10 reps	10 reps	10 reps		
Zott press	10 reps	8 reps (add weight)	6 reps (add weight)	6 reps (same weight as set 3)	
Hypers	12 reps	12 reps	12 reps		
Hamstring curl with band	12 reps	12 reps	12 reps		
Leg extension	15 reps	15 reps	15 reps		

Friday					
	Set 1	**Set 2**	**Set 3**	**Set 4**	**Set 5**
Incline press with band	10 reps at 30% 1RM*	8 reps at 45% 1RM*	5 reps at 50% 1RM (band)	5 reps at 50% 1RM (band)	5 reps at 50% 1RM (band)
Dumbbell military press on disk	8 reps each arm	6 reps each arm	6 reps each arm		
Dumbbell clean	6 reps	6 reps	6 reps		
Shrug	12 reps	12 reps	12 reps		
Front and side raise	12 reps	12 reps	12 reps		
	12 reps	12 reps	12 reps		
French press	12 reps	10 reps (add 10 lbs)	8 reps (add 10 lbs)	6 reps (add 10 lbs)	
Curl	12 reps	12 reps	12 reps		

* Warm-up exercise.

PLAYER EVALUATION AND PLACEMENT

Evaluating a player's athletic ability as well as his attitude, work ethic, and other important factors help coaches motivate and teach him. We dedicate a two-hour meeting before we begin fall meetings and practice to simply discuss and strategize about our players. Each coach on the staff evaluates each player and assigns him a ranking from 1 (most valuable) to 40 (least valuable). Criteria for this evaluation includes player ability, attitude, work ethic, coachability, versatility as a player, and just a little gut feeling from each coach. After every coach ranks each player, the total score is tallied and then ordered from smallest (most valuable) to greatest (least valuable).

This evaluation is a valuable tool. Coaches who know and understand certain players better than other assistants can share motivation and teaching tactics for those players that will help the entire staff get more out of them. Some coaches may have a completely different perspective on players than other coaches, and truthful discussion will lead to a better understanding between coaches and players, leading to improved performance on the field.

GAME SCHEDULE

Most teams are married to a conference and must play a high percentage of their football games against predetermined opponents. Our conference games are the last seven games of the regular season, but our first three ball games are against nonconference opponents.

Preconference opponents need to be chosen carefully. At the beginning of each season every head coach in the nation is giving the same pep talk. Every team is undefeated and has a chance to go one and zero if the first game is a victory. Momentum is huge early in the season, and getting out of the blocks is very important when developing a football team and preparing for a tough conference schedule. I try to schedule first-rate opponents that will help our team improve. I don't want a patsy on the schedule so that we come out of the game feeling overconfident with a false sense of security, but I don't want to schedule the NFL champions either and take a chance of getting crushed by a stronger, more dominant team. I shoot for competitiveness with all things being equal, same classification, enrollment, and ability level.

Work directly with your athletic director and put careful thought into your nonconference schedule. The athletic director's perspective will also include television, radio, season tickets, and other revenue-generating opportunities—all of which are great—but never forget that your job and livelihood depend on program development and success. With program success will come revenue-generating ability, so make sure you schedule with your program's best interests in mind.

Some coaches like to schedule blockbuster games against great teams. These games create a great football environment and test a football program on a national scale. Just remember to focus on making sure your football team is playing the best football possible when playoff time rolls around. Playing a brutal schedule can lead to team improvement provided your team stays both mentally and physically healthy during the season. Often the stress of having to play great each week can take a mental and physical toll on players and coaches. Normally, teams that are healthy and confident perform the best in tough ball games. I believe our 2000 T-shirt said it best when it comes to scheduling philosophy: Focus on the journey. Nobody remembers who was ranked number one in September or October. What really matters is who is ranked number one in December after the championship playoffs. Take every season practice by practice, game by game.

For the most part, players are smart and read the Internet and newspaper daily. They know which teams are supposed to be talented and which are not. I have found it beneficial to present the team with a season overview and plan. I go over the schedule opponent by opponent and reinforce our

Early in the season, every team is looking to get out of the blocks quickly. Schedule preconference games so they will be competitive but won't crush your team's confidence going into the conference schedule.

journey philosophy with players. Weekly improvement and team development are the keys to being ready for conference play and the playoffs. No matter who we play, we will prepare and practice with great effort. Remind players that program success is not measured by opponents and scores, but in daily effort and team improvement. This approach allows for daily goals and evaluation and a chance for your team to reach their full potential.

STAFF PLANNING

There is no substitute for great organization within the coaching and support staff. It should all begin with the head coach. I include every possible responsibility on our staff duty list, define my expectations for each duty, and select a staff member who is capable and willing to perform the task. By clearly defining staff roles, responsibilities, and expectations, you will help staff appreciate each other and take pride in being part of a well-organized, focused unit. I include the following positions in preseason planning and preparation:

- Head coach and assistant coaching staff
- Player strength and conditioning staff
- Sports medicine staff and student trainers
- Team doctors and chiropractic staff
- Equipment managers and student managers
- Statisticians
- Videotaping and editing crew

Coaching Staff

Football has evolved into such a specialized game that selecting and organizing a top-quality group of assistants is vital. The size of a football staff is usually governed by the institution's budget and can vary greatly. We have a nine-man coaching staff. An additional strength coach and our head track coach assist us with the year-round conditioning program and handle the running back responsibilities as well. Our booster club provides the funds to hire these additional vital assistants. However, I have worked on three-man staffs and five-man staffs and still gotten the job done with great planning, organization, and teaching. The bottom line remains that football is a highly specialized game, and the more individualized instruction you can provide players, the better the chance that they will improve.

Figure 4.1 shows the coaching staff broken down into specific positions and hierarchy, based on individual responsibility levels. The offensive coordinator is the quarterbacks coach and the defensive coordinator is the safeties coach. Special teams coaching assignments are established by the special teams coordinator, using the head coach and the remaining assistants in their specific areas of expertise.

Normally, one week before fall camp, I assemble my entire coaching staff for our initial fall camp meeting. A coaching staff must be a well-oiled machine, able to work together in harmony. Therefore, it is vital to discuss staff vision, purpose, and mission. A thorough reminder of our coaching philosophy and expectations will help each staff member's compass return to true north as we prepare for the upcoming practice sessions. I want all my staff members to have equal footing when it comes to ideas and concepts, so our initial meetings are always open to questions and answers to ensure that everyone has their say about fall staff organization and planning.

I prefer to use a duty list and allow my assistant coaches to choose the responsibilities they are comfortable with or want to branch out and try (figure 4.2 shows a sample duty list). I hand out the duty list and go over it, giving my expectations about each assignment, then have each staff member add or delete areas as needed. We begin the next morning's staff meeting by going over the list again and adding names in the proper assignment area. The duties that are not covered I assign to the coaches I feel have the ability to excel in those specific areas. After the list is complete, we finalize the responsibility list with a final question and answer period and then continue the meeting in other areas. I

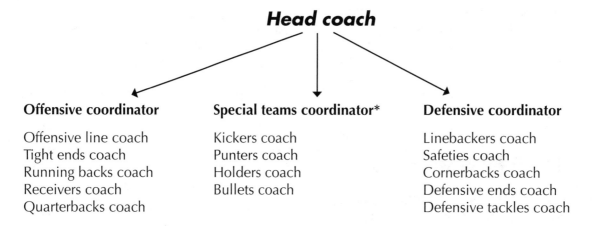

Head coach

Offensive coordinator	**Special teams coordinator***	**Defensive coordinator**
Offensive line coach	Kickers coach	Linebackers coach
Tight ends coach	Punters coach	Safeties coach
Running backs coach	Holders coach	Cornerbacks coach
Receivers coach	Bullets coach	Defensive ends coach
Quarterbacks coach		Defensive tackles coach

* The special teams coordinator assigns special teams coaching duties to all members of the coaching staff.

Figure 4.1 Coaching staff tree.

really stress teamwork to my staff when it comes to handling all the responsibilities of the program. If a coach falls behind in his duties or has a conflict and cannot finish a project, I encourage every staff member to join in and assist each other until the work is done.

Your preseason coaches meeting should also include planning and discussing roles, responsibilities, and expectations of coaches and players in the areas of practice times, locations, and formats; practice field setup and breakdown; in-season lifting and conditioning times; personnel evaluation; video times, locations, and exchanges; practice video schedule; scouting and scouting report generation; transportation; team meals and hospitality; media relations; official statistics reports;

Coaching Responsibilities

Defense		Special teams		Offense	
Position responsibilities		Kickoff		Position responsibilities	
Tackles		K, R5, L5		Line	
Ends		R4, R3		Tight ends and line	
Linebackers		L4, L3		Quarterbacks	
Secondary		R2, R1		Receivers	
		L2, L1			
Scouting report				Scouting report	
Breakdown		Kickoff return		Defensive fronts	
Board		Front 5		Coverages	
Tendencies		Tight ends		Game plan	
Running game		Back 4			
Passing game				Extra duties	
Personnel		Punt		Team script	
Special teams		C, RUB, LUB		5-on-5 script	
		RG, LG		7-on-7 script	
Extra duties		RT, RE		Soph OC	
Practice schedule		LT, LE		JV OC	
Team script		PP, punter		Soph assistant	
5-on-5 script				Sideline equipment	
7-on-7 script		Punt return		Video exchange	
Soph DC				Video prep	
JV DC				Chart 1st downs	
Soph assistant		PAT		Formation and play info	
Defensive stats				Awards	
OPS				Stats	
Lifting		PAT block			
Transportation					
Meals					
Itinerary					
Forms					

Figure 4.2 Assistant coaching duty list.

data entry for self scouting; locker room supervision; grade checks; player awards and discipline; and weekend schedules for coaches and players. Offensive, defensive, and special teams should all be covered and thoroughly planned. We discuss these areas in depth in chapter 6.

Sports Medicine Staff and Student Trainers

The head trainer is in charge of organizing all team doctors, assistant trainers, and student trainers along with maintaining a sufficient level of medical and training supplies. I coordinate directly with the trainer each morning and inform him of the practice time and schedule, the intensity level, and the number of breaks the team will take. In turn, the trainer organizes the support training staff for each area of practice to ensure that each area of the team is covered by a member of the training staff. The head trainer submits a daily training room report to each coach so that they are aware of injuries that will limit or prevent a player from practicing. Coaches are then capable of planning personnel adjustments for each practice.

Keeping the lines of communication open with the sports medicine staff allows proper planning and organization of personnel and practice. Start every day and end every day with a conversation with your head trainer. Ask him to check for signs of overtraining or dehydration and use his position to the fullest. Utilize this staff's expertise and trust their judgment to do what is best for the player and for the team. Keeping your players on their feet and on the field will make your football program more successful, so take great care of your training staff.

Student Managers

Good equipment managers are invaluable, so recruit trustworthy students who are willing to dedicate their time to being part of your program. These young people must be self-starters who are honest, hardworking, and comfortable in a team environment. Players sometimes look down on managers, which can tarnish their attitude and pride, so take care of your managers and give them your support.

In our preseason meeting with the team I introduce each manager and demonstrate the type of treatment our team should provide our managers. I also include managers on our team apparel list and deck them out with the same clothes our support staff wears. Although this is a small gesture, giving student managers team colors to wear makes them feel like an integral part of the program and leads to stronger loyalty and performance.

Our head trainer is also our head equipment manager. He is in charge of organizing our student managers. He gives them their assignments and several responsibilities to ensure that they fully develop in all areas as student managers. Laundry, video setup, equipment repair, inventory, and field setup and breakdown are all areas that fall under our student managers' responsibilities.

Statisticians

Keeping in mind our philosophy of playing with maximum effort and weekly improvement, stats are not that important on my list, but you can learn a lot about your team's performance by studying accurate statistics. I am fortunate to have a couple of gentlemen who have volunteered to keep the game stats for our program and then report them to the proper media outlets and assistant coaches.

We purchased a software system that works on personal digital assistants (such as Palm Pilots) and allows statisticians to download information into our main computers for permanent records and weekly statistic reports for the coaches and players. The software is capable of generating a multitude of reports and information for the staff to review, but we limit ourselves to rushing, passing, and special teams reports. Our staff reviews the accuracy of the reports while watching the game video to ensure accurate records for archiving. I meet weekly with statisticians to make sure that they are aware of our travel plans or special arrangements that need to be made for them to enter a stadium or to meet with the people who will get them in position to do their job. Include team apparel or hats for your statisticians; they are people you can't live without.

Video and Editing Crew

High-quality video and video cutups are vital for evaluation of and improvement in your football program. The video duties at Jenks are divided into three areas: recording, editing, and data entry.

Practice video is shot by our student managers and then duplicated onto videocassettes for the coaches to study and evaluate with players. Three professional cameramen who are paid by the game for their professional services record game video. The quality of our game video is normally very good, and our student managers are able to assume a more important role during the game by attending to players' and coaches' needs.

The master game video is then downloaded and digitally edited into our main computer system by a special fraternity of men. Our Friday night film crew is a group of dads who dedicate every Friday or Saturday night to editing the Trojan's game video. The group of dads is limited to a four-man crew made up of two senior dads and two junior dads who go through a training session during the summer and truly enjoy their labor of love and hanging around the coaches' war room like they did when they played. I have enjoyed the camaraderie developed over the years with some of the most dedicated fathers, and the Friday night film crew has developed into a proud tradition. Select them carefully because some parents can't handle the player scrutiny and privacy required to be a member of a fraternity that works out of the coaches' war room.

PLAYER RECRUITING

Our program at Jenks has produced nearly 30 NCAA Division I football players in the past eight seasons and numerous Division IAA and Division II players as well. The recruiting process can be an enjoyable experience at times, and it can be a miserable experience in some situations. The key to ensuring a smooth recruiting journey for players is careful planning and a solid grasp of recruiting guidelines, qualifications, and rules.

Athletes can be grouped into four basic categories: blue chips, midlevel Division I, bubble players (Division I recruitable under special circumstances or in special offensive or defensive systems), and sub-Division I players.

Division I blue-chip players are athletes who, because of their great ability and performance, have already proven their potential as impact players no matter which university they plan to attend. The recruiting process for blue-chip players involves tracking their eligibility for the NCAA clearinghouse beginning in their freshman year of high school and making sure that the student-athlete takes the SAT or ACT exam and sets a qualifying standard on these required entrance tests. Make sure that you and your school counselor are aware of the qualifying standards of the universities that the athlete is interested in attending and monitor his progress throughout his high school career. Usually, the hardest decision for a blue-chip player is deciding which university he wants to attend because all of his choices are great ones.

The midlevel Division I player has a little more on his plate than the blue-chip athlete during the recruiting process. On top of the same academic requirements, the midlevel player must also accomplish something on the playing field that will separate him from the other midlevel players. The recruiting process is one of cat and mouse; recruiters rank the midlevel players at each position and simply check them off until they can get the highest-ranked player on the list. It's a tough process for an athlete and his family because it is a subjective process. The athlete is swimming in a barrel of the same kind of fish and must do something that will make a difference in the recruiter's eyes and cause him to make an offer. In these cases, I encourage athletes to attend summer camps at the universities that they want to attend and try to gain the attention and interest of recruiters. I also remind them that summer camps are tryouts; their performance needs to be very good or their recruiting stock could easily go down in value.

Finding a Place

Garrett Mills was one of the best tight ends to ever play at Jenks. He had more than 1,000 yards receiving in his senior season alone. His build, 6 feet, 2 inches and 225 pounds, made him a difficult athlete to recruit out of high school. Garrett was a little short for a true tight end and a little light for a true fullback, which made the recruiting process very frustrating for Garrett and me. Garrett was really an H-back, a versatile player who could block, catch, and run with the ball in the open field. Truly a weapon in the right offensive system against less athletic linebackers or safeties who were too small, Garrett simply had to find the right school, one that could utilize his abilities in their package.

Late in the recruiting process the University of Tulsa offered Garrett a scholarship. Proud to carry on a family tradition (Garrett's dad, Mike, was an offensive lineman at TU), Garrett signed with the Golden Hurricane. In his sophomore season, Garrett led the nation in touchdown receptions for a tight end, not bad for a player who couldn't get an offer anywhere.

Bubble players are unique players who still have a chance to play Division I football, only under special circumstances. For example,

an option quarterback who is an extremely gifted runner but might be considered a nonpasser because of the offensive system he played in could be a bubble player. This player could easily add value to a college option program but may not be of value to a passing college unless he is willing to switch positions. Getting the proper exposure is vital for the bubble player, so assist the player in identifying the universities that could use his abilities and would be interested in recruiting him.

As the head coach, you can assist players throughout the recruiting process in many areas, but remember that the final decision must come from the player. Be open and honest with recruiters and maintain your program's integrity at all times. Painting a false picture of an athlete not only jeopardizes your program and the interested university's program but can also place the athlete in a situation where he may have trouble succeeding. Never steer an athlete to a university for personal reasons. If a player comes to you for advice, be open and honest and try to highlight the advantages and disadvantages of each university.

The player should involve his parents throughout the recruiting process. Be there if they need you for advice or as a liaison to the recruiter. Players who are not fortunate to have parents involved may need your help to a much greater extent. My policy has always been to treat each young man as I would my own son and try to place him in the best possible support system so that he has a chance to succeed on the field and in the classroom. Encourage athletes to be honest with recruiters about their interest (or lack of interest) in their particular school and to always be open minded about each school.

CHAPTER 5

WORKING TOGETHER AS A STAFF

The biggest challenge about writing a chapter on working together as a staff is considering the multitude of management styles head coaches use within their individual football programs. Everyone is different in the way he wants his football staff to operate and ultimately succeed. Some head coaches want to be involved in every phase of the operation and, in many cases, micromanage the operation, making nearly every decision related to the program. Although many coaches have been successful with this approach, others prefer to delegate responsibilities and simply support and assist in the program's operation, using a more open and flexible management approach. This approach empowers personnel and develops assistant coaches into the best coaches they can be. Many different management styles and approaches have been successful. Select one that fits your personality and organizational skills and produces championship results.

Working together effectively as a staff can be accomplished in many ways, and ultimately this is what puts the icing on the cake of being a coach. Working in an environment in which one is respected and truly a part of a successful team can lead to an enjoyable and fulfilling career. A sense of belonging and importance is key to bring the best out of any staff.

In some environments I've worked in, I could not wait to get out of the office or off the practice field just to get away from the friction and tension created by a staff that was not functioning as a productive unit. The feeling of being on pins and needles was a huge distraction and limited my ability to use my creativity and personality. Ultimately this type of environment inhibited me from developing into the best coach I could possibly be. This kind of an uncomfortable working environment overflowed and spilled down to the players, who in some cases were completely aware of internal staff relationship issues because of the obvious tension in the air at meetings and during practice sessions.

Staff continuity, loyalty, and cohesiveness are all important ingredients that make us better coaches and allow us to thrive in our profession. If we feel good about what we are doing and enjoy going to work every day, our productivity is likely to improve dramatically.

The keys presented in this chapter—team-work, communication, expectations, and ambassadorship—are ones I feel are important when developing a quality environment for a coaching staff. Remember to give your staff members enough slack on the rope to be flexible and effective but not enough rope to hang themselves with.

CREATING A PRODUCTIVE STAFF ENVIRONMENT

Consistency is important in your approach to coaching. Make the most of every opportunity in practice. I encourage coaches to visit with and coach their players during stretching. It's a great time to set the tone for practice and remind players what will be emphasized during specific drills. It is important to teach all of the time whether it's in a high pressure intense part of practice or during a relaxed stretching period. Be a great educator.

Make every play a learning experience. Let your players know what they did well and let them know what they can improve. Each play is an opportunity for improvement and learning. This situation also lets players know that they are being evaluated constantly. I want all players and coaches to understand that we are all constantly trying to improve and stay focused during our practice time together.

Organization and preparation are vital components when trying to optimize our time together as a staff. Whether we are at practice or in staff meetings we need a plan to guide us and allow us to maximize our time together and channel our efforts in the direction that will lead to success. Organization in practice builds confidence and efficiency. Lack of organization breeds futility. Script everything during practice and meeting times and leave nothing to chance, but be flexible and don't let a play list or an itinerary limit your imagination or creativity.

At staff and team meetings, use time wisely. Nothing leads to boredom or loss of attention faster than being in a disorganized or non-pertinent staff meeting. Communicate the important items and move on to the next important issue. Eliminate as much trivia as possible and focus on what will make your organization better.

Begin and end all meetings and practices on time. I demand punctuality from my coaches, my players, and myself. I believe in sticking to the schedule posted even if we have to reduce some areas of practice to squeeze in everything. It is important to be consistent and timely or risk losing the staff's confidence in your organization skills.

Leave nothing to chance when preparing for a game. Lack of game preparation will get you fired faster than anything else. If you wing it during a game, you are taking unnecessary chances that could be detrimental to your team. Remember our purpose—the constant pursuit of excellence is our driving force to pay careful attention to details and be prepared for every challenge.

Remember your mission. You may be the best influence a player has in his life. Players believe and respect what you say and do. Never take that for granted or compromise your position.

Educate against drug, alcohol, and tobacco use. Athletes cannot possibly play at peak performance if they use drugs or alcohol. We encourage athletes to place the team ahead of any personal issues with drugs, alcohol,

Don't just wing it on game day. The pursuit of excellence requires hours of preparation.

and tobacco. We test all players and coaches for drugs to drive home the point that I really believe in living a life free of drugs, alcohol, and tobacco.

I do not allow profanity from players or coaches in my program. I want our program to be all class. Emotion, anger, and intensity are part of our profession, but we don't use them as excuses to use profanity. If profanity from players becomes an issue, I prefer to use extra conditioning or drill work to reinforce the need for a more positive verbal approach along with a one-on-one discussion regarding my players' use of profanity. Use of profanity by my coaches is unacceptable.

Control emotional outbursts. Teach with emotion and spirit. Angry outbursts can be detrimental to players. Players focus so much on the tone and intensity that they sometimes forget to listen to the message the coach is trying to convey. I constantly remind players to listen to the message, not the tone. I also remind coaches to control their emotions. Even when emotions are running high, coaches need to teach players and exude confidence in them.

Dress professionally. Although many believe football coaches in general are lazy and poor educators who do not put education in the right perspective, I would counter and say some of the best educators I've known have been my assistant coaches. I encourage all members of my staff to look the part and be the part by dressing professionally.

Be an ambassador for your program. Work diligently with the faculty and staff at your school. At all times show that you are an integral part of the school's educational team. Great coaches are great teachers both in the classroom and on the ball field. I try to assign a member of my staff to each academic department for communication purposes and to keep the teamwork chain connected between the football program and the school's faculty and staff. The lines of communication are always open between the faculty and coaching staff. Teachers are fully aware of the support they will receive from our program in academic and discipline areas.

Be a mentor. In staying consistent with our mission, I encourage coaches to be rocks—pillars of confidence, discipline, and knowledge—that players can look up to and pattern their lives by. Young people need a lot of attention in a lot of areas. The respect they have for their coaches creates a fertile ground for teaching important life lessons.

Being a self-starter is one of the most important traits of effective coaches and players. If we are truly developing young people for the real world, we must empower them and develop self-motivation. No one is going to shove you out of your bed or house in the morning and make you become successful. You have to do it yourself. If it is to be, it's up to me.

I try to have an open-door policy for all my coaches and players, meaning I am approachable. Coaches are in the business of developing people, so dealing with problems is inevitable. The key is communication and prompt, program-oriented action. To maintain and build the cohesive unit you want, every member of the staff and team must pool their knowledge and be great problem solvers.

However, remember to voice solutions, not complaints. Everyone in the organization has the right to voice his or her opinion provided it is program oriented. If you have a complaint or problem, give me a better way to do it or solve it, and we'll see if we can implement the new idea. I don't want complainers or whiners, just problem solvers and improvers.

When problems do come up, act like a professional. Developing a sense of ownership in the program for every member is important. When problems arise, and they will, handle them with professionalism. Always ask the big three questions: What is best for the team? What is best for the player? Am I thinking long term?

Be a shining light to those around you. You are a reflection of the football program to everyone you come in contact with. Be sure you represent the program's philosophy at all times. The press has recently crushed football programs with amazing traditions because of the shallow actions of a few men associated with them. Be positive and be proud of your profession as a coach, and represent our profession to the fullest.

Share your knowledge with others. My staff makes at least one visit every spring to another school to share knowledge and to stay as current as possible on instructional techniques and concepts. Sharing football knowledge makes the sport better every year. You can always improve and give back to your profession.

Everyone can always get better. Constantly seek new knowledge in your profession. You are either improving or not—there is no middle ground. Even the smallest improvement is improvement and will have a positive impact on the program.

Attend workshops, camps, and clinics. Coaching football involves many different areas. Remember to be diverse in your studies and broaden your knowledge of football. Set goals and priorities and take note of when you need to move on and keep growing.

Be loyal to the head coach, the staff, and the school. Remember that the program is bigger than any one person. Jenks High School football has been good for a long time, long before I got here, and it will be good long after I'm gone. In our run of seven championships in eight seasons, we employed three different offensive coordinators, four defensive coordinators, and three special teams coordinators. The program is bigger than any coach or player. The teamwork, the tradition, and the system never graduate or move to another job. The team lives on forever. Tradition doesn't graduate.

We need each other in order to be successful. I constantly tell players that the most important thing they can do to achieve personal success is to do everything in their power to make sure that the team succeeds. If every player and coach gives his best effort in the name of team success, everyone will perform at a higher level than anyone could on his own.

Keep family matters in the family. Coaches and players understand that we are a family. Many people who have never been involved in a close family or organization cannot relate to many of the things that we do together. Tough

situations that we must all deal with will arise in the football family. Everyone outside the family doesn't necessarily need to know about our problems. Our locker room and staff room are safe havens for our family, places to go to receive support when times are tough.

When communicating with staff, be open and honest. Honesty is the most important component of communication. People must understand exactly where they stand and what you expect of them. Improvement can be made when communication is sincere and personal.

I remind myself that this is our program, not mine. I want every member of the program to accept ownership of the organization, to make decisions as if he owned the company and it was his own money he was investing. I never limit myself to just my perspective on something. Yes, I make the final decision, but I always surround myself with wise counsel who take the same amount of pride in the program that I have.

Assistant coaches are encouraged to make a family out of their position players. I want my assistant coaches to build solid relationships with their position players. We have Tuesday night group dinners every week during the season just to get players and coaches together in a relaxed environment away from the gridiron. It's a great opportunity to gather feedback and build relationships outside the pressure of practice.

Just as you are open and honest with your staff, be open and honest with your players. Let players know exactly where they stand. They will respect you for your honesty and your team-oriented approach. Every player is different and must be dealt with in a unique way. Players should know that you say what you mean and you are sincerely concerned about their continued improvement and development.

In your daily routine, take care of the little things. Treat the facility and equipment as if they were your personal belongings. Lock the doors when you leave, turn off the lights, and shut down your computer. Taking care of the little things makes life easier on everyone involved in the organization and teaches your players valuable life lessons. When players and coaches leave my program, I want them to be leaders and pacesetters, people who take pride in doing things the right way, men of character who will make a difference in society through the leadership principles they acquired by being involved in our football program.

Be a team player. Help fellow coaches become better coaches. I take pride in developing young coaches into better coaches. Program success, great players, and talented assistant coaches have helped develop many outstanding head coaches. It all boils down to being a team player and giving your best effort to ensure program success. You get out of coaching exactly what you put into it. Always help your fellow coaches improve.

Build each other up. Coaching football is an emotional job. The dependence of young people performing under great pressure and the expectations of a championship program can take their toll on all of us if we're not careful to keep our priorities in order. Be positive and upbeat as often as possible. If a member of my staff is having a bad day or week, I pick up

the phone and call him, or I take him to lunch and let him know how much I appreciate him and how valuable he is to our organization. A simple handwritten card to a staff member can work wonders in the pursuit of excellence. Take the time to build each other up.

Help each other with daily tasks and projects. Look for things that need to be done. Volunteer to assist coaches with projects or cover their duties to let them spend a few extra hours with their families. There are always things that need to be done. Do your part and help your fellow staff members complete their tasks.

Always do what is best for the program. I tell my assistants, "Be where you are." Many coaches want to be somewhere else for the sake of being somewhere else and climbing the coaching ladder. The grass is not always greener on the other side of the fence. Work hard to make your program the best it can be and great things will come from your efforts, not only for your football organization but for your professional career as well. In the past nine years, six of my assistant coaches have moved on to become head coaches. I believe

Coaching a championship football team is a team effort. Assistants need to work together to support each other and build each other up.

that their continued success was directly linked to their hard work and dedication to our football program and their willingness to grow as coaches here at Jenks. Understand and believe that program success will lead to personal success, so put everything you have into the program and great things will come.

FINDING THE RIGHT PEOPLE

Surrounding yourself with great people is not only part of our philosophy, it's essential to program growth, improvement, and success. Identify people who share a common program philosophy and who are willing to be team players. Men who meet as many components of your coaching philosophy as possible will allow you to develop your coaching staff into a solid team capable of accomplishing great things.

I involve trusted veteran members of my staff in the interview process to make sure everyone has a positive feel for a potential employee and confidence he will get the job done. Ask questions regarding the applicant's

personal coaching and teaching philosophies as well as offensive, defensive, and special teams philosophies. Create scenarios and ask the applicant how he would solve a particular problem or how he would react to a certain situation. Include personnel and team scenarios as well as game and practice situations when developing an interview routine. Be thorough in your evaluation process and select those who are passionate, capable, and willing to work hard and work with purpose. A precise, successful initial selection can solidify a powerful staff and prevent a multitude of problems later.

Empower coaches with your philosophy. I remember being a young assistant in a staff meeting and wanting to raise my hand and interject my opinion on what we needed to do to enhance our offensive success. I just knew that we needed to run 48 toss from the I-formation to improve our running game, but I also knew that the head coach was a veer man and the odds of lining up in the I-formation were slim to none, and slim had just left town. I told myself then that I would be an empowering head coach and make a great effort to bring out the strengths of my staff.

Every member of my staff—from assistant coaches to trainers to student managers—is empowered with our program philosophy and encouraged to pursue excellence in all their activities.

As coaches we have more control over what types of systems we run than what types of players we have. Therefore, it is much easier to mold a system to a group of players than it is to mold players to a system. Producing a system that allows players to utilize their strengths must be the focus.

Whether initiating a new football program or initiating a new football season, renew and discuss your program's vision, purpose, and mission. As discussed in chapter 1, a common vision, purpose, and mission can empower an entire organization and make it a strong, productive team.

I assemble every member of my staff for the initial meeting of the season, including trainers, managers, assistant coaches from each level, team doctors, secretaries, booster club leaders, and even the leaders of my youth football organization. Some members of my staff are veterans, and we have worked many seasons together; others are new and still developing. Everyone involved in this initial meeting will feel empowered and a part of something bigger. I want everyone to sit around the same table and talk about what we want to accomplish as a staff for the upcoming year and the years to come. I want everybody to completely understand what the organization stands for and will try to accomplish.

At the meeting, I review our vision, purpose, and mission and gather as much feedback as possible. Remember it is important to constantly evaluate your mission as you evolve in your career. We discuss the great tradition of Jenks Football and the success that can be accomplished through teamwork. We discuss expectations and talk about ways to organize our approach.

Most importantly we share how we want players to believe and understand that we are all in this boat together for one common purpose—the pursuit of excellence. When a player goes to the trainer for rehabilitation, I want the trainer to pursue excellence in helping the athlete. When our secretary assists a college recruiter or parent, I want her to pursue excellence. When our janitor is cleaning the locker room, I want our locker room to exude excellence. Create an environment of success by making sure everyone in the organization does his or her part to the fullest. This environment is contagious and will spread to everyone remotely involved in your football program. Empower great people and great things will happen.

CHAPTER 6 PLANNING AND CONDUCTING PRACTICES

The most vital component of developing a team is practice. Execution of plays, attitude, intensity, mental and physical toughness, conditioning, and game preparation can all be enhanced through a well-planned and executed practice.

Because you must cover all practice components in a limited amount of time and must cover them thoroughly through repetition, meticulous planning and preparation must go into a practice regimen. Attention to every detail is required for getting the most out of a practice session.

More practice doesn't mean better performance. Instead, be very organized and thorough when planning practice and cover all the important areas with great detail. Many coaches fall into the trap of believing that the quantity of time spent practicing determines to the quality of performance during games. Remember, it is the quality of practice and teaching that determines the quality of performance on the field.

The NCAA has a 20-hour-per-week rule to limit the amount of practice time, but most high school practice guidelines are governed only by the head coach's judgment. Consider the mental and physical condition of your players when developing the practice itinerary. There is a law of diminishing returns, and as coaches we flirt with it all the time. At some point, the amount of time you practice will no longer lead to team improvement, but reduce team performance through mental and physical overtraining. Thoroughly evaluate the effort and focus of your team during workouts. If the team finishes sluggishly or inconsistently, try structuring your practices differently or shortening some of the drill sessions to enhance team performance and attitude. Mentally and physically tired teams will not perform up to their potential. A mentally and physically healthy team has a chance to compete at its highest potential, while a tired or injured team doesn't.

Effective practice is the lifeline of team performance. Our job as coaches is to create a learning environment during practice that is as close to a game situation as possible. I want the game to be the easiest part of the week. I want the game to be the night when the players can cash in the chips they have invested throughout the week and reap the rewards of being thoroughly prepared.

The Gamer

Great effort in practice is a simple way to justify playing time to players. When I took over the job at Jenks, we had a great linebacker who was a returning starter and a fine player. As we worked our way into the season and started reviewing practice tapes, we discovered that he was a poor practice player who did not work very hard during technique drills and then did not play with much intensity during group and team periods. I put the linebackers coach in charge of motivating him to become a better leader on the practice field and to set a higher standard for his practice performance. My linebackers coach did everything he could to get the effort we wanted out of the player but to no avail, so I called the player into my office to talk to him about his poor practice habits. After a lengthy discussion about what we expected from him on the practice field, he finally told me that he was just a gamer, a player who played better during games but not practice, and that's the way he had always been. I told him that players who don't practice well not only don't play well, but they don't play at all. I explained to him that his coach was going to grade his practice plays each day and if he didn't score better than the linebacker who was playing the same position, he would not start. The first week the other linebacker graded higher, and I started him in front of the better player. We won the ball game, and fortunately, the defense turned in a gem. From that day forward, the gamer was also a great practice player.

We place a high value on practice time. Coaches nominate practice players of the week, the young men who gave great effort during practice and made themselves and their team better. We give practice players of the week T-shirts and a coupon for free food at a local sandwich shop. It is our way of making practice important and praising players who go the extra mile to improve the team and themselves.

I encourage coaches to constantly find players who practice well and recognize them in any way possible. On the other hand, when the team or a player does not respond and put forth the mental and physical effort we expect, we respond with different types of reinforcement. Sometimes I repeat the drill or the play and emphasize the expectations we have for the team or player. Other times we add a conditioning element to the drill to teach players the importance of giving their best mental and physical effort during practice.

PRESEASON PRACTICE

Our state association allows practice to begin the second Tuesday of August each year and requires three days of noncontact practice before pads can be used on the fourth day (see sample defensive and offensive schedules in tables 6.1 and 6.2). We use the three noncontact days to install the majority of our offense, defense, and special teams systems. We schedule an intrasquad scrimmage on the fifth day of practice, or the day after we put the pads on for the first time, so we plan our installation schedule carefully this first week. After the intrasquad scrimmage, we have five more days of practice until our first scrimmage against another opponent, so our installation procedure continues throughout the second week of practice as well. We complete the installation process the third week before our third and final preseason scrimmage and spend the rest of the time focused on our opening opponent.

The majority of athletes who participate in the summer conditioning program report to practice in tremendous shape, allowing us to spend time working on installing our system instead of conditioning. It is important to emphasize the teaching progression you want to incorporate during this first week of practice. Start with the basics and build toward the more complex. Our offensive and defensive systems build off our standard alignments and plays, and then we build or add more each practice session until the system becomes flexible and adaptable for players and coaches.

Table 6.1   Defensive Implementation Schedule for Week 1

	August 10 Helmets	August 11 Helmets	August 12 Helmets	August 13 Pads	August 14 Scrimmage
Emphasis	Huddle Teaching Base tite	Base split Teaching Motion adjustments	Stack Teaching Blitz package	Review	
Personnel	Regular Nickel Bear	Regular Nickel Griz	30 Dime Quarter	Victory	
Formations and motions	Rt/lt H-motion AG/BG Slot Trade/Jet Tex	Flex Ace Tight Twins Poke/Hoss Z-motion	Shoot Bunch Trips Cal/Dot Stack	Rex/Lex Arc	
Runs	14/15 18/19 12/13	44/45 28/29	24/25 20/21	70/71 Around, dummy Reverse	
Tags	Loose Out Stack 22	Loose Solid Stack 22	Razor Blade Zone dogs	Boot	
Blitzes	Dbl LB Dbl LB X 22s	Dbl LB Dbl LB X 22s	Buick Chevy Cobra	Redskin Ice Buc/Pirate	
Coverages	83/9 Red/white/blue Signals	0, 1, 5 Red/white/blue Signals	2, 2 man 4 Spy 1 dbl	7 7 read 9 read	
Tags	Flat Seam Hitch	Wheel Curl Bend	Dbl, out Wheel Switch		
Screens	Doppler Now Bubble	Wind Breeze	Tornado	Cyclone Quake	
Fronts	Tight Bear	Split Griz	Stack		
Coverages	8 3 9				
Other	I, O, S Green Over	G Deuce	W, T Deuce	Pass	

Table 6.2 Offensive Implementation Schedule for Week 1

	August 10 Helmets	August 11 Helmets	August 12 Helmets	August 13 Pads	August 14 Scrimmage
Emphasis	Tempo Teaching Base O	Tempo Teaching Base O	Tempo Teaching Base O		
Personnel	Regular Spread	Ace Tight Diamond	Shoot		
Formations and motions	Rt/lt H-motion AG/BG Slot Trade/jet 1/2, 3/4, 5/6	Flex Ace Tight Twins Poke/Hoss Z-motion	Shoot Bunch Trips Cal/dot Stack	Rex/Lex Arc	
Runs	14/15 18/19 12/13	44/45 28/29	24/25 20/21	70/71 Around, dummy Reverse	
Tags	Read Toss, spread WR	G, Utah Q, Bluff Boss	Crack		
Protections	80/90 Naked Bomber	50/60 Fk 2/3 Fk 4/5	500/600	Boot	
Passes	All quicks Naked Bomber	51/61, 52/62 59/69 56/66	53/63, 54/64 58/68 55/65		
Tags	Flat Seam Hitch		Dbl, Out Wheel Switch		
Screens	Doppler Now Bubble	Wind Breeze	Tornado	Cyclone Quake	
Fronts	Tight Bear	Split Griz	Stack		
Coverages	8 3 9				
Other	I, O, S Green Over	G Deuce	W, T Deuce	Passes	

The athletes who take advantage of the summer conditioning program report to preseason practice in great shape, allowing us to focus on implementing the system rather than conditioning in the first few weeks of practice.

As a player, I went through two-a-day and three-a-day practice sessions and didn't enjoy them very much. My main concern was the ordeal of leaving my comfortable room and going back to the stadium to stretch and warm up again and do many of the things over that we had just done a few hours before. I realize that two- and three-a-day practice sessions are popular, but at Jenks we have adopted one four-hour practice session per day (table 6.3).

We divide the team into varsity players and junior varsity players as accurately as possible. The practice session begins with varsity players working on the offensive side of the ball and junior varsity players working on defensive skills. When drills require a scout team, junior varsity players work against varsity players, allowing both sides the high-quality practice looks they need for improvement. After the varsity players complete their two-hour block of offensive practice and the junior varsity players finish defensive practice, we take a break to allow players to cool down while coaches meet with their individual players to go over the areas and concepts that must be worked on during the next practice session. After the break, the varsity and junior varsity switch sides of the ball and we repeat the practice, allowing the varsity two hours to work on defense and the junior varsity to work on offense. Special teams practice is incorporated at the end of each two-hour block and worked on each day just like offense and defense.

This system has led to improved practice performance and attitude. Both players and coaches know that when practice is over, it is over. They can work on other important tasks without having to worry about reporting for another practice that day.

Coach's Keys

1. Careful planning is vital when developing a successful practice schedule.

2. Use an installation schedule for preseason practices to ensure that systems are installed correctly and thoroughly.

3. Evaluate often and optimize practice time in the areas your team needs it the most.

4. Consider a once-a-day practice format. See if players' and coaches' outlook and performance improve.

5. The daily practice plan should include drills and teaching from each practice component: athletic enhancement, individual technique, special teams, offensive and defensive groups, and offensive and defensive teams.

6. Be a great planner and a great teacher. These traits work hand in hand. One won't work without the other.

7. Don't be afraid to modify and adjust during practice to get the most out of your time and your players. Find the positive as often as you can. If you must scold, provide a plan for improvement as well.

Table 6.3 Preseason Practice Schedule

Time	Station	Offense	Defense	Notes
8:00	Stretch	All coaches		One coach per line
8:05				Take roll off list
8:10	Form run			
8:15				
8:20	Agility	Circuit	1.5 min per station	1 min rest
8:25		See sheet	Line up and sprint on whistle	
8:30				
8:35				
8:40	Break			
8:45	Indy/tempo	Varsity: O screen	JV: D pursuit	
8:50	Individual	Varsity: Individual O	JV: Individual D	
8:55				
9:00				
9:05				
9:10	Group/individual	7-on-7	O line/D line individual	Water on the run
9:15		South 20 out		
9:20				
9:25	Group/individual	5-on-5	WR/DB individual	Water on the run
9:30				
9:35				
9:40	Break			
9:45	Team	Varsity: Team O	JV: Team D	
9:50		Two huddles	Service	
9:55				
10:00	Break			
10:05	Indy/tempo	JV: O screens	Varsity: D pursuit	
10:10	Individual	JV: Individual O	Varsity: Individual D	
10:15				
10:20				
10:25				
10:30	Group	7-on-7	O line/D line individual	Water on the run
10:35				
10:40				
10:45	Group	5-on-5	WR/DB individual	Water on the run
10:50				
10:55				
11:00	Break			
11:05	Team	JV: Team O	Varsity: Team D	Water on the run
11:10				
11:15				
11:20	Special teams	Kickoff return on AT	Individual	O line/D line
11:25	Rotate snappers and kickers			QB/receivers/RB
11:30		Returners Riggs		Shotgun
11:35	Everybody up			
11:40		Notes:		
11:45		Hydration	Fundraiser money	
11:50		Stim-O-Stam	Pads tomorrow	
11:55		Paperwork		
12:00				

When preseason practice ends and the focus turns to game preparation, players should have a firm grasp on your team's offensive, defensive, and special teams systems. They should be able to execute at a high level against the looks they will see from their first few opponents. Remember, do what you do well. A team that can execute its system effectively will be successful. Put players under pressure in practice often and prepare them thoroughly for the upcoming season.

WEEKLY PRACTICE

With preseason practices behind us, we look forward to getting into the groove of the season and establishing our regular weekly preparation routine. We incorporate a weekly itinerary when preparing practice plans for each opponent. We look at last year's game plan and information if they are still pertinent as well as current scouting information compiled from preseason scrimmages and films of our upcoming opponent.

Some coaches completely forget about their own team when the regular season begins and instead focus on their opponents. Certainly, your preparation must involve researching your opponent and making plans for how to defeat them, but don't forget the importance of making sure that your team improves daily. I would hate to go into the season knowing the only offensive and defensive plays we could use were the ones we installed the first three weeks of the preseason. Make sure you are still cultivating your own team's growth and improvement even though your thoughts are also focused on your opponent.

With preseason behind us and looking ahead to the regular-season routine our focus goes to preparing for our opponent while continuing to develop our own team, both athletically and mentally. Building practice schedules around a game plan is covered in chapter 14, but here is a day-by-day breakdown of how we build our practice plans.

Monday

Practice begins each day during the sixth-hour athletic period. I hand out game plans, and we view scouting video of our opponent. Monday's practice is much more mental than physical. Because players are rehabilitating injuries and recovering from soreness from the previous weekend's game, we work hard mentally, but minimize the amount of physical contact on Monday.

On the practice field, players wear shoulder pads and helmets with shorts. They work to fix last week's mistakes and install the initial game plan. We cover all phases of special teams, go over the preliminary defensive adjustments we plan to use against the opponent by personnel group and by formation, and work hard on the timing in our passing game while the offensive line goes over blocking adjustments and schemes. Players spend a great deal of time in individual stations, working on fundamentals and clearing up mistakes made the week before.

Junior varsity players play their games on Monday nights, so they are excused at the end of practice to eat a pregame meal and prepare for the game.

Monday concludes with conditioning drills for all varsity players to work out the last bit of stiffness and soreness and prepare them physically for the intensity of Tuesday's practice. All linemen, linebackers, fullbacks, and tight ends lift weights after practice.

Monday's practice includes 30 minutes of prepractice meetings and films to go over the three phases of the game plan and 45 minutes postpractice conditioning and lifting. On-field practice usually takes an hour and a half to complete. Most reps on Monday are less intense. Our focus is on correcting last week's mistakes, getting our legs back, and installing our game plan.

Tuesday

Tuesday is our big workday. First, in prepractice the offensive and defensive lines work on pass protection and rush, and the punt team works on protection. Afterward, the team suits out in full gear. Practice is at full speed and physical. We carefully control the amount of contact, but every drill and play is executed at maximum effort and intensity.

We run all drills and plays against the looks we think our opponent will give us on game day. We videotape all segments of practice to get a feeling of what we like and what we don't like against the various looks so that we can make adjustments in Wednesday's practice.

I don't necessarily look for perfect execution on Tuesday because we are in the very early stages of the game plan and preparation, but I do look for great concentration, effort, and enthusiasm. Tuesday is our toughest practice day, not only physically but also mentally because of the new looks the players will face against a new opponent.

Try to make Tuesday as positive as possible. Make sure players are open minded about Tuesday's practice. Adjustments will be made, and things will be changed for Wednesday's workout, but effort and intensity will not be compromised. The goal is to make Wednesday's practice run more smoothly as a result of enhanced understanding of the adjustments and looks covered on Tuesday. There are no conditioning drills after Tuesday's practice, although skill players lift weights.

Wednesday

Wednesday is another hard workday, but we normally reduce the amount of hard contact to avoid the risk of practice-related injury or pain with the game only two days away. We make adjustments after watching Tuesday's practice tape as we finalize the finer points of the game plan in all areas.

Practice begins with a team period for the defense so that they can review all of their adjustments in alignment and assignment before practice begins. The offensive team works on a blitz period and the two-minute drill as well. All the special automatics on both sides of the ball are covered during the team segments of practice as well as special teams adjustments or plays. We emphasize tempo on Wednesdays to ensure that players are responding under gamelike situations. Prac-

Conditioning drills keep players agile, flexible, and fit.

tice ends with high-intensity sprinting drills to ensure quick leg turnover and freshness on game day.

Thursday

Thursday is the dress rehearsal. Practice lasts about an hour and a half. All adjustments on offense, defense, and special teams are covered one last time. I am picky on Thursdays, and the players are completely aware of it. I expect complete and total focus on Thursday; anything less than perfect will not be tolerated. There are no physical challenges on Thursday, only mental challenges, and players must respond positively to be successful on game day. Players wear only practice jerseys, shorts, and helmets for Thursday workouts. The day ends with a short film study and written test for all players. The film and testing are our way of finalizing the week of preparation and exposing the players to the important information one last time.

PRACTICE STRUCTURE

We divide the practice schedule into a series of five-minute sessions. I encourage you to organize your practice schedule in the manner you believe will optimize your time spent on each component of practice. By organizing practices with time segments, you can add time to the areas in which you need more work and reduce time in the areas in which your team is performing well. Time segments also allow you to stay on schedule and organize and utilize your players' and coaches' abilities by planning ahead. Organization breeds confidence and success, disorganization leads to inconsistency and frustration.

I post the practice schedule on the bulletin board so that players will know we will begin and end on time. For the most part, I stick to this commitment. On certain days, the time allotted for a certain drill or component does not allow for enough teaching, and players simply do not grasp the concepts you are trying to communicate. Nothing kills a good practice faster than having to stop and reteach a concept when you have the whole team together and want to cover a lot of information in a hurry. Do you go overtime and extend practice, or do you just move on and hope to resolve the problem during the next practice session? Fortunately, great organization in practice planning will almost always prevent this situation. If it does arise, try one of the following ideas to preserve practice tempo while teaching the concepts that players are struggling with.

First, try to substitute the plays on the script that players have mastered with more of the new plays they are wrestling with, even if you must repeat some of them. You still get the same number of plays in the same amount of time, except the time is spent where the players really need it. Second, go ahead and finish practice on time and cover all the material you normally would. After practice, have players take off their gear then return for a special 15-minute jam session in a less

stressful environment in which you reteach the concepts that they struggled with. Finally, increase prepractice time both on the field and in the film room to give the players a firmer grasp of the information before they get out on the practice field.

Include components from offense, defense, and special teams in every practice session. There is not enough time to cover every component in every practice, but in the scope of a week you should cover as many components as possible. Every practice should include components from the following areas:

- Athletic enhancement (strength, conditioning, flexibility, speed, and agility)
- Individual technique (basic skill development)
- Special teams
- Offensive and defensive groups
- Offensive and defensive teams

Athletic Enhancement

We begin every practice session with a variety of athletic-enhancing exercises and drills. These drills also cross over into the individual drills that players do. For example, every day the defensive ends coach works on takeoff with the defensive ends. Takeoff is the explosive movement used in a game to rush the passer. (The takeoff drill is also used by our conditioning coach to enhance each player's ability to accelerate off the line of scrimmage and develop overall speed and agility.)

Carefully study your practice plans to make sure that you do not overemphasize a particular exercise or body part. This research will also allow you to include more enhancement exercises during practice because you can do different exercises during other segments of practice.

Flexibility and strength are vital for reducing injury and maintaining a high level of team performance throughout the long season. Building team speed and agility is important because the teams you will have to defeat during crunch time will be fast and agile. We try to develop these areas daily.

Players begin every practice with a four-minute jog to enhance circulation and prepare for the warm-up routine. Players complete the form running and dynamic stretching routine before moving on to the flexibility routine to make sure that their muscles are completely warmed up and ready to stretch.

Players build strength not only by lifting weights, but also by doing dynamic and explosive stretches. These special exercises place athletes in football-playing positions and force them to use great technique to complete the exercises. The dynamic routine increases both strength and conditioning levels while enhancing the athlete's flexibility, providing a great advantage in injury prevention and recovery.

Dynamic flexibility and form running routine

1. Sprinter's lunge with A-skip
2. Sprinter's lunge plus skip with B-skip
3. Lateral shuffle with high-knee carioca
4. Ankle flips with goose steps
5. Power skips with bounders
6. Backpedal with turn and run
7. Pop-up with sprint
8. Reverse pop-up with sprint

Dynamic flexibility and form running are completed using 20 yards on the practice field. The first phase is done during the first 10 yards with the second phase completed in the final 10 yards. Each exercise is done twice, or down and back. Tempo and technique are coached and stressed by each coach, who is in charge of his own line of players.

The daily flexibility routine is done immediately after the dynamic routine from the stretching lines. Players align 5 yards apart, and each line leader is in charge of leading the team through its individual exercise. This is a great opportunity to communicate with players as a team because they are all together in one area. I encourage coaches to talk to their individual players about important components of practice and use this time to focus the players on practice.

Flexibility routine

1. Hamstring stretch
2. Sprinter's lunge
3. Butterfly stretch
4. Hip-flexor stretch
5. Isometric neck stretch
6. Sumo squat
7. Quad stretch
8. Low back stretch
9. Rock and roll stretch
10. Shoulder flexibility routine

Individual Technique

Teaching players how to play football occurs during the individual component of practice. Players spend one-on-one time by position with their position coaches and work on the individual techniques of their positions.

During this phase, we cover position-specific drills and tackling techniques or other position-related teaching. During the season, individual work also includes teaching players techniques that will help them be successful against the upcoming opponent.

Take pride in this component of practice. Great technique will allow players to succeed even though they may be physically outmatched by an opponent. Many coaches get caught up in the scrimmaging and team part of practice and forget about teaching technique to players. Be great teachers of technique, and your team will always have a chance on the field.

Special Teams

We emphasize special teams just like we do offense and defense. We want special, special teams.

We work all phases of special teams on Mondays and Thursdays. On Tuesdays and Wednesdays we work certain phases of the kicking game into the team and group regimens. I am present at each special teams event during practice and at all special teams meetings and film sessions because I want coaches and players to understand how vital this component of practice is. Much of our success and many of our playoff victories are directly related to having outstanding special teams units. After all, if special teams are one-third of a normal game, shouldn't we practice them one-third of the time?

Flexibility exercises such as the sumo squat are incorporated into practice to keep players loose and prevent injuries to the muscles and joints.

Offensive and Defensive Groups

We incorporate a lot of offensive and defensive group work into practice planning. Group work includes what we call five-on-five and seven-on-seven. When we want to emphasize the running game and run defense, we simply practice with the offensive and defensive fronts, linebackers, and running backs. There is no reason to practice corners or receivers in the running game because they are rarely involved in this portion of the game. Receivers and defensive backs take advantage of this time to work on their special skills in an individual period or other group drill.

Group work is a way of specializing players' practice responsibilities and emphasizing certain responsibilities within a given practice time frame. It works the same for the passing portion of group work as well. Defensive backs and linebackers practice the passing game with quarterbacks, tight ends, and receivers. Linemen take advantage of this part of practice to work on pass rushing and blocking or other individual areas that will enhance their performance.

Offensive and Defensive Teams

In most situations, the varsity team practices against the junior varsity team. However, if we need a better look or more intensity, we choose a "best of the rest" scout team to give the varsity team the best look we can get. We pick and choose carefully when and where to practice good-on-good to make sure that we keep the risk of injury as small as possible.

The team component of practice creates a gamelike atmosphere to prepare players to execute under the pressure of game conditions. We also build into the team component of practice blitz periods, goal line periods, third-down periods, and any other situation we feel might benefit our team's preparation for the upcoming opponent.

Try to leave the practice field as positive as possible. Even if things didn't go as well as you had planned and you need to work on certain areas, do your best to find the good in your team's effort. I'm the first to bring to light a player or team's deficiencies or shortcomings, but I also give them a plan for improving performance and the hope of getting better during the next practice session. Don't think I want players and coaches to be comfortable all the time. However, be aware of the demands you place on them and the outcomes you expect. Remember that they want to be good, so praise often and scold with a plan of improvement attached to the scolding.

PART III INSTRUCTION

CHAPTER 7
OFFENSIVE POSITIONS AND FORMATIONS

This chapter briefly covers the attributes needed by offensive football players for individual positions plus a few formations you might use to put players in position to be successful on the offense.

The strategy and creativity required to place offensive personnel in position to maximize their athletic potential is both enjoyable and challenging. Remember, though, using the information covered in the previous six chapters is as important as how you place and use personnel. The ability to build a team atmosphere and get everyone in the program on the same end of the rope is vital to performance no matter what offensive system you use or where you place your players.

All of this said, success is also aided tremendously by placing the best athletes in positions to use their individual skills in a team environment. Just remember your principles and your mission and make all your decisions with the team's best interest in mind. Even the best-thought-out plan will fail if some in the organization are on a different page.

PLAYER POSITIONS AND SKILL SPECIALTIES

In the modern game of football every player has specialized skills unique to his position on the field. The days of the single wing and straight T are almost over. Players must possess and develop specific skills, techniques, and responsibilities for each position.

An example of this specialization is the use of the fullback in our offensive system. We are an I-formation offense for several reasons. We want the best runner to rush the ball every time we run the ball; in our offensive system, that's the tailback. The fullback is used as a lead blocker and a pass receiver, attributes that are at times hard to find and hard to develop. Our fullback must be an unselfish, athletic, physical player who can block a variety of defensive players including linebackers, safeties, and even defensive linemen. Not only must our fullback be very physical in the running game, but he also must be a solid pass route runner with great hands like a receiver.

We use our offensive running game to take advantage of aggressive defenses with our play action passing game to the fullback. Our fullback is truly a specialized player. Tune in on any Sunday and watch any NFL team. You will see a highly organized group of specialists on the field.

Quarterback

The quarterback is the leader of the offensive team. In the offensive huddle, our players look into the eyes of the quarterback and see a player with great poise, confidence, and leadership. The quarterback is the glue that holds everything together in the huddle. When the team needs to be fired up, he's the guy who lights the fire. When the team is uptight, he's the guy who calms them.

Quarterbacks lead in different ways. Some are very athletic and make great plays when their team needs them the most. Some are very smart and can change a bad play into a great play by calling an audible. Truly great quarterbacks have great athletic ability, great leadership skills, and great intelligence. They are students of the game who study hours of film with the offensive coordinator. During a game, they think just like the coaches do.

In a perfect world, our quarterback would be 6 feet, 3 inches or taller so he could see

The multiple responsibilities of the quarterback—calling plays, setting the cadence and snap count, and executing both pass and run plays—require a player who is intelligent, athletic, and a great leader.

over the linemen while in the pocket. He also would be very intelligent and have the ability to change plays at the line of scrimmage when he recognizes special defensive alignments and strategies. He would have great leadership qualities and traits. I have never coached a perfect quarterback, but in seven championship seasons I have had quarterbacks who led their teams in a variety of ways. All were different, but all were effective.

Forming and Breaking the Huddle

The center sets up the huddle 5 yards from the ball (figure 7.1). The huddle consists of two rows. The offensive line forms the front row; they stand upright with hands to their sides. Skilled position players form the back row; they stand upright with hands to their sides.

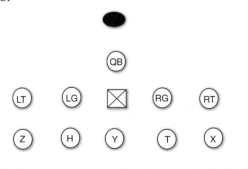

Figure 7.1 Huddle formation.

The quarterback has complete control of the huddle when he enters it. Everyone looks at the quarterback. The quarterback gives the formation, the shifts and motion, the play, and the snap count. A player who didn't hear the quarterback indicates this by calling, "Check."

After the quarterback gives the snap count, receivers leave the huddle. The quarterback repeats the snap count and says, "Ready, break." All players clap their hands and leave the huddle. The offensive line hustles to the line of scrimmage. Backs follow the linemen to the line of scrimmage.

Communicating Offensive Formations

A system that controls 11 people through hundreds of alignments and movements must be easy to understand and consistent throughout multiple personnel groupings. The system must allow you to communicate with 11 people, but be simple, straightforward, and not too wordy—remember, time is very important in the huddle. The communication system must distinguish assignments among different players in the huddle, linemen, receivers, and backs. The communication system should also cross over through the multitude of different offensive formations and alignments. In other words, you shouldn't have to change your communication system just because you want to run the veer instead of the wishbone or the shotgun instead of the wing-T.

The communication system we use is based on a few basic alignments that can be controlled with a group of letters and numbers that pertain to positions on the field and personnel groupings (table 7.1 and table 7.2).

Table 7.1 Nomenclature of Formations

Q	Gun	QB in shotgun
Y	(No call)	Regular split next to OT to call side
	Rex/Lex	Regular split next to OT off the ball
	Flex	Split 4-8 yards from OT
	Wide	Align as outside WR
H	(No call)	Behind QB 4-5 yards deep
	1/2	Straddle OT's inside leg to call side
	3/4	In up position to call side
	5/6	Regular WR alignment to call side
	7/8	Align as middle WR to call side
	9/10	Align as outside WR to call side
	Split	Straddle OT's inside leg to formation strength
	Flip	Straddle OT's inside leg away from formation strength
Z	(No call)	Align in regular WR alignment to call side
	Slot	Align inside of X away from call side
	Twins	Align outside of X away from call side
	Wing	Align next to TE/OT to call side
	Hip	Align next to TE/OT away from call side
	Strong	Align in power-back position to call side
	Weak	Align in power-back position away from call side
X	(No call)	Align in regular WR alignment away from call side
	Tight	Align as TE away from call side
	Exit	Align in regular WR alignment to call side
T	Abe/Bess	Straddle OT's inside leg to call side
	Cal/Dot	In up position to call side
	Ed/Flo	Regular WR alignment to call side
	Guy/Hope	Outside WR alignment to call side
	Split	Straddle OT's inside leg away from formation strength
	Flip	Straddle OT's inside leg to formation strength
WR	Bunch	WRs compress on both sides
	Crunch	WRs compress on right side
	Clump	WRs compress on left side
	Stack	WRs stack on both sides
	Rod	WRs stack on right side
	Line	WRs stack on left side
	Pair	Z- and H-stack

Table 7.2   Personnel Groupings

	Running backs	Tight ends	Wide receivers
Tight diamond	3	2	0
Diamond	3	1	1
Tight	2	2	1
Regular	2	1	2
Open	2	0	3
Ace	1	2	2
Spread	1	1	3
Shoot	1	0	4
Empty	0	1	4
Star	0	0	5

We label our skill players with letters to help organize the system. The quarterback is Q, the tailback is T, the fullback is H, the flanker is Z, the wide receiver is X, and the tight end is Y. When we change offensive personnel and the fullback goes out and another receiver comes in, he becomes the H

Figure 7.2 shows the basic alignments and numbering system for the fullback (H). The quarterback simply calls one of the basic formations and adds a number to align the H. The position is also tagged with a number to motion the H from one position to another. For example, the quarterback might call "Right 5, H 6." In this formation, the H would begin

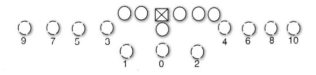

Figure 7.2   Fullback (H) alignments. For odd-numbered plays, align to the left; for even-numbered plays, align to the right. 0: Behind quarterback 4 to 5 yards deep. 1/2: Straddle offensive tackle's inside leg to call side. 3/4: In up position to call side. 5/6: Regular wide receiver alignment to call side. 7/8: Align as middle wide receiver to call side. 9/10: Align as outside wide receiver to call side.

aligned in a 5 position, then at the quarterback's direction, H would motion across the formation to the 6 alignment.

Using Cadence and Snap Count

We use a nonrhythmic cadence that incorporates a combination of numbers, words, and huts. This system enables the quarterback to audible and call plays at the line of scrimmage. It also keeps the defense off balance.

In the huddle, if the quarterback calls, "On first sound," it means the snap will take place on his first sound. There will be no motions, shifts, or audibles. When he's ready for the snap, the quarterback simply calls, "Hut."

If the call in the huddle is "on one," the quarterback is using the normal snap count. The play will make full use of motions, shifts, and audibles. At the line, the quarterback says, "Red 13, red 13, hut," to signal the snap.

When the quarterback calls, "On two," in the huddle, it means that the snap count will be on the second "hut." The quarterback uses this plot when the defense is getting a jump on the snap count. At the line, it sounds like "red 13, red 13, hut, hut."

If the quarterback calls, "Freeze," in the huddle, this means that no play will be called. You are trying to get the defense to jump. If they don't fall for it, the quarterback either will call a play at the line or will call a time-out. At the line, the quarterback calls, "Red 13, red 13, hut, hut, hut."

Running Back and Fullback

Running back is a general description of the players who rush the ball after being handed or pitched the football. In our offensive system, the term *running back* refers to our I-back.

Our running back's (tailback's) normal alignment is 7 yards deep directly behind the ball (figure 7.3). In other offensive systems, running backs line up in a variety of backfield positions in order to utilize their individual skills. The veer offense uses two running

backs aligned approximately 5 yards deep directly behind each guard. Some offensive sets offset the running back to the left or right of the fullback.

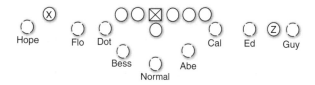

Figure 7.3 Tailback (T) alignments. Boy-named plays are to the right; girl-named plays are to the left. Normal: Behind quarterback 7 to 8 yards deep. Abe/Bess: Strad-dle offensive tackle's inside leg to call side (note: A-gun/B-gun same as Abe/Bess). Cal/Dot: In up position to call side. Ed/Flo: Align as inside wide receiver to call side. Guy/Hope: Align as outside wide receiver to call side.

A good running back can exploit any hole and freeze the defense with his speed and aggressiveness.

No matter what offensive system you incorporate or what alignment your running back uses, great running backs have the following traits and skills. Speed and elusiveness are vital traits in a running back. Select a player who has the ability to defeat defensive players one on one. Great running backs have a knack for making people miss them, plus they have the speed to outrun defensive players in pursuit to turn a 5-yard gain into a huge offensive gain. Because the running back is the workhorse in most offensive systems, he must be very durable. Find running backs who attack the defense with their speed and aggressiveness. Football seasons are long, and the running backs who can endure the long season of tackles and contact are the ones who will help your organization win championships. Running backs come in all shapes and sizes, but the great ones all have speed, power, elusiveness, and durability.

The fullback is a member of the running back family. He usually aligns 3 to 5 yards deep in the backfield directly behind the ball (see figure 7.2). The fullback must be a physically tough player who can get tough yardage up the middle and make point-of-attack blocks to spring the running back. In many systems, the fullback must be able to do all this plus run great pass routes and catch the ball. Great fullbacks are unselfish tough guys who put the team first. The ball is seldom handed to them, and their blocking assignments are always physically demanding. Fullbacks believe they can throw the game-winning block every time the ball is snapped.

Wide Receiver, Split End, and Flanker

The wide receivers, split ends, and flankers make up the receiving corps. Wide receivers align outside away from the ball and play a specialized position (figure 7.4). Look for players who have great hands, speed, and athletic ability. A great wide receiver can scare the average defensive back with his

Figure 7.4 Wide receiver (X) alignments. Normal: Align in regular wide receiver alignment away from call side. Ace: Align in regular wide receiver alignment away from call side but off the ball. Nasty: Cut split in half away from call side. Tight: Align as tight end away from call side (usually second tight end is substituted). Exit: Align in regular wide receiver alignment to call side.

ability to run downfield with great speed and make game-changing plays. Wide receivers must have great footwork and be able to get away from pass defenders. This ability to create space between themselves and the defense is vital for getting open to have the opportunity to catch a pass.

Another important trait of wide receivers is their willingness and ability to block downfield for other offensive players with the ball. The difference between a good play and a great play is often determined by the wide receiver's blocking ability against the last defender downfield.

Great wide receivers come in different shapes and sizes and have unique abilities that allow them to get open and catch balls. They may be tall and strong, short and fast, quick and elusive—whatever their skills may be, they always get open, they always catch the ball, and they are willing and able to block downfield defenders.

We like to use tall receivers against shorter defensive backs and look for formations and situations in which we can gain a physical advantage over the defense. (Figure 7.5 shows wide receiver terms and formations. Figure 7.6 shows flanker (Z) alignments.) Another common technique is to move or align receivers in positions in which linebackers or defensive players with lesser ability have to cover them. Be diligent in finding ways to use your wide receivers against the defense and always teach and emphasize the game-breaking importance of their blocking skills.

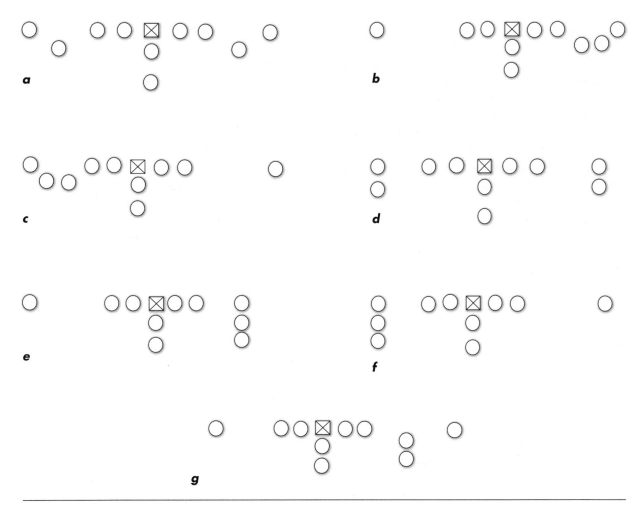

Figure 7.5 Wide receiver alignment terms: *(a)* bunch—wide receivers compress on both sides; *(b)* crunch—wide receivers compress on right side; *(c)* clump—wide receivers compress on left side; *(d)* stack—wide receivers stack on both sides; *(e)* rod—wide receivers stack on right side; *(f)* line—wide receivers stack on left side; *(g)* pair—Z and H stack.

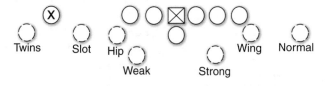

Figure 7.6 Flanker (Z) alignments. Illustration shows call side as right. Normal: Align in regular wide receiver alignment to call side. Wing: Alignment next to tight end or offensive lineman to call side. Strong: Align in power-back position to call side. Weak: Align in power-back position. Hip: Alignment next to tight end or offensive lineman away from call side. Slot: Align inside of X away from call side. Twins: Align outside of X away from call side.

Tight End

The tight end is a hybrid position: he must have the strength and size to play as an offensive lineman but have the speed and pass-receiving skills of a wide receiver. Tight ends need to be physical and tough like offensive tackles and be dominating run blockers. They also need to be better athletes in the passing game than the linebackers who are trying to cover them.

Your system will determine which tight end skills you need. A run-oriented team may want a bigger blocking-type player. If you prefer a passing approach, you may want a smaller, more athletic receiving tight end.

Great tight ends have the skills of a lineman and receiver. Another important trait in a good tight end is his ability to learn the rules for both the running game and the passing game. In most offensive systems the tight end is involved in all phases of the offense. He must be a student of the game to be successful.

Our tight ends align outside the offensive tackle most of the time, but we also like to move them around by removing them from the line of scrimmage and motioning them across the formation to assist with playside and backside blocking assignments (figure 7.7). We also use them in the passing game.

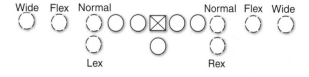

Figure 7.7 Tight end alignments. Normal: Regular split next to offensive tackle to call side. Rex/Lex: Regular split next to offensive tackle to call side but off the ball. Flex: Split 4 to 8 yards from offensive tackle to call side. Wide: Align as the outside wide receiver to call side.

Tackle

Tackles align outside the offensive guards. They have important responsibilities in both the running game and the passing game.

We prefer tall, athletic players who are aggressive by nature but have the ability to remain under control. Most errors happen when offensive tackles are being too aggressive and get out of position or lose leverage on the defender and fall to the ground. Tackles draw the assignment of pass-blocking the best defensive rushers on every snap. Defensive teams always have great athletic ends with tremendous speed, so offensive tackles must use great blocking technique and control in order to protect the quarterback in the pocket. When done well, the tackle's blocks go completely unnoticed by the crowd. When done poorly, the whole stadium scoffs when the quarterback gets hit from the blind side by a speeding defensive end.

Two other great attributes are a good reach (long arms) and great hands (a good grip) in order to control pass rushers. Tackles must also be physical run blockers who can play in space, block defenders with better ability, and play against the biggest, meanest defensive tackles.

Guard

Aligned on either side of the center, the guards are faced with blocking the biggest and most physical players the defense has to offer. Not only that, but guards must also be great pass blockers with the athletic ability to pull and block defenders on the run.

Many approaches have been taken to finding the perfect size and shape for an offensive guard. We have found the following traits to be equally important. Power, agility, and size are vital when finding and developing guards. Guards line up on every snap across from the biggest players on the field and must control them on run-blocking schemes. Guards also must be athletic enough to pass-block different defensive pass rushers. We sometimes sacrifice size to gain power and agility, but keep in mind the mass of today's defensive linemen and your particular offensive system's demands on your offensive guards.

Center

The center is the general of the offensive line. He makes the protection calls in the passing game and also assists in identifying special defensive alignments and strategies. Because every play in football except the kickoff begins with a center exchange, the center must be able to skillfully snap the ball either in a hand-to-hand exchange or shotgun (lateral) exchange with the quarterback.

The center must concentrate on several things before, during, and after an offensive play. First, he must remember the snap count the quarterback gave him. Second, he must make the proper defensive calls to the offensive line, exchange the football between his legs to the quarterback, and carry out his blocking assignment. After the play is over, the center establishes the huddle location and gets the group under control until the quarterback joins the huddle with the play. This entire scenario looks easy, but a shortfall in any area can be tragic. Look for a very athletic, powerful, cerebral player. The center is the hub of the offensive line. Without a good one, your offensive team will suffer and never reach its full potential.

Some of the great centers who have played in our system were masters at anticipating the quarterback's snap count and centering the ball almost in advance of the quarterback's cadence. Although it sounds simple, it is important to the offense. Many quarterback–center exchanges are botched because the center loses his concentration and the ball arrives at the quarterback's hands later than the quarterback expects. I encourage everyone to practice quarterback–center exchange and timing every day in practice until it becomes automatic.

Coach's Keys

1. The only limitations on offensive formations are the offensive coordinator's personality and the players' ability to execute out of each alignment.

2. The communication system should be consistent, simple, and understandable to all 11 players in the huddle. The system should cross over to all offensive systems, personnel groupings, and philosophies.

3. To ensure that you're placing players in the best possible position to be successful, focus on your own offensive philosophy and research the ways opponents will defend certain alignments.

4. Formations should be diverse. Be able to pass from condensed formations and run from spread formations. Develop the ability to be balanced from each formation. Don't allow defenses to gang up on you.

5. Study position-by-position player attributes and place players in position to use their individual offensive skills and abilities. Do not ask players to perform tasks they don't have the ability to accomplish.

6. Creativity without execution is futile. Execute, execute, execute.

OFFENSIVE FORMATIONS

Offensive formations are virtually limitless in scope. If you can imagine it, you can line up in it. Use offensive formations to put offensive personnel in position to be successful. Once the center, guards, and tackles line up in standard position, the other six players can align anywhere the offensive coordinator wants them to in order to defeat the opponent. Figure 7.8 shows our four called formations.

Our offensive system involves a limited number of running and passing plays that we can execute out of hundreds of formations. The blocking rules and schemes don't change, the formations do. Because the formation can change, the defense feels the stress to align and defend a variety of formations.

On videotape, our offensive system looks amazingly complex. In fact, we run a limited number of schemes out of many different looks. In theory, 10 running plays that can be executed from 20 different formations and alignments look like 200 different plays to an opponent's defensive coordinator. We gain an advantage by taking our opponent out of his comfort zone and making him concentrate on alignment and assignment issues.

Try polling your defensive staff to find out which formations and plays they have trouble defending. I have always found that our defense plays much better when they can

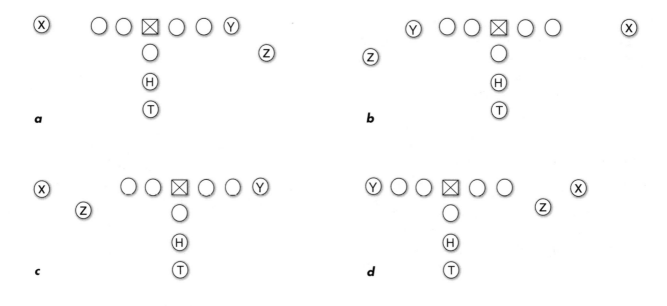

Figure 7.8 Called formations: *(a)* right; *(b)* left; *(c)* right slot; *(d)* left slot.

just line up against the same group of formations over and over. Their focus is much easier to maintain when they don't have to worry about where to line up. Be creative and plan carefully when deciding which formations to use in your offensive system.

Consider a variety of issues when developing an offensive system and selecting offensive formations. First, consider your offensive philosophy. Does your philosophy lead you to be a power-running ball club, a balanced offensive team, or a wide-open passing offense? Make sure your formation selection allows you to stay consistent with your philosophy.

Also consider the personnel on your squad when determining where players should line up. It would hurt a team to align in a four-wide receiver system if the program didn't have many solid wide receivers who had great speed and ability. Do you have big, physical offensive linemen? Do you have a couple of great I-backs? Ask yourself these questions when contemplating formations.

A third issue to consider when developing and choosing formations is how your opponents defend certain formations and personnel groups. Study film of your opponents and develop a strong understanding of their

defensive alignments and philosophy. How do your offensive players match up with your opponent's defensive players in certain formations? The more you study, the more ideas you will develop, and the more likely you will be to select offensive formations that will help you succeed as an offensive unit.

Successful formations should allow the offense to be multidimensional. In other words, the formation should allow the offense to be balanced or at least make the defense think it is balanced. Great teams can run or pass effectively out of nearly every formation and alignment they incorporate.

Purpose is also very important. We line up players in certain positions for certain reasons, not just to look like we have multiple formations. Put players in position to use their abilities and to take advantage of the defensive approach applied to the formation. It does your squad no good to throw the ball for the sake of throwing the ball or to run the ball just to say you ran the ball. Have a purpose for every snap. The offensive team can execute your system at a high level if you have taught them exactly what to do, where to line up, and why they do what they do. I know it sounds simple, but be very good at what you choose to do.

Many coaches assume that in order to run the football, the team must condense formations and load up the box with big, physical blockers and runners. This is one approach many coaches take to physically running the football, and many have been successful using this approach. However, I would like you to consider spreading the field with three or four receivers and making the defense spread out to cover your receivers (figure 7.9). Snap the ball to the quarterback in the shotgun formation and let the running back be the lead blocker against the defense. Through formation and personnel, you have created natural space for your running back (the quarterback in this case) to run the ball and you have used a lead blocker (the running back) against a defensive team who is used to the running back carrying the ball. Is this a power running game? You bet!

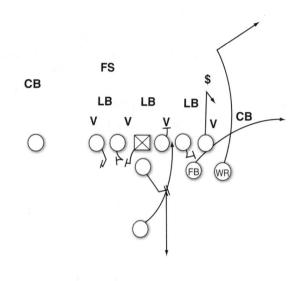

Figure 7.10 Compressed action pass.

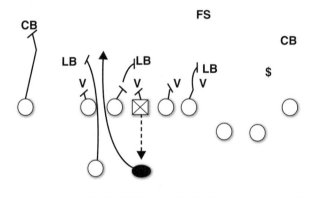

Figure 7.9 Power run.

Now condense your formation by bringing in the wide receivers in a tight alignment along with the fullback in a wing formation (figure 7.10). This reduced-wing formation is ideal for running the football offtackle or outside. The defense must adjust and align their players closer to the ball and closer to the line of scrimmage to stop the run threat. What a perfect opportunity to run an action pass off your favorite running play and work your receivers and fullback downfield against a defense that is reduced, condensed, and expecting a run. Use a running formation to throw the ball? You bet!

Hybrid and Gimmick Formations

Use your imagination and creativity to come up with a variety of formations and alignments. Many coaches have done amazing things with formations, but let me share with you the truly important components of a hybrid formation.

No matter how cool a formation looks or how complex it is, can your offense effectively execute plays from it? If your offense can't execute successfully, then the formation is of no use. Make sure to remember the bottom line when being creative. Also consider the idea that a confused defense can sometimes confuse your offense. In other words, your offensive team may not see the same defensive alignments you worked on during practice, and this could lead to a lack of offensive execution. When developing special formations, take the same approach you would with your regular offensive formations and plays. Make the players and coaches believe that the hybrid formation will be successful and then practice until you can execute it at the same level as other offensive plays.

Motion System

In our motion system, we simply call the number of the player that we want to go into motion and the position in the formation to which we want him to go (figure 7.11). For example, if the H starts in right 5, but we want to motion him across the formation to the 6 position, the quarterback calls, "Right 5, H 6," in the huddle.

If we are in a two–tight end set, we use the words *red* or *blue* to indicate which tight end should go in motion. Red refers to the tight end on the right, and blue refers to the one on the left.

There are a few exceptions to these rules. If we tell a player to go in jet motion, he will

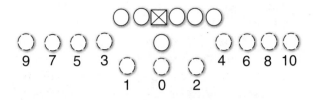

Figure 7.11   Motion positions.

motion across the formation at running speed. We will either run the speed sweep with him or fake it depending on the play call. When a player is called to perform U-motion, he will motion to the center and back to his original alignment. When a player is in arc motion, he will motion deep into the backfield.

CHAPTER 8

TEACHING OFFENSIVE SKILLS

The ability to teach and develop football technique is the key to being a successful football coach and developing a successful football team. From a fan's point of view, great play calls or high-flying, wide-open offense and defense make the difference in close games, but the key to developing a consistently winning team is the coach's ability to teach his players sound technique and skills.

Great technique and position skills can help a smaller or less-talented athlete succeed against athletes who have more size and ability. Teaching young men to be technicians at their individual positions is the most important aspect of the game. A player with great technique has a chance to be successful. A good athlete with great technique will almost always defeat a great athlete with average technique.

In this chapter I explain the most important offensive techniques that will make players successful at their individual positions. Keep in mind, before an athlete can master complex position skills, he must first have the solid foundation of basic position tech-

nique. It is useless to teach a receiver how to catch a football if you don't teach him how to release and get open from the defender. Teaching technique is a building process that separates the great coaches and teams from the merely good.

OFFENSIVE LINEMAN

A firm foundation in fundamentals is vital when building a solid offensive lineman. Before the front five come together to execute technical schemes flawlessly, a lot of individual teaching must take place. Begin with a great stance and progress into many different skill areas.

Stance

Make sure all drill work begins with the linemen in great stances. Don't let them be lazy or unfocused and get sloppy with their stances. Sometimes big guys take shortcuts that can hurt their technique.

Figure 8.1 Offensive lineman's stance: *(a)* lineman bends at the waist; *(b)* he reaches to the ground with his dominant hand.

In our program, a great offensive lineman's stance begins with his feet shoulder-width apart or a little less. Once his feet are the proper width apart, the lineman moves his dominant foot back until the toes are approximately even with the instep of his front foot. Next, the lineman bends at the hips and waist and places his elbows just above his knees (figure 8.1a). If he is doing it correctly, the lineman will feel his quads, hip flexors, and hamstrings begin to flex.

This position will be a little different for each player, but is critical for placing big guys in an athletic position. Taller, longer players may need to widen the stance a little and be a little taller in this presnap position. Shorter, more compact players may have to narrow the stance and be a little shorter. The bottom line is that the stance needs to be functional for the player.

Once the elbows are on the thighs and the knees are flexed, the lineman rocks forward until his heels are slightly elevated. (We test this by seeing if we can place a credit card under his heels.) This position adds additional flex to the lineman's legs and puts him in position to extend his dominant hand to the ground (figure 8.1b). With his fingertips and thumb supporting his weight, the other hand slides down the thigh with the hand cupping the knee. The lineman's back should be flat, and he should have his head up, looking comfortably at the defense.

Make sure the athlete is comfortable and balanced. If he has too much weight forward, the lineman will not be able to assume the pass-blocking position. If insufficient weight is forward, he will not be able to fire off the line and attack the defense with authority. A good test of weight balance is to ask the lineman to push up with his dominant hand. If the lineman can't push up with his hand and stand, he has too much weight forward and needs to move his hand closer to his body. Another good indicator of stance balance is to see if the lineman can take a six-inch step with either foot. If he has too much weight forward, he will be unable to step with his nondominant foot. Remember the importance of comfort and remember that every player is different and won't have the same stance as the next guy.

We teach the left guard and left tackle to play in a left-handed stance and the right guard and right tackle to play in a right-handed stance. (Left-handed stance and right-handed stance refer to the hand the player has on the ground and the leg that is offset behind the other.) The center and tight end play with their dominant hands down. The center must assume a stance that allows him to center the ball to the quarterback and allows him to step with either foot to execute his blocking assignment. By using these stance techniques, our offensive linemen always have their outside legs back, which gives them an advantage in pass protection and other areas discussed later.

Base Block

Commonly referred to as the one-on-one block, executing the base block requires great technique because the offensive lineman must defeat the defensive lineman without help. Often the defensive lineman is a better athlete than the offensive player, so again I emphasize the importance of technique.

The offensive lineman assumes a good stance. He needs to remember the snap count because getting a jump on the defensive player is a big advantage. Offensive linemen use either the defender's inside number or outside number as the aiming point, depending on the blocking rules of the play.

At the snap, the offensive lineman begins the base block by taking an approximately six-inch power step with the foot closest to the aiming point (figure 8.2a). The six-inch step allows the offensive lineman to take off and get in position then get his feet back to the ground for power at the point of impact with the defender. If the defender makes contact while the offensive lineman's feet are in the air, the fight is over before it gets started.

Figure 8.2 Base block: *(a)* lineman takes a six-inch power step; *(b)* lineman's eyes are focused on the aiming point; *(c)* lineman maintains a wide base and uses his hands throughout the block.

The offensive lineman focuses his eyes on the aiming point while exploding off the line under control (figure 8.2b). He delivers a powerful blow with his hands inside the framework of the defender's body. The offensive lineman naturally establishes good position on the defender by focusing on the defender's chest number and leading with the hands.

After contact, the offensive lineman stays in control by maintaining a wide base and taking short powerful steps while shoving with the hands (figure 8.2c). Great offensive linemen have strong hands and practice blow delivery over and over until they master the technique. Remember, the lineman who establishes and maintains hand control will win the battle.

We teach base-blocking technique against other players, not bags or dummies. The base-blocking fit is vital in developing offensive linemen. We start by putting the offensive lineman in the position we want him in after the six-inch power step. The lineman places his face mask on the aiming point number and places his hands on either breastplate of the opponent and initiates his block from this position so that he will get the feel for the fit we want. Once he becomes comfortable with the fit, we back him up and allow him to take the power step and execute the block.

Combo and Double-Team Block

The combo block is by far the most important block in football. The offensive linemen who understand the technique and execute combo blocks well are the linemen whose teams rush the football effectively. The word combo is short for combination, which means using two offensive linemen to block two defenders who are on different levels.

To execute a combo block, two offensive linemen must work together to block the first-level defender with a double-team technique while watching for the second-level defender to approach and blocking him at the last minute. The advantage of using a combo is the ability to place two offensive linemen on one defensive player to secure the block and then release one of the offensive linemen to block a second-level player.

To teach the combo block, start with the double-team portion of the technique. Place a defender between the two offensive linemen you want to work the double team. Both offensive linemen will use the defender's chest numbers as aiming points to execute the double team (figure 8.3a). Both offensive linemen's initial steps will be directly at their respective chest numbers while each lineman blocks his half of the defender. Get movement of the defensive player off the line of scrimmage as each offensive lineman gets his eyes on the second-level player.

While driving the first-level player off the line, the offensive linemen prepare to engage the second-level defender when he shows on either side of the first-level player. If the second-level defender shows on the inside of the double team, the inside offensive lineman comes off the double team and blocks the second-level player while the outside offensive lineman continues the block on the outside half of the defensive lineman (figure 8.3b). If the second-level player shows on the outside of the double team, the outside offensive lineman comes off the double team and blocks him while the inside offensive lineman continues to block the inside half of the defensive lineman (figure 8.3c).

Figure 8.3 Combo block: (a) double team; (b) inside lineman comes off double team to block second-level player; (c) outside lineman comes off double team to block second-level player.

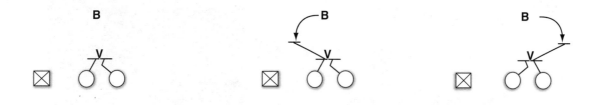

Figure 8.4 Combo blocking scenarios.

The combo block is the lifeline to any effective rushing offense. We practice this particular blocking technique dozens of times each day. Figure 8.4 shows a few of the combo blocking scenarios you can practice for your offensive system.

Pull-and-Trap Block

Our offensive system requires each offensive line position to execute various trapping techniques in both directions. Some plays require the lineman to pull either right or left and to trap a defensive lineman or even a linebacker or safety on the second level of defense.

The most important component of pulling is maintaining a balanced stance, a stance that allows the lineman to drop step with his lead foot and pivot and drive off his back foot. If too much weight is forward, the lineman cannot execute an effective pull technique without wasting movement to make up for imbalance. We also remind linemen not to rock back in the stance and transfer their weight back before the snap. Although this move would allow an offensive lineman to pull with better efficiency, the change in stance tips off the defense and gives them the advantage of knowing that the play involves a pull.

Our method for teaching offensive linemen to pull is the same method a manager uses to teach a baseball player to steal second base.

The offensive lineman assumes a proper stance (figure 8.5a). On the snap, he takes an open drop step with the lead leg while the lead elbow swings back and around to help position the body to run laterally (figure 8.5b). The open drop step turns and opens the lineman's hips so that he can drive off the backside pivot foot and run downhill at his blocking assignment (figure 8.5c).

The lineman is aware of his blocking assignment. He must visually locate his target while on the run. It is imperative for the offensive lineman to maintain his ability to see the defender, especially on second-level defenders such as linebackers and safeties.

Players repeat their technique until the technique and movement become natural and comfortable. Linemen have landmarks on trap blocks just like on base blocks. The play may require the puller to block the defender outside or kick him out. In this case, the lineman aims for an inside hip or number. He tries to hit that point with control and to drive the defender to the outside. Other plays may require the lineman to pull and reach or seal the defender to the inside so that the ball carrier can run to the outside. This technique is called a *log*. The lineman aims at the outside number of the defender. On contact, he runs to accelerate around the defender and seal, or log, him to the inside.

Figure 8.5 Pull-and-trap block: *(a)* linemen assume their initial stance; *(b)* lineman takes an open drop step and runs laterally; *(c)* he turns and runs downhill to his blocking assignment.

Fold Block

The fold-blocking technique is a common, effective way to gain leverage over a defender by taking advantage of blocking angles. The first fold technique is an outside fold (figure 8.6). On an outside fold, two offensive linemen work together, with the lineman on the outside blocking down and sealing, or pinning, the defender to the inside while the lineman on the inside executes a pull technique to the outside to block an outside defender

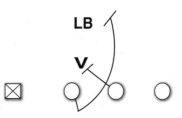

Figure 8.6 Outside fold block.

(figure 8.7). In essence, the two offensive linemen trade responsibilities and use angles to their advantage.

Figure 8.7 On an outside fold block, the offensive linemen work together and use the blocking angles to their advantage.

The outside lineman assumes a proper stance and takes an approximately six-inch power step inside at the defender's hip. It is crucial for the lineman to understand what kind of technique the defensive player prefers to use. Is he a charger who tries to penetrate the backfield at any cost, or is he a reader who simply reacts to the blocking scheme in front of him? If he is a charger, the outside lineman must adjust by placing his head in front of the charging lineman and pinning, or sealing, him to the inside. If the defender is a reader, the pin block becomes more of a base block, a block of position and footwork, to ensure that the defender doesn't gain outside position on the execution of the block. The inside offensive lineman is the puller. He executes the pulling technique discussed earlier.

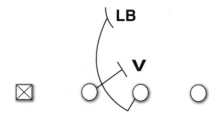

Figure 8.8   Inside fold block.

The inside fold block (figure 8.8) is taught the same way as the outside fold block except that the offensive linemen's roles are switched. The inside lineman blocks out to seal, or pin, the defender while the outside lineman executes the pull technique back to the inside (figure 8.9).

Figure 8.9   On an inside fold block, the offensive linemen switch roles. The inside lineman seals the defender, and the outside lineman executes the pull technique to the inside.

Pass Block

Pass protection is the most unnatural and difficult football technique to master. We have to teach the least athletic players on the field to master feet and hand placement on some of the most gifted athletes in football. Pass blocking is unnatural because it requires offensive linemen to be powerful yet move their feet constantly to maintain leverage. Run blocking requires power and aggressiveness; pass blocking requires maintaining position and power without moving forward while keeping balanced.

Teaching pass blocking begins with the pass *set,* the initial placement of the offensive lineman's feet on the snap of the ball in relation to the quarterback's position and the defenders' angle of rush (figure 8.10a). For the pass block, the offensive lineman finds an aiming point or landmark based on the defender's alignment. We want the offensive lineman's outside foot to be inside the defensive lineman's outside foot.

I know this sounds complicated, so let me explain. Our tackles normally block outside rushers who are trying to turn the corner with speed to sack the quarterback. We teach tackles to set with the outside foot back and inside the rusher's outside foot to maintain inside leverage and position. As the rusher drives upfield, the tackle delivers an explosive blow with his hands and arms, extending them into the defender's chest while concentrating on not getting too much weight forward and overextending (figure 8.10b), which can lead to a loss of leverage and balance and a sack from around the edge of the pocket.

Figure 8.10   Pass block: *(a)* pass set; *(b)* block.

Our guards and center normally block rushers who are aligned closer to the quarterback and who must rush more directly upfield to get to the quarterback. In concept, the pass set of the guards and center is like the tackle's; in technique, however, it is a little different. We teach interior lineman to set just like the tackle except with a shorter and firmer attack strategy. Because the quarterback is directly behind the interior linemen, they must maintain the front of the pocket and not allow penetration of any kind so that the quarterback can step up and deliver the ball from inside the pocket. We want the linemen to maintain inside position with power and balance, but they must be strong and firm and never allow penetration up the middle of the pocket.

Offensive linemen are taught these keys to pass blocking:

- Never get beat inside by the pass rusher.
- Never overextend by leaning forward or leaning on the defender.
- Use explosive blows with the hands and maintain separation by locking out the pass rusher with extended arms.
- Imagine you have a broom handle running down the length of your spine. This will paint the mental picture of standing tall as a pass blocker.
- Be aware of the quarterback's position within the pocket.
- Protect the quarterback at all costs.

Three-on-Three and Five-on-Five Drills

Both the three-on-three drill and the five-on-five drill are excellent ways to place your offensive line in a position to learn, drill, and execute all of the blocking styles and techniques we have discussed plus additional special situations your offensive system may need.

Three-on-Three Drill

Our three-on-three drill begins by isolating three offensive linemen in their normal line positions. In some situations, we begin the drill with the center, right guard, and right tackle; in other situations, we use the center and both guards on either side. In a third situation, we use a guard, tackle, and tight end. Whatever the situation, make sure the linemen are practicing in their actual offensive line positions next to the linemen they normally work with in a game situation.

Once the offensive players are in position, place two defensive linemen in position on the line of scrimmage with one second-level player aligned in the look you will see on game day. From this alignment, you can drill any of the blocking techniques and schemes you need to cover. The environment tends to lend an advantage to the defense because of the limited number of gaps to control and the limited area the drill actually covers. As an offensive line coach, I used these conditions to test the offensive linemen under tough conditions to see who could play in the trenches. With the area reduced in size, the coach can easily see the offensive unit working together and rapidly make adjustments and present coaching points during the drill.

Five-on-Five Drill

Run the five-on-five drill the same as the three-on-three drill, but place your front five offensive linemen in the drill together. Use a variety of defensive alignments and generate any defensive environment you want. This is a great drill to teach, drill, and evaluate both ability and toughness. We also add our tight ends to this drill with an additional defender to use all of our blocking schemes and techniques. The five-on-five drill is a little more offensive friendly than the three-on-three drill because of the number of techniques, schemes, and plays the offensive unit can practice.

1. Skill and technique allow an average player to defeat a good player. Make sure every offensive player has a firm foundation in the fundamentals of his individual position. Play calling and game planning will fail without technique and execution.

2. Great offensive lines work well together as a finely honed group. Practice footwork, body position, hand placement, and explosion. Place players in tough situations in practice to find out who the real tough guys are.

3. Running backs must develop great ball-handling skills through drill work. Once they are sound in their fundamentals, teach them the concepts of the running plays without overcoaching. You never want to limit a great player's ability by not allowing him to use his skills to the fullest.

4. Receivers must be able to do four things very well: release cleanly from the line of scrimmage, run great pass routes, catch the ball with their hands, and stalk-block. Develop these skills by placing receivers in gamelike situations in practice.

5. The quarterback is the offensive triggerman. Develop his ball-handling and throwing skills as well as his leadership and confidence. Teach him to be comfortable and confident in the pocket.

TIGHT END

The tight end is a hybrid position. He needs the blocking skills of an offensive lineman and the ability to run pass routes and catch balls like a receiver. In our offensive system, we look for players who have good size and strength and above-average athletic ability. The tight end will rarely be as big as the defensive lineman he is assigned to block, so we look for strength and athletic ability to make up for the size disadvantage.

The size disadvantage in the blocking scheme can lead to an advantage in the pass-receiving portion of the tight end's responsibility. In many cases, the tight end will be bigger and stronger than the defensive back who is trying to cover him in the passing game. The tight end may be faster than a large, physical linebacker who is trying to defend the pass. The tight end is a skilled position, one that is vital to offensive production in both the running and the passing game. In short, the tight end must have all the skills discussed in the offensive lineman section plus the skills discussed in the next section on wide receivers.

One tight end skill that must be perfected is the ability to release from the line of scrimmage into a pass route. The tight end usually lines up in close quarters with the defensive player he must avoid or defeat in order to run down the field and catch a pass. The release or escape technique we teach is a *juke release*. In the juke release, the tight end attacks the defender's alignment then cuts rapidly away from the direction of the original movement. By attacking the defender's alignment and technique, whether inside or outside, the tight end forces the defender to adjust his alignment in order to maintain his gap responsibility. This creates a natural space and opportunity for the tight end to escape and get into his pass route. This is an effective technique for an athletic tight end.

Other escape techniques that can be used by larger, more physical tight ends are the slam or butt technique and the rip or swim technique. The tight end attacks the defender he must defeat just as if he were attempting to run-block while gaining hand position and control on the side of the defender from which he will escape. Once hand control is established, the tight end pulls the defender toward himself while executing a swim or rip move with the other arm, powering through the defender's shoulder and sprinting away into the pass route. Pass-receiving skills will be covered further in the next section.

At least once a day, drill tight ends with the wide receivers to hone the tight ends' eye–hand coordination, improve their route-running skills, and continue to improve their timing and consistency in the passing game. Carefully coordinate where the tight ends spend their practice sessions, balancing their time and efforts between their lineman responsibilities and their receiving assignments.

WIDE RECEIVER

Wide receivers play a variety of important roles in a successful offensive system. They must provide solid downfield blocking in the running game, and they must run great pass routes and catch the football consistently. These skills are key no matter what system the wide receiver plays in.

Stance and Release

Our wide receivers use a two-point stance with the foot closest to the ball forward and the outside foot offset behind. This stance allows us to build in consistent release steps and techniques for running certain pass routes along with enhancing the timing of the passing game. Just like offensive linemen, our receivers must learn both a right-handed and left-handed stance.

A wide receiver assumes a two-point stance by first digging his front, or inside foot, into the ground then offsetting his outside foot in a comfortable position behind the inside foot (figure 8.11a). The receiver assumes an athletic position with a slight bend in the hips, waist, and knees and elbows slightly bent with hands out front in the ready position. The receiver needs to be in position to release from the line of scrimmage in an athletic manner whether he gets a free release or has to defeat a press defender. With the inside foot up and planted (figure 8.11b), the receiver can drive off the front foot and not take false or backward steps with his back leg. This is important in developing explosive speed on the snap of the football.

After receivers can get into a comfortable and functional two-point stance, we progress to teaching release techniques. First, receivers learn the simple explosive speed release

Figure 8.11 Wide receiver *(a)* stance and *(b)* release.

used when no defender is in position to inhibit their release from the line of scrimmage. The receiver assumes a steady stance and simply drives off the line of scrimmage with his inside foot, accelerating to maximum speed as soon as possible. The receiver must practice the speed release over and over to ensure he is not only fast but also under control and is able to execute his pass route effectively.

The second release is designed to defeat a defender who is directly in front of the receiver on the line of scrimmage and who is trying to disrupt or prevent the receiver's release. The receiver assumes the same stance, but the release is much different. The receiver's first step is to attack the alignment of the defensive back. In other words, if the defender is aligned outside, the receiver attacks outside; if the defender is aligned inside, the receiver attacks inside. This technique forces the defender to move his feet and his alignment to stay in the receiver's path. When the defender moves, it creates space and opportunity for the receiver to change his initial direction and escape the defender by moving in the opposite direction of his initial release. The movement and setup

help the receiver initiate a clean release from the defender.

After mastering the press release, the receiver learns a rip or swim move (figure 8.12) in which the receiver's arms further enhance and assist the release. If the defender gets his hands on the receiver during the release, the receiver can rip or swim through the defender's arms to create more space to release from him. The receiver's ability to master these release techniques is critical in the passing game. If a receiver can't get open, he is really not a receiver because the quarterback cannot safely throw him the ball.

Stalk Block

Receivers who are willing and able to be great blockers make the difference between good running plays and great running plays by blocking the last line of defense. We teach our receivers the stalk block (figure 8.13), a technique that involves taking one of the releases discussed earlier and convincing the defensive player that the play is a pass. The play is called a stalk block because the

Figure 8.12 *(a)* Rip and *(b)* swim.

receiver does what the defender does or mirrors the defender.

The receiver makes every effort to sell himself as a pass threat to the defensive player. Once the defender recognizes that the play is a run, the receiver positions himself directly in front of the defender and assumes an athletic position with his feet firing rapidly, getting ready to react to the defender's initial charge to the ball carrier. When the defender reacts, the receiver attacks the defender by delivering a blow with his hands on the defender's chest, trying to maintain surface and position on the defensive player.

Figure 8.13 Stalk block: *(a)* receiver sells himself as a pass threat; *(b)* receiver engages the defender once the defender sees that the play is a run play; *(c)* receiver blocks the defender to allow the ball carrier to run by.

The receiver must let the defender make the first move. Then the receiver attacks and maintains a blocking surface for as long as possible without holding or clipping the defender. The running back always runs off the position of the wide receiver, so position doesn't matter. As long as the receiver blocks, the running back will go the right direction. Stalk blocking takes a lot of effort and intensity but is vital to a successful rushing football team.

Route Running

Route running involves two situations. Against zone coverage, the receiver must recognize the coverage and have great vision to find the open area in the zone so that the quarterback can deliver the ball to the open area. Against man-to-man coverage, the receiver must be able to create space between himself and the defender covering him. Many techniques, such as a head fake, a juke with the receiver's footwork, and a change of tempo when running the route, can be used to create space.

When teaching route running, make sure the receiver gets many repetitions against both zone and man coverage so he will be confident in recognizing and defeating each coverage. Make sure the receiver has at least a couple of different route stems or setups so that the defensive back must guess and won't catch on that the same move is being repeated. Predictability can be fatal in the passing game.

Receivers learning to run routes and get open need to study the video of their opponents to learn which moves are effective against defenders and what weaknesses the defender may have. Does the defender give up the hitch? Does he bite on a double move such as a hitch-and-go? What type of release will give the receiver inside position or outside position? All of these questions can usually be answered by studying video.

Catches

Once the receiver masters release techniques and route running, he must master catching the ball as well. It does no good for a receiver to be wide open if he cannot catch and secure the football.

Concentration is a critical component of developing consistent hands. Most of the great receivers I have known had great focus on the ball no matter what was going on around them. They had the ability to block out everything in the environment except themselves and the ball.

Constantly work with receivers. Teach them to catch the ball in their hands without using their body or pads. We call this technique *catching the ball cleanly* (figure 8.14a). Receivers who can catch the ball with their hands will be much more consistent and successful than those who can't.

Finally, receivers and tight ends make sure every catch made is completed by securing the ball against the body in what we refer to as the *safe position* (figure 8.14b). In the safe position, the ball is tucked away in the arm that is away from the nearest defender and secured using the same technique we teach running backs. Thumb, fingertips, and palm firmly grip the ball. The forearm and biceps press the ball against the ribs. Ball security is vital for receivers because they often are in vulnerable positions while catching the ball.

Receiver Drills

We use the following drills to develop the skills of wide receivers and tight ends. You know what you expect receivers to accomplish, so develop and adjust drills to fit your teaching needs.

Blind Catch

For the blind-catch drill, start with the receiver about 10 yards away from the coach with his back turned to the coach. The coach throws a pass then tells the receiver when to turn and face the ball. This drill forces the receiver to concentrate on eye–hand coordination because he only sees the ball in its last few feet of flight. This is a great drill for working on focus and forcing the receiver to concentrate. The coach can control the level

Figure 8.14 *(a)* Catching the ball cleanly. *(b)* Securing the ball in the safe position.

of difficulty by allowing less reaction time for the receiver to turn and by throwing the ball into different areas so that the receiver will have to intensely focus to visually find the ball and secure the catch. Finish the drill by making the receiver secure the ball against his body in the safe position.

Buddy

A receiver and a defensive back line up side by side to simulate a man-to-man pass situation. The receiver runs a route straight down the field with the defender running alongside him. This scenario creates a realistic man-to-man environment for the receiver. The defender can do anything within his power to disrupt the receiver's concentration such as place his hands on the receiver's body or wave his hands in the receiver's face, bump the receiver with his body, or anything he can think of to take the receiver's mind off the ball. The receivers coach throws the ball, and the receiver must leap and catch the ball in his hands then secure it against his body in the

safe position. This drill is beneficial for many reasons and is one we do nearly every day.

RUNNING BACK

With a diverse number of offensive systems, the running back's techniques and role may differ a great deal. Many running back skills are universal, but it will be necessary to teach position-specific techniques that fit your individual offensive system.

Stance

The tailback or I-back assumes a two-point stance so that he can have a clear view of the defensive alignment and see the offensive-blocking schemes develop in front of him. The tailback places his feet shoulder-width apart or a little narrower, depending on his body size. His weight is on the balls of his feet, and his hands are on his thighs for balance and stability. The tailback's stance must allow effective movement in every direction because he has several responsibilities in our system.

The fullback uses a three-point stance similar to the stance used by our offensive linemen. The three-point stance allows the fullback to step with either foot and look at the defense to locate his blocking assignment. In some systems, the fullback is an attacking runner and blocker and may assume a four-point stance that allows maximum acceleration in a forward direction. This technique is used in wishbone offenses as well as trapping offenses. Develop and teach stances that allow each backfield member to execute all of his offensive responsibilities without having to change or adjust, which would give the defense the advantage.

Handoffs and Defensive Reads

I teach the same handoff technique to all members of the backfield. We use the two handed–cradle method of accepting handoffs (figure 8.15). The running back places the elbow closest to the quarterback up with the forearm parallel to the ground and across his chest. The palm of the hand should be open and turned forward. The arm opposite the quarterback should be flexed at the elbow with the forearm across the waist and parallel to the ground. The palm of the bottom hand should be open and turned up. When the quarterback places the ball between the running back's forearms, the running back cradles the ball with both hands, one over each end of the football, which allows maximum ball protection while in traffic and also allows the running back to place the ball in either hand after he clears the first wave of defense.

Great running backs have a natural sense of where to rush the football and how the defense will react. Teach the running back the concept of each blocking scheme and what the running play is supposed to accomplish against the defense. Is the play designed to go outside, inside, or cut back against the grain?

I have always been careful not to over-coach the running back position. Don't coach beyond basic skills or you might limit the run-ning back's great ability by forcing him to run in a certain spot. Teach the running back concepts and let his ability do the rest. Make sure the running back protects the ball with both hands while in traffic and puts the ball in the arm away from the defense in the safe position discussed in the receivers section. These simple principles will prevent turnovers and make your offense more consistent.

It also is important to develop running backs as blockers. Many of our quarterback running plays and pass protections require the running backs to be productive blockers. We incorporate practice time for our tailbacks to practice run- and pass-blocking techniques just like linemen.

If your running back also works as a receiver, be sure you schedule practice time to develop route-running and receiving skills as well. Running backs who have the ability to catch passes can be tremendous weapons and open up countless offensive opportunities.

Figure 8.15 Receiving a handoff using the two handed–cradle method.

Running Back Drills

We incorporate a variety of specific running back teaching methods. Every running back should practice the following drills to ensure they take care of the football and develop a strong awareness of body control and ball security.

Endless Handoffs

Running backs form two lines about 5 yards apart facing each other. The running backs in the front of each line jog toward each other. One hands off the ball to the other who then hands off the ball to the next running back. After handing off the ball, the running back goes to the end of the line and the drill continues.

This drill teaches proper hand and arm placement for receiving the handoff and securing the ball. As players become comfortable with the ball-handling drill, pick up the tempo until they can execute the drill at game speed.

Ball Exchange and Cutting

This drill teaches the running back to cut off of his outside foot and to secure the ball away from the defender. Place cones in a zigzag position 5 yards apart. Start with the ball in the running back's outside arm. The running back runs toward the first cone and plants on his outside foot while shifting the ball into his other hand. He travels to the next cone and repeats the process.

For variety, have the running back spin back to the inside while exchanging the ball at each cone. Again, this teaches the running back to be conscious of protecting the football from the defense and proper footwork techniques for cutting and accelerating.

QUARTERBACK

As with running backs, your offensive system will determine what stance your quarterback will assume. The quarterback needs to be in

position to accept the snap from the center while stepping back and away from the line of scrimmage to avoid the offensive linemen and then to hand the ball to the running back or set up to throw a pass. Our quarterback offsets his dominant foot back slightly behind the other foot for balance and ease of stepping backward after the snap.

Snaps

The center–quarterback exchange looks simple and automatic, and it can be if you are willing to teach proper technique and drill it until it becomes second nature. Keep in mind the environmental factors that can affect the center–quarterback exchange. The center's footwork at the snap, rain or snow, perspiration, and anticipation of a blitz are all factors that must be considered when teaching proper exchanges.

Have the quarterback assume his stance behind the center (figure 8.16). The quarterback's throwing hand, the top hand, is placed against the center's buttocks (figure 8.17a). The quarterback must always apply pressure against the center's buttocks so that the center will sense where the target hand is located. The quarterback places the palm of the other hand against the top hand facing up to form a pocket for the ball. The quarterback should bend his knees and elbows slightly so that he can extend and ride the center during the snap as the center takes his initial steps. The center must know where to place the football laces in his grip so that the football is exchanged to the quarterback with the laces in perfect position for the quarterback to throw the ball (figure 8.17b). Once the ball is exchanged, the quarterback pulls the ball into his body with both hands for control and then executes the next operation in accordance with the play responsibilities.

Handoffs

To exchange the football, spacing and timing must be practiced over and over. Backfield alignment and spacing must be consistent to ensure proper quarterback–running back

Figure 8.16 Quarterback's stance under center.

Figure 8.17 Center–quarterback exchange: *(a)* quarterback's hand placement under the center; *(b)* snap.

handoffs. Most exchange problems happen when collisions occur in the backfield caused by poor spacing, or when the mesh between players is too far apart and the quarterback can't place the ball into the running back's belly. These exchanges need to be rehearsed again and again to ensure quality and consistency.

The quarterback secures the exchange from the center and takes the proper steps to be in position to mesh with the running back. He then places the ball into the running back's pocket or belly. The quarterback maintains possession of the ball until he feels the

running back's arms and hands take control of the ball. The quarterback then releases the ball and carries out the rest of his play-faking responsibilities.

Play Action Fakes

Play action passing can be a tremendous weapon when used in conjunction with a solid running attack. We want our action passing game to look exactly like our running game as far as the backfield action is concerned. We want the defensive players who are in charge of stopping the run to believe that we are running the ball when in actuality we are throwing it. We accomplish this by strongly emphasizing our quarterback and running back mechanics to create a visual perception of the running play we are faking.

Pitchouts and Tosses

Option teams commonly use the pitchout as the last leg of the option game. We teach our quarterback to hold the ball as if he were going to make a forward pass. Then when the time comes to pitch the ball to the running back, he laterals the ball straight down the line of scrimmage by extending the ball and rotating the wrist and thumb toward the running back, ending the motion with the palm facing the running back. The ball should tumble end over end and fly in front of the running back so that he can maintain maximum speed around the corner while catching the ball.

The toss play is also a very popular way of getting the ball in the running back's hands

Figure 8.18   Tossing the ball: (a) quarterback reverses out from center exchange with the ball in both hands; (b) quarterback turns and tosses ball to the running back; (c) the ball is tossed with no spin or spiral to allow the running back to make the catch while maintaining speed around the corner.

rapidly so that he can attack the defense around the end. The quarterback receives the center exchange and reverses out with the ball in both hands (figure 8.18a). He tosses the ball in front of the running back with no spin or spiral; he just floats the ball (figure 8.18b). This dead toss is easy to field and allows the running back to secure the ball quickly and attack the defense (figure 8.18c).

Passes

In today's game, the quarterback's ability to pass the football effectively is essential for offensive effectiveness. The quarterback must develop many skills to become a consistent and effective passer. One of the skills is footwork. When the quarterback sets up in the pocket, he must be on his toes with his weight balanced in ready position to deliver the ball on time. The pocket is a loud, violent area, and the quarterback who can deliver the ball in this environment is one who can win.

Timing passes and three- and five-step drops are important parts of any offensive system. Repetition is the key to developing a quarterback's footwork, technique, timing, and execution of the timed passing game. Several timing passes are included in chapter 9.

Develop timing by having the quarterback throw the ball to the receivers who will play during the game. The speed of the receiver is a big factor in developing consistency in the passing game. When the quarterback decides who to pass the ball to, he must release the ball quickly and accurately so that the receiver can remain open and make a play on the ball. Plus the quarterback must throw the ball through a passing lane within the line of scrimmage. We develop our quarterback's release point by having him throw the ball over the top or up by his ear. This technique is much more accurate and forgiving when throwing from the pocket.

The quarterback's ability to read the defense (zone or man) is just as critical as the receiver's ability when deciding where to throw the ball. Develop a reading progression of the defense for each pass play to ensure that the quarterback and the receivers are all on the same page (figure 8.19). A reading progression begins by finding a defender who is responsible for covering a certain area such as the flat or the curl. The read and the delivery of the ball is predicated from what the defensive man does after the ball is snapped. A misread can lead to a turnover or a big hit on the receiver. Study your opponent thoroughly with your quarterback and practice, practice, practice.

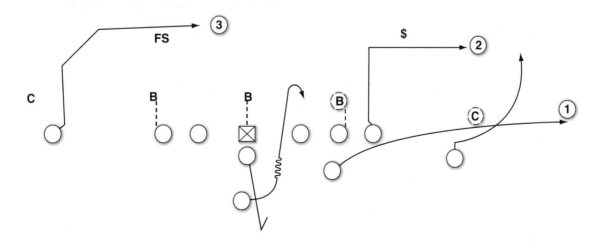

Figure 8.19 Reading progression for pass play. If C is flat, throw high/low off the C. If C is deep, throw high/low off the B or $. If $ rolls to flat, throw the dig (3).

Quarterback Drills

Design drills that develop the quarterback skills needed in your offensive system. If you are a pocket passing team, use drills that teach the quarterback pocket poise and skill. If you are a rollout or bootleg team, teach the quarterback the skills required to throw and read on the run. Quarterback mechanics and ball-handling skills are vital for offensive success and consistency.

Pocket Wave

The pocket-wave drill begins with the quarterback simulating a center snap with the ball in his hand. The quarterback takes a three- or five-step drop and gathers his feet with the ball in the ready position. The quarterback coach then points right, left, forward, and backward and directs the quarterback to slide in the pocket while maintaining the proper throwing posture. This drill is ideal for teaching the quarterback how to adjust to the shape of the passing pocket and deliver the ball under normal circumstances. Rarely does the quarterback have time to drop back and set his feet, find the receiver, step up, and throw. The quarterback will find that 90 percent of throws from the pocket will be thrown while sliding or drifting. This is a great drill for teaching poise and feel in the pocket.

Goal Post

Have quarterbacks throw their individual cuts from the end line over and through the goal posts. I know this sounds crazy, but this drill is ideal in developing a nice high release of the ball and wrist snap to generate velocity and spin. Start with easier routes such as post and fade routes then progress to curls and comebacks, which require more snap to get the ball over the crossbar and turned over to the receiver. This is a great drill for teaching the quarterback to throw over the defensive line and for developing wrist strength.

Throwing Net and Trash Cans

Use a six-by-ten-foot net with color-coded target holes in various places to drill throwing accuracy. The holes are color coded so that the quarterback can drop back and the coach can call out which hole to throw the ball through. This requires great concentration and develops accuracy in the pocket.

Trash cans are used for deep ball-accuracy drills. We place a trashcan in the location we want the ball to land on special red-zone plays and downfield passes against certain defenses. The quarterbacks try to land the ball inside the trash can. When the receiver knows exactly where the ball will be, he can be in position to make a play because the defense doesn't know where the ball will be thrown.

CHAPTER 9 TEACHING RUNNING AND PASSING GAMES

When developing running and passing game philosophies, your only boundaries or limitation are your imagination, personnel, and ability to teach. National championships have been won with the wishbone offense, and they have also been won with the run-and-shoot offense—two systems that are polar opposites. The bottom line is that to be successful in any offensive system, you must have a complete understanding of the system, have the players necessary to execute the system, and have the ability to effectively teach the system to your players. Knowledge of a system is of little value without the ability to communicate it and execute it.

At Jenks, we want our offensive system to be diverse so that we can adapt the system to fit our players year in and year out. We cannot go out and find players to fit our system, so we must be able to tweak our offense to fit the players we have. For example, one year we may have an outstanding running quarterback and may want to incorporate option plays and sprint-out passes to utilize his abili-

ties. Another year we may have a pocket-type quarterback, in which case we would implement several types of passes to complement our player's abilities.

Another important variable to consider is the climate your team plays in. Is the weather always warm and nice, cold and rainy, or a combination of them all? In Oklahoma, we play in all four seasons—hot, dry summers; rain and thunderstorms in the spring and fall; and cold, windy winters. We must be able to execute our offensive system in all types of environmental conditions or we will not be successful.

In this chapter I share my thoughts on developing running-game and passing-game philosophies as well as present many of our offensive plays that have stood the test of time and been solid over and over. I'm not claiming that this is the best or only offensive system in the world, but this is the one we have chosen, developed, and used to win championships at Jenks.

RUNNING GAME

I believe in a physical, punishing running attack. There is no substitute for the ability to rush the football effectively. Football teams that can effectively rush the football win more consistently than teams that pass the football effectively. History and statistics prove it. Rushing the ball effectively allows offensive teams to control the ball and control the clock. Both areas are vital in wearing down an opponent and winning a close football game. Look at the sports page on any given weekend and you'll see teams that pass for 300 yards and lose the ball game. However, a team that rushes for 300 yards rarely loses the game.

Take great pains to establish a rushing system. I use the word *system* because the ability to be successful rushing the ball depends directly on your ability to teach players how to execute a series of running plays that work together. Rushing plays have to work together and work off each other to be successful. Running plays can rarely stand alone and be effective because defenses are too good at defending the rush unless they are faced with other variables and other combinations of plays that come off the existing rushing plays. When teaching the rushing system to our players, I try to create a mental picture for them, including formations, blocking schemes, and concepts behind different running plays. The bottom line is that you as the coach must believe in your system and be able to teach players how to excel within your rushing system.

Coach's Keys: Rushing

1. A formation is just a formation. Formations are simply alignments of personnel.

2. Rushing systems vary greatly, but most include power plays, misdirection plays, zone plays, quick hitters, and delay schemes.

3. Well-devised formations are of little benefit unless a team can execute from them.

4. Increase rushing continuity by adding subtle changes in each running scheme and plays that complement each other. Continuity allows you to make quick adjustments and take advantage of what the defense gives you.

5. Teach players the blocking rules and the concepts and philosophies of rushing plays. This approach eliminates stagnation and allows opportunities for continued improvement.

Rushing Formations

The following classic running formations have proven to be successful. Keep in mind that these are formations and not offensive systems. The wishbone, veer, wing-T and I-formation are all offensive systems, but in this particular section I address the strengths and weaknesses of these four formations.

Rushing formations are unlimited as long as you have seven players on the line of scrimmage. The other four can align virtually anywhere. Place personnel in positions to use their abilities to the fullest. As long as your squad executes well, you will be successful.

Wishbone Formation

The wishbone formation (figure 9.1) was made famous by the great Texas and Oklahoma teams in the 1970s and 1980s. The wishbone formation is not nearly as popular as it used to be, but it still has merit as a great running formation. Use of the wishbone in the NFL and in Division I college ball is practically over except in some goal line–running situations. The formation is still used by some smaller division colleges and high schools across the country.

One advantage of the wishbone formation is that it allows the quarterback to hand the ball or pitch the ball to four different players. The quarterback is the triggerman in the wishbone formation. He not only must have great running ability but also great judgment when running the triple-option play the wishbone formation made famous. The wishbone is great for teams that have athletes with good

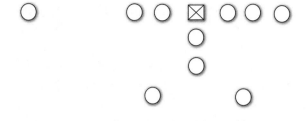

Figure 9.1 Wishbone formation.

speed but may be small in stature because most of the blocking schemes are angle blocks and cut blocks.

One of the disadvantages of the wishbone is the condensed nature of the formation—10 or 11 players are aligned very close to the ball. The defense can take advantage of the formation by overloading the running box with extra players because of the limited number of wide receivers.

Veer Formation

The split-back veer formation (figure 9.2) was the rushing craze in the late-1960s and throughout the 1970s. The formation featured great halfbacks on either side of the quarterback, which made defenses become much more sound and disciplined. The quick-hitting dive plays that spring from the formation and the veer teams' ability to run the option in each direction made the veer the formation of choice in the 1970s.

The veer formation usually employs huge splits between the offensive linemen, naturally spreading the defensive team. This spreading of the defense and the ability of the offense to isolate defenders have a tendency to allow the veer formation to produce big gains in the vertical running game.

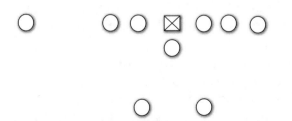

Figure 9.2 Veer formation.

The disadvantage of the veer formation, with its backs split in the backfield, is the limited number of power running plays that can be incorporated. The spread backfield also makes misdirection plays easier to read for defensive players because all the ball carriers are directly in front of the linebackers.

Wing-T Formation

The wing-T formation (figure 9.3) was made most famous by the University of Delaware. The formation also won several national championships for coach Bob Reade at Augustana College. The wing-T formation uses an offset split-back alignment made up of a physical fullback and an athletic halfback. The wingback is the big play weapon in the offense.

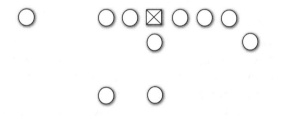

Figure 9.3 Wing-T formation.

The advantage of the wing-T formation is that it allows the offense to have three very distinct personalities. The wing-T allows a great power running game as well as a great speed offense with sweeps and counters. The biggest advantage of the wing-T is the ability to use misdirection with the wingback and the halfback. Counter plays and reverses are difficult for defenses to recognize and can lead to big plays on the ground.

The drawbacks to the wing-T are similar to the drawbacks of the wishbone and veer formations. The lack of wide receivers ensures that the wing-T offense will be up against overloaded defensive fronts that will make every attempt to force them to pass the football to win.

I-Formation

The I-formation (figure 9.4) evolved out of the desire to get the ball to the best offensive athlete deep in the backfield, giving him enough

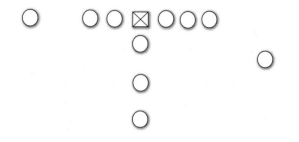

Figure 9.4 I-formation.

time to use his great ability and vision to make the defense miss him. The great running teams at the University of Southern California and University of Nebraska were the premier college programs that put the I-formation on the map.

The I-formation allows the I-back to rush the ball in either direction, a major advantage of the formation. The I-back can run misdirection in either direction, which is also a nice addition to the formation. The versatility in the I-formation is a huge advantage—the power running game, the speed running game, and the misdirection running game all can be accomplished by incorporating this formation. By far, though, the biggest advantage of the I-formation is that the best player gets the ball every time. However, this is also the formation's biggest disadvantage. The defense knows that the best guy on the offense will get the ball and will do everything within their power to overload the line of scrimmage and stop him.

Types of Running Plays

Before we discuss specific nuts-and-bolts plays and formations, I want to detail the different types of running plays. No matter what system or formations you incorporate, you need to be aware of the various types of running plays and the mentality that goes along with them:

- Power plays are attack-style plays with schemes and lead blockers at the point of attack.
- Misdirection plays, counters, and reverses use directional deception.

- Zone plays use a universal blocking scheme that blocks areas instead of men.
- Quick hitters are plays that utilize speed and allow the defense little time to react.
- Delay schemes are plays that develop by allowing the defense to react to a perception.

On the next several pages are diagrams of several examples of the types of plays just explained. At Jenks, we package out of the I-formation because we prefer to feature our best runner on most of our running plays. The blocking rules for each position are included, and the play is shown versus different defensive alignments to ensure that you understand the blocking rules of each play.

These plays are not isolated to the I-formation and can be run from a variety of other formations and alignments. These are the plays that, when executed well, can be successful against many defensive schemes and alignments. This system of running plays is versatile and has helped us win seven championships at Jenks in the last eight seasons. The rules are precise and have the ability to encompass a variety of defensive systems.

12-13 play (fullback zone dive)

The fullback dive play (figure 9.5) incorporates zone blocking rules, and we use it as a quick hitter against the defense. We like to use this play when linebackers are reacting to fast flow against our outside running game or against a reading-type defensive line if our fullback can cut the ball back against the grain and take advantage of overpursuit by the defense.

Frontside T: If covered, stretch. If uncovered, combo with TE to force player or LB.

Backside T: If covered, double with backside G to LB. If uncovered, climb to second level. Press to a 5 and 9.

Frontside G: If covered, stretch. If uncovered, combo with tackle to force player or LB.

Backside G: If covered, stretch. If uncovered, combo with C to force player or LB.

C: If covered, stretch. If uncovered, combo with playside G to force player or LB.

Frontside TE: Stretch.

Backside TE: Block cut-back player.

Frontside WR: Inside run rules.

Backside WR: Backside rules.

QB: Reverse out, ride FB, fake TB toss away.

TB: Fake toss away from play.

FB or other: Aiming point outside leg of guard. Read first-covered OL's block to daylight.

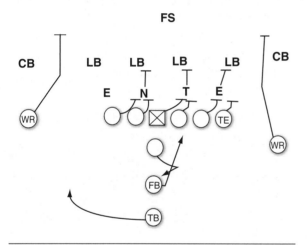

Figure 9.5 12-13 play (fullback zone dive).

14-15 play (tailback inside zone)

The tailback inside-zone play (figure 9.6) has been the most consistent rushing play in our offensive system for more than eight years. The zone scheme allows offensive linemen to be aggressive and confident about their assignments against nearly every front we face. It allows the tailback to get the ball deep in the backfield with great vision and a lot of options. This is another play that forces the defense to be gap sound and play the cutback from the tailback.

Frontside T: If covered, stretch. If uncovered, combo with TE to force player or LB.

Backside T: If covered, double with back-

side G to LB. If uncovered, climb to second level. Press to a 5 and 9.

Frontside G: If covered, stretch. If uncovered, combo with tackle to force player or LB.

Backside G: If covered, stretch. If uncovered, combo with C to force player or LB.

C: If covered, stretch. If uncovered, combo with playside G to force player or LB.

Frontside TE: Stretch.

Backside TE: Block cut-back player.

Frontside WR: Inside run rules.

Backside WR: Backside rules.

QB: Open at 5/7 to call side. Get ball as deep as possible to TB. Bootleg fake away from call.

TB: Lateral step. Aiming point is outside leg of OT. Read first-covered OL's block.

FB or other: Block first man to show off backside tackle.

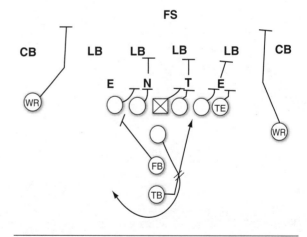

Figure 9.6 14-15 play (tailback inside zone).

16-17 play (tailback G)

The tailback-G play (figure 9.7) was designed to take advantage of the pro 4-3 defense by allowing the tackle to aggressively block down for the pulling guard. This provides a great angle to seal the tackle and create a running lane for the tailback with the pulling guard. Our rules allow us to run the play against many fronts, but our best look is against the

4-3. Make sure the tailback runs this play inside out to set up the guard's block on the end.

Frontside T: On or down.

Backside T: Scoop rules.

Frontside G: Pull for end man on line of scrimmage or playside LB.

Backside G: Scoop rules.

C: Scoop rules. Versus shade strong, overtake.

Frontside TE: 5 and 9, down. 6/9 technique, best release to inside LB. 7 technique, pin.

Backside TE: Scoop rules.

Frontside WR: Inside run rules.

Backside WR: Backside rules.

QB: Open at 5/7 to call side. Get ball as deep as possible to TB. Fake play pass.

TB: Lateral step. Aiming point is outside leg of tackle. Read pulling guard's block.

FB or other: Read guard's block to force.

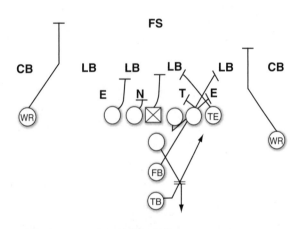

Figure 9.7 16-17 play (tailback G).

18-19 play (outside zone to TE)

The outside-zone play to the tight end (figure 9.8) has been a very consistent play as well. The zone scheme is a catchall because the play can be executed against a variety of defensive looks. We use a lot of motions and formations with this play to gain leverage on the defense. Have the tailback stretch the defense with his speed and look for creases created by the defense's overpursuit.

This play uses the TAC call. The TAC call is a call made between the tackle and tight end that tells the tight end to block down and the tackle to pull around. It is a switch call between the tackle and tight end.

Frontside T: If covered, rip, reach, escape to second level. TAC call by TE, pull for LB. If uncovered, pull and overtake man on TE.

Backside T: Scoop rules.

Frontside G: If covered, rip, reach, escape to second level. If uncovered, pull and overtake man on tackle.

Backside G: Scoop rules.

C: If covered, rip, reach, escape to second level. If uncovered, pull and overtake man on playside G.

Frontside TE: Rip, reach, escape to second level. Versus 7 technique, make TAC call, pin 7 technique.

Backside TE: Scoop rules.

Frontside WR: Outside run rules.

Backside WR: Backside rules.

QB: Open at 4/8 to call side. Get ball as fast and deep as possible to TB. Fake play pass.

TB: Lateral step. Chase spot 3 yards outside of TE.

FB or other: Block force.

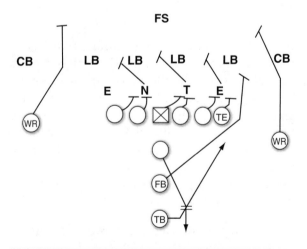

Figure 9.8 18-19 play (outside zone to TE).

18 toss-19 toss (tailback outside zone)

Frontside T: If covered, rip, reach, escape to second level. If uncovered, pull and overtake man on TE.

Backside T: Scoop rules.

Frontside G: If covered, rip, reach, escape to second level. If uncovered, pull and overtake man on tackle.

Backside G: Scoop rules.

C: If covered, rip, reach, escape to second level. If uncovered, pull and overtake man on playside G.

Frontside TE: Rip, reach, escape to second level.

Backside TE: Scoop rules.

Frontside WR: Outside run rules.

Backside WR: Backside rules.

QB: Reverse out and toss ball to TB.

TB: Lateral step, receive toss, and secure the ball. Aiming point 1 yard outside TE.

FB or other: Block force.

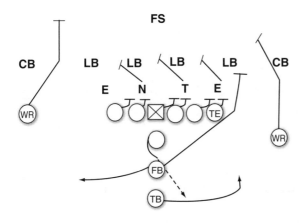

Figure 9.9 18 toss-19 toss (tailback outside zone).

18 O-19 O (speed option)

The speed-option play (figure 9.10) incorporates the same blocking scheme as the tailback outside-zone play, only the quarterback keeps the ball and isolates the support defender. When executed correctly, we get a two-on-one situation against their support defender and our quarterback has the option to keep or pitch the ball, depending on what

the defender chooses to do. We also like to run this play against man-to-man defenses to take advantage of the mismatch between the tailback and the opponent's linebackers.

Frontside T: If covered, rip, reach, escape to second level. If uncovered, pull and overtake man on TE.

Backside T: Scoop rules.

Frontside G: If covered, rip, reach, escape to second level. If uncovered, pull and overtake man on tackle.

Backside G: Scoop rules.

C: If covered, rip, reach, escape to second level. If uncovered, pull and overtake man on playside G.

Frontside TE: Rip, reach, escape to second level.

Backside TE: Scoop rules.

Frontside WR: Outside run rules.

Backside WR: Backside rules.

QB: Gain a little depth and sprint to force. Pitch off force.

TB: Pitch relationship with QB.

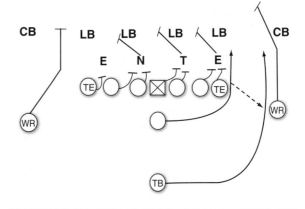

Figure 9.10 18 O-19 O (speed option).

18 WR-19 WR (outside zone to WR)

Another play we use to take advantage of the wide receiver's speed and agility is the outside-zone play (figure 9.11) in which the quarterback hands off to one of our skill players. We use the same outside-zone blocking scheme as always and take advantage of certain formations and motions that produce leverage against the defense. We also fake the ball to the receiver and set up other plays in our offense from this play scenario.

> Frontside T: If covered, rip, reach, escape to second level. If uncovered, pull and overtake man on TE.
>
> Backside T: Scoop rules.
>
> Frontside G: If covered, rip, reach, escape to second level. If uncovered, pull and overtake man on tackle.
>
> Backside G: Scoop rules.
>
> C: If covered, rip, reach, escape to second level. If uncovered, pull and overtake man on playside G.
>
> Frontside TE: Rip, reach, escape to second level.
>
> Backside TE: Scoop rules.
>
> Frontside WR: Outside run rules.
>
> Backside WR: Backside rules. Ball carrier, jet motion, secure handoff, get depth, and run outside.
>
> QB: Snap ball when WR is at tackle. Reverse out and hand ball to WR. Fake toss away.
>
> TB: Fake toss opposite playside.
>
> FB or other: Block force.

Figure 9.11 18 WR-19 WR, right 5 H jet 18 H (outside zone to WR).

20-21 play (influence trap to TB)

One of our most consistent quick-hitting plays is the influence trap to the tailback (figure 9.12). It's one of the oldest plays in football, yet one that is still effective. Be sure to teach the tailback to read the tackle's second-level blocking on the linebacker. When the tailback

learns to run off these second-level blocks, the trap play can be a great weapon against an aggressive defense.

> Frontside T: First LB inside.
>
> Backside T: Scoop backside LB.
>
> Frontside G: Influence to end man on line of scrimmage.
>
> Backside G: Pull and kick 3 technique.
>
> C: On or back for pulling guard.
>
> Frontside TE: Inside release to outside LB/support. Versus 7 technique, outside release.
>
> Backside TE: Scoop.
>
> Frontside WR: Inside run rules.
>
> Backside WR: Backside rules.
>
> QB: Reverse out away from call. After handoff, fake option away.
>
> TB: Dive at C's backside hip. Run trap path off pulling guard's block.

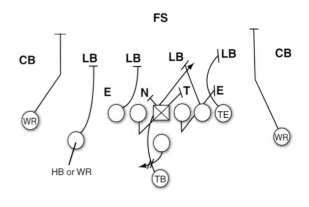

Figure 9.12 20-21 play (influence trap to TB).

24-25 play (linebacker trap)

We use the linebacker trap play (figure 9.13) to complement the read zone play out of the shotgun. Through research and formation, we can manipulate the defense and get one-on-one blocking assignments for our offensive linemen and force the defense to be very disciplined to stop this play. We also allow the quarterback to read the end that is aligned over our pulling tackle and pull the ball if the end is pursuing and stopping the tailback play. This play is a must-have in any shotgun offense.

Frontside T: If covered, stretch. If uncovered, down.

Backside T: Pull for playside LB. Enter off double team.

Frontside G: On or down.

Backside G: Backside cutoff.

C: Scoop.

TE: Stretch.

Frontside WR: Inside run rules.

Backside WR: Backside rules.

QB: Face out to call side, secure handoff, and boot away.

TB: Jab step away from call. Press A-gap to daylight.

FB or other: Fill for pulling tackle.

Frontside T: On or down to backside LB.

Backside T: Pull for playside LB. Read backside G's block.

Frontside G: On or down to backside LB.

Backside G: Pull and kick/log end man on line of scrimmage.

C: Block back for G.

Frontside TE: If T covered, down. If T uncovered, best release to support.

Backside TE: Scoop.

Frontside WR: Inside run rules.

Backside WR: Backside rules.

QB: Open like 14-15 away from call side. Get ball deep to TB, fake naked away.

TB: Lateral, cross over, plant. Follow tackle and cut off his block.

FB or other: Fill for pulling tackle.

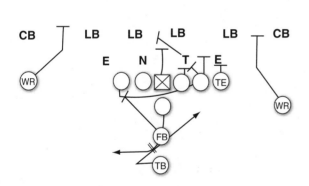

Figure 9.13   24-25 play (linebacker trap).

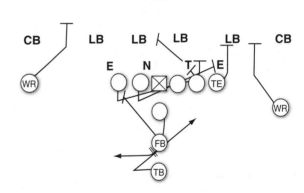

Figure 9.14   28-29 play (counter).

28-29 play (counter)

One of my favorite plays is the counter play (figure 9.14) made famous by Joe Gibbs and the Washington Redskins. This play combines great blocking angles and misdirection, and we have been able to run it against nearly every defensive front. Emphasize having great movement at the point of attack and sealing the defense to the inside. Be sure that the pulling tackle reads the block of the pulling guard for his fit against the defense. This play has withstood the test of time at every level of football.

30-31 play (influence trap to FB)

Identical to 20-21, the influence trap to the fullback (figure 9.15) hits the defense hard and fast. Emphasize the same coaching points with the fullback and teach him to read the second-level blocking by the tackle. Also look at the quarterback option play off the fullback trap as a solid complement to the play.

Frontside T: First LB inside.

Backside T: Scoop backside LB.

Frontside G: Influence to end man on line of scrimmage.

Backside G: Pull and kick 3 technique.

C: On or back for pulling guard.

Frontside TE: Inside release to outside LB/support. Versus 7 technique, outside release.

Backside TE: Scoop.

Frontside WR: Inside run rules.

Backside WR: Backside rules.

QB: Reverse out away from call. After handoff, fake option away.

TB: Fake option away.

FB or other: Dive at C's backside hip. Run trap path off pulling G's block.

Backside G: Scoop rules.

C: Scoop rules.

Frontside TE: 6/9 technique, best release to inside LB. 7 technique, pin.

Backside TE: Scoop rules.

Frontside WR: Inside run rules.

Backside WR: Backside rules.

QB: Reverse out, secure handoff to FB and fake option with TB.

TB: Fake option to call side.

FB or other: Aiming point inside leg of tackle. Read guard's block to daylight.

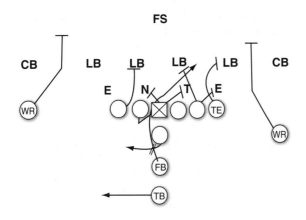

Figure 9.15 30-31 play (influence trap to FB).

Figure 9.16 36-37 play (fullback G).

36-37 play (fullback G)

The fullback-G play (figure 9.16) has the same blocking scheme as the 16-17 tailback-G play. This fullback version hits faster and opens the door for the quarterback to use the G-option play by keeping the ball after faking the handoff to the fullback. The fullback becomes a lead blocker on the inside linebacker, allowing the quarterback to option the third-level defender. We also use this blocking scheme in the shotgun and allow the quarterback rather than the fullback to carry the ball.

Frontside T: On or down.

Backside T: Scoop rules.

Frontside G: Pull for end man on line of scrimmage or playside LB.

42-43 play (TB isolation)

The tailback-isolation play (figure 9.17) is a classic and is still used by nearly every successful football team at every level. This play is designed to attack the defense by getting a double-team block at the point of attack and using a lead block by the fullback on the linebacker, forcing him to take a side. The tailback simply runs off the fullback's block. The 42-43 play is a real "bloody your nose" football play.

Frontside T: On or down.

Backside T: Scoop. Versus 3 and 5, press.

Frontside G: On or down.

Backside G: Scoop. Versus 3 and 5, press.

C: On or scoop.

Frontside TE: Stretch.

Backside TE: Scoop.

Frontside WR: Inside run rules.

Backside WR: Backside rules.

QB: Open at 5/7 to call side. Get ball as deep as possible to TB. Fake naked away.

TB: Lateral step. Aiming point is open gap playside.

FB or other: First LB past C.

Backside TE: Scoop.

Frontside WR: Inside run rules.

Backside WR: Backside rules.

QB: Reverse out, get ball deep to TB. Fake frontside rollout.

TB: Jab step away from call. Press A-gap to daylight.

FB or other: Kick end man on line of scrimmage.

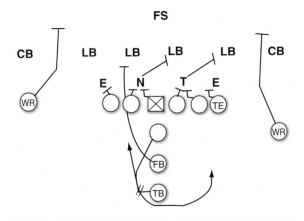

Figure 9.17　42-43 play (TB isolation).

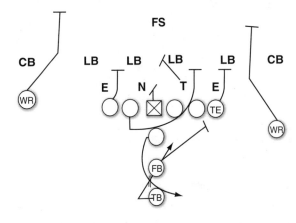

Figure 9.18　44-45 play (power-O).

44-45 play (power-O)

The 44-45 play is commonly referred to as the power-O (figure 9.18). The O stands for the offside guard who pulls for the playside linebacker. This play is the modern version of the counter play and has become one of our staple running plays. The fullback must be a great blocker and kick out the end man on the line of scrimmage for this play to be successful. For a change of pace, have your backside guard and fullback switch responsibilities and run this play like the 28-29.

Frontside T: On or down to backside LB.

Backside T: Scoop.

Frontside G: On or down to backside LB.

Backside G: Pull for playside LB. Enter off double team.

C: Playside A-gap to backside A-gap.

Frontside TE: If T covered, down. If T uncovered, best release to support.

46-47 play (offtackle goal line)

The 46-47 play is simply an offtackle goal line play (figure 9.19). Get great movement at the point of attack and have the fullback kick out the end man on the line of scrimmage. The main coaching point is to make sure the frontside double team seals the frontside second-level player and doesn't allow him to get over the top and make the play on the tailback.

Frontside T: On or down.

Backside T: Scoop.

Frontside G: On or down.

Backside G: Scoop.

C: On or scoop.

Frontside TE: Down or playside LB/support.

Backside TE: Scoop.

Frontside WR: Inside run rules.

Backside WR: Backside rules.

QB: Reverse out, get ball deep to TB. Fake naked away from play.

TB: Lateral step, press ball in C-gap.

FB or other: Kick end man on line of scrimmage.

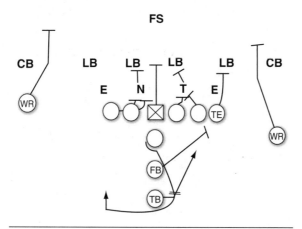

Figure 9.19   46-47 play (offtackle goal line).

48-49 play (toss sweep)

The toss sweep (figure 9.20) that Nebraska made famous is still a great football play. The playside guard pulls for the playside linebacker, and the fullback blocks the force defender. This scheme provides the tailback several opportunities to take advantage of the defensive team's gap changes. This is a play in which you can switch the pulling guard's and fullback's responsibilities and have another great play.

> Frontside T: If covered, reach. If uncovered, down.
>
> Backside T: Scoop rules.
>
> Frontside G: Pull for playside LB.
>
> Backside G: Scoop rules.
>
> C: Scoop.
>
> Frontside TE: Reach.
>
> Backside TE: Scoop rules.
>
> Frontside WR: Outside run rules.
>
> Backside WR: Backside rules.
>
> QB: Reverse out and toss ball to TB.
>
> TB: Lateral step, receive toss, and secure the ball. Aiming point 1 yard outside TE.
>
> FB or other: Block force.

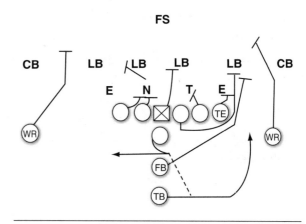

Figure 9.20   48-49 play (toss sweep).

Continuity in the Running Game

The five basic types of running plays are: power plays, misdirection plays, zone plays, quick hitters, and delay schemes. Thousands of different running plays fall into these five categories. The key element to success and continuity is your team's ability to execute them.

Our offense uses 10 to 12 different running plays. Each play has several different options or scheme adjustments. Because 10 plays that have two adjustments each turn into 20 plays, remember that the number of plays you have in your system is not nearly as important as your team's ability to execute the plays you have.

Building your running plays to complement each other is the key to great rushing continuity. Our inside-zone play (figure 9.21) is our favorite running play both statistically and philosophically. We run the inside-zone play more often than any other play.

Our counter play (figure 9.22) is the complement to the inside-zone play. To the defense, the counter play looks exactly like the inside-zone play for the first three steps by the tailback and the quarterback. This similar backfield action forces the defense to play our best play before reacting to the misdirection play. We believe that the way the inside zone and the counter play complement each other gives our offense continuity.

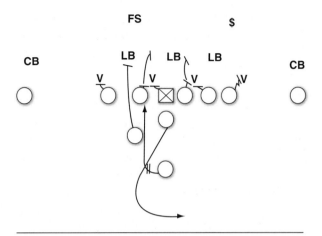

Figure 9.21 Inside zone.

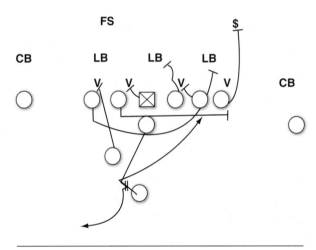

Figure 9.22 Counter play.

In each year that I have been the head coach at Jenks, we had an I-back average more than 5 yards per carry. People often ask what our secret is to having such a consistent running attack, and I always respond the same way. There aren't any secrets. The ability to instill in your players the same understanding of the running game that you have as the coach is the key. If the players understand not only the blocking rules but also the concepts and philosophy of the play, they will continue to improve as the season goes on.

We strive to make our players into coaches on the field. If you only teach blocking rules in the running game, players become stagnant because they are not challenged daily once they master the rules of the play. Players will thrive when they become conscious of the concepts and philosophies of a running play. This process doesn't happen the first week or two of the season; it takes time and great teaching. Make your players coaches on the field.

PASSING GAME

In our offensive philosophy, we set up the passing offense by using the running game. We force defenses to be aggressive and over-load the line of scrimmage to stop the ground attack, creating many opportunities for the passing game.

Just because we want a physical rushing game doesn't mean we can't or won't pass the football. We work extremely hard to develop the passing game so that our offense can take what the defense gives. If the defense wants to stop the run by gambling and overloading, we take advantage by throwing the football down the field against one-on-one coverage.

Championship football teams are able to run and pass the football effectively. Your philosophy and personality will lead you in developing and implementing your own passing system. The ability to pass the ball effectively will always give a team the chance to win ball games, so work hard to execute the passing game at a very high level. The ability to pass the ball effectively places additional stress on defensive units by forcing them to be sound in the secondary in order to prevent giving up the big passing play.

Passing efficiency is vital even for teams who throw the ball only 10 times a game. The University of Oklahoma threw the ball just 10 times a game while using the wish-bone rushing offense, but the great tight end Keith Jackson averaged huge yardage for each reception he made because the defense forgot about him while trying to defend the Sooners' powerful running game.

1. An effective passing game is essential for offensive success because defenses cannot gang up on the running game if the passing game is a threat.

2. Have a variety of timing routes, action passes, sprint-out passes, and naked passes that your offense can execute. This variety will allow you great flexibility as a play caller.

3. Practice the passing game with the same receivers and quarterbacks every day to ensure timing. A well-executed timing route is very difficult to defend.

4. Emphasize protecting the quarterback. No matter how great a player he is, the offense will not be successful unless the quarterback is protected.

5. Use formations that utilize your players' talents. If you have great skill players, spread the field and get as much speed and ability on the field as possible so that the defense must match your talent level or give up big plays.

6. Run and pass the ball out of the same formations.

Types of Pass Plays

We package our passing offense into four basic areas: timing routes; play action passes; sprint-out passes; and naked, bootleg, and waggle passes. We teach each package of the passing game separately so that every player understands his individual responsibilities within each package. For each passing package, linemen learn their protection rules and the quarterback learns his responsibilities, as do the tight ends and receivers.

Timing routes, including three-step drop, five-step drop, and some seven-step drop passes, utilize timing and synchronization between the quarterback and receiver. Timing routes require a great deal of repetition between quarterback and receiver to develop the timing and execution level needed to beat defenses. A well-executed timing route is very difficult for the defense to stop because the quarterback and the receiver know exactly what the other will do, while the defender must react to the play after the snap. I encourage every offensive system to develop efficient timed passing routes. Examples of timed routes appear later in this chapter.

Play action passes are used to fool the defense. We fake one of our favorite running plays to get the secondary to commit to the run then throw a pass downfield against a confused or out-of-position defense. The play action passing game can be a huge weapon if the offense runs the ball effectively, providing a big-play threat. Defenses that are willing to walk up and overload to stop the run take a big chance of giving up a big play. If the defense chooses to stay back and reduce the risk of the big, play action pass, the running game will be even more effective.

Sprint-out passes allow the offense to stress the defense by rolling the quarterback out of the pocket and placing him in position to run or pass the football. Rolling the quarterback out of the pocket also relieves some of the pressure that defenses can place on the quarterback when he is in the pocket. If you have a quarterback who can throw well on the run, implement some of the sprint-out passing plays presented later in the chapter.

Naked, bootleg, and waggle passes are lumped together in our system because the pass protections are included in the names of the routes. All three passes are hard play action and involve special offensive line, quarterback, and receiver rules. These built-in, play action passes fool the defense into believing that the offense is running the ball. Also, they allow the quarterback to move out of the pocket to reduce the defensive pressure on the pocket.

Naked tells our offensive line and quarterback that we will fake the running play called and there will be no pass protection on the backside pass rusher. In other words, the quarterback is naked, or on his own, once he reverses field to deliver the ball.

Bootleg is another play action passing scheme that requires one of our guards to pull to lead the quarterback as he completes the play fake, reverses direction, and rolls out to pass the football. Another great way of tricking the defense is to use a solid play action fake, change the quarterback's direction, and roll out against the grain of the defense.

Waggle is another form of play action pass that involves aggressively turning the offensive line in the direction of the play fake while pulling a backside lineman to the backside to block the remaining defensive lineman. Waggle protection is a very effective way to draw linebackers into the trap of believing that the offense is running the ball when they are actually throwing it.

In our offensive terminology, 80s and 90s are our three-step timing routes and 50s and 60s are our five-step timing routes (table 9.1). The first number in the call tells offensive linemen and the running back the protection; the second number tells receivers what routes to execute. For example, if the quarterback calls, "54," the 5 tells the offensive line and the running back that they must execute an odd, five-step protection, and 4 tells the number one receiver to run a comeback and the number two receiver to run a flag route. Any adjustments are made simply by tagging additional routes or tagging additional pass protectors such as the tight end or fullback. This system gives the offensive play caller the flexibility to attack virtually any defense he comes across by making simple, yet precise, communications to every player.

Table 9.1　Pass Route Combinations

Play	FS1	FS2	FS3	BS1	BS2	Tags
80s and 90s						
81-91	Fade	Seam		Fade	Seam	Hitch, flat
83-93	Hitch	Hitch	Hitch	Hitch	Hitch	Seam
84-94	Out	Slant	Slant	Out	Slant	Hitch
86-96	Slant	Slant	Slant	Slant	Slant	Flat/hitch
88-98	Fade	Flat/stick	Stick/flat	Slant	Slant	Non-mirrored
50s and 60s						
51-61	Fade	Seam read	Seam	Fade	Seam	Auto opposite seam 3 × 1
52-62						
53-63	Curl	Quick out	Spot	Curl	Quick out	#2 sneak, #3 swing
54-64	Comeback	Curl	Out	Comeback	Curl	
55-65	Corner	High mesh	Bubble	Post	Low mesh	
56-66	Post	Dig	Quick out	Comeback	Drag	Wheel
57-67	Corner	Quick out	Seam read	Corner	Quick out	
58-68	Fade	Out/quick out	Out	Fade	Out	3 WR #2 quick out, #3 out
59-69	Hitch	Flag	Seam read	Hitch	Flag	#3 flag, #2 hitch

Whatever communication system you incorporate, make sure it addresses all 11 players effectively. Offensive linemen don't need to know what the receivers are doing, and receivers don't care what the linemen are doing. Make sure the communication is precise and effective.

Protections

Sound pass protection is vital to a consistent passing game for a variety of reasons. The quarterback must be protected at all costs because the triggerman is the key to a successful offensive system. The quarterback's ability to step up in the pocket and throw the football with good timing is also crucial to the passing game, and the protection must be solid in order to accomplish this. Variety and diversity are also critical components of pass protection because defensive coordinators constantly study offensive schemes and devise ways to get to the quarterback.

Make sure your system has sound three-step, five-step, sprint-out, and bootleg protections in place. Incorporate a flexible system so that you can adjust protections during the game if the opponent breaks out something new against you. As with every play in your system, make sure your squad can thoroughly execute the protection schemes. Your success and your quarterback are depending on it.

80s and 90s passing plays

The 80s and 90s plays (figure 9.23) are three-step timing routes that require the middle of the pocket to be firm so that the quarterback can step up and throw the ball quickly. Make sure lineman know that they need to be aggressive and under control to keep the defensive players' hands down and out of the passing lanes. We incorporate an aggressive approach and allow offensive lineman to either cut-block defenders or aggressively attack them to keep the pocket firm and keep the defenders' hands down.

Frontside T: Aggressive. Cut number 2 down lineman.

Backside T: Aggressive. Cut backside C-gap. End man on line of scrimmage.

Frontside G: Aggressive number 1 down lineman.

Backside G: Aggressive backside B-gap.

C: Aggressive backside A-gap.

Frontside TE: Route unless max call. (Max call keeps TE in to become part of pass protection scheme instead of running called pass route.)

Backside TE: Route unless stay call.

TB: Two RBs, number 2 LB to outside heat. One RB, number 1 LB, number 2 LB to outside heat.

FB/other: Two RBs, number 1 LB. One RB, number 1 LB, number 2 LB to outside heat.

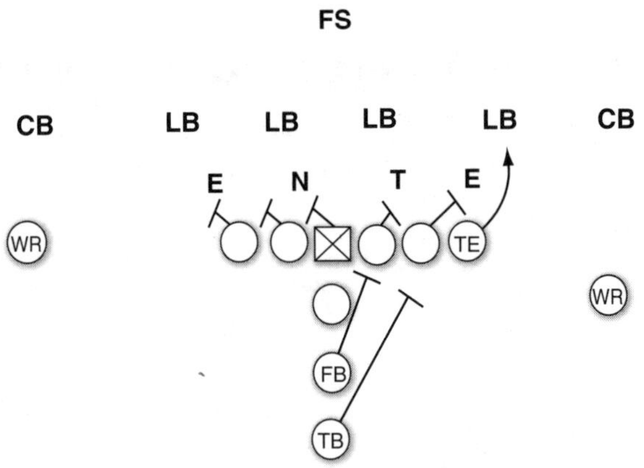

Figure 9.23 80s and 90s passing plays.

50s and 60s passing plays

The 50s and 60s (figure 9.24) are five-step timing routes that require more of a pure pocket than the three-step system. The quarterback takes a five-step drop so that he is deeper in the pocket and more vulnerable to the outside rush of the ends. Tackles must be aware of the quarterback's depth and position in the pocket and not allow the defensive ends to turn the corner and get to the quarterback around the edge. The guards and the center must be firm so that the quarterback can step up in the pocket and deliver the ball with good timing. We use pocket pass protection techniques and protect the quarterback at all costs.

Frontside T: Number 2 down lineman.

Backside T: Backside C-gap. End man on line of scrimmage.

Frontside G: Number 1 down lineman.

Backside G: Backside B-gap.

C: Backside A-gap.

Frontside TE: Route unless max call.

Backside TE: Route unless stay call.

TB: Two RBs, number 2 LB to outside heat. One RB, number 1 LB, number 2 LB to outside heat.

FB/other: Two RBs, number 1 LB. One RB, number 1 LB, number 2 LB to outside heat.

Figure 9.24   50s and 60s passing plays.

500s and 600s passing plays

The 500s and 600s (figure 9.25) are sprint-out routes in which the quarterback rolls outside the pocket. Linemen use a post-and-turn technique and seal the defenders inside and away from the quarterback. This protection is really a zone concept because linemen are responsible for the defenders who rush through their inside gaps. Running backs are responsible for any edge pressure or scraping linebackers.

Frontside T: If covered, post, backside gap. If uncovered, backside gap.

Backside T: If covered, post, backside gap. If uncovered, backside gap.

Frontside G: If covered, post, backside gap. If uncovered, backside gap.

Backside G: If covered, post, backside gap. If uncovered, backside gap.

C: If covered, post, backside gap. If uncovered, backside gap.

Frontside TE: Route.

Backside TE: D-gap.

TB: Two RBs, second to show past T. One RB, first to show past T.

FB/other: Two RBs, second to show past T. One RB, first to show past T.

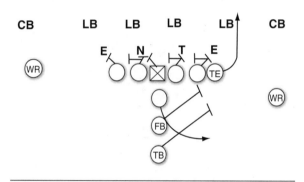

Figure 9.25   500s and 600s passing plays.

Naked at 8/9 passing play

The word *naked* tells the quarterback that no one in the protection scheme is assigned to the backside perimeter rusher (figure 9.26). The word also tells offensive linemen that they are in a full playside zone protection. This protection is used to draw the defense inside with a play action fake to the tailback and to allow the quarterback to burst outside the pocket and deliver the ball. We utilize naked protection off a variety of running plays. The main coaching point is aggressive action by the offensive line and backfield.

Blocking: 414/415, 442/443, 418/419.

Frontside T: Full flow.

Backside T: Full flow.

Frontside G: Full flow.

Backside G: Full flow.

C: Full flow.

Frontside TE: Route (naked route).

Backside TE: Route (under number 1 over number 2).

Frontside WR: Route (25-yard comeback).

Backside WR: Route (post).

QB: Great run fake, get depth. Head and eyes around first. Run first, pass second.

TB: Fake run and block first opposite-colored jersey.

FB/other: Route (naked to playside, drag backside).

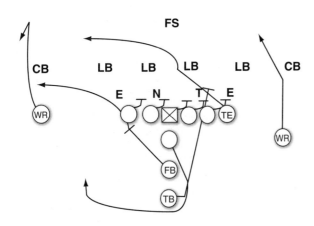

Figure 9.26 Naked at 8/9 passing play (414 naked at 9).

Nude at 8/9 passing play

Nude protection (figure 9.27) tells everyone in the scheme to block the running play called. In other words, we want the play to look and sound exactly like the running play we called to lure the defense away from their pass defense responsibilities. This protection can be risky against a blitz, but it can be rewarding if it fools the defense. Most of the running plays we nude off of allow the quarterback to be on the move, running away from the defense.

Blocking: 424/425, 428/429, 444/445.

Frontside T: Block play.

Backside T: Block play.

Frontside G: Block play.

Backside G: Block play.

C: Block play.

Frontside TE: Route (naked route).

Backside TE: Route (under number 1 over number 2).

Frontside WR: Route (25-yard comeback).

Backside WR: Route (post).

QB: Great run fake, get depth. Head and eyes around first. Run first, pass second.

TB: Fake run and block first opposite-colored jersey.

FB/other: Route (naked to playside, drag backside).

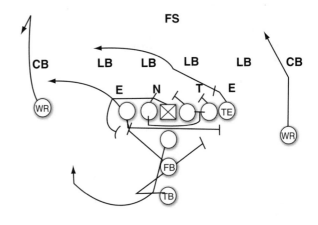

Figure 9.27 Nude at 8/9 passing play (428 nude at 9).

Boot at 8/9 passing play

Boot is another play action protection that utilizes a pulling backside guard to block the perimeter defender (figure 9.28). We normally boot off of a 42-43 scheme, but we can boot from other running plays as well. This action gives the quarterback the option of setting up in the pocket or rolling outside off the pulling guard's block.

Blocking: 442/443.

Frontside T: Block playside gap.

Backside T: Block playside gap.

Frontside G: Pull and lead for QB.

Backside G: Block playside gap.

C: Block playside gap.

Frontside TE: Route (naked route).

Backside TE: Route (under number 1 over number 2).

Frontside WR: Route (25-yard comeback).

Backside WR: Route (post).

QB: Great run fake, get depth. Head and eyes around first. Run first, pass second.

TB: Fake run and block first opposite-colored jersey.

FB/other: Fill for pulling guard.

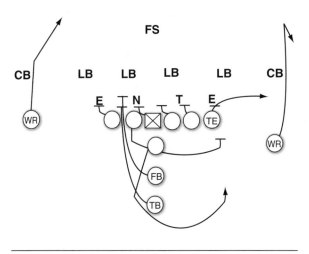

Figure 9.28 Boot at 8/9 passing play (443 boot at 8).

Fake passing play

We add the word *fake* to pass protection to add a simulated quarterback-to-running-back exchange in the backfield while using our standard 50-60 pass protection up front with the linemen (figure 9.29). Fake is just another way to distract the defensive backs who are looking for keys in the backfield while allowing offensive linemen to be in one of our secure protections.

Blocking: 0/1 (70/71), 2/3 (42/43), 4/5 (14/15).

Frontside T: 50/60 pass protection.

Backside T: 50/60 pass protection.

Frontside G: 50/60 pass protection.

Backside G: 50/60 pass protection.

C: 50/60 pass protection.

Frontside TE: Route.

Backside TE: Route.

Frontside WR: Route.

Backside WR: Route.

QB: Flash fake, setup in the pocket.

TB: Fake run, 50/60 pass protection.

FB/other: Fake run, 50/60 pass protection. Possible route.

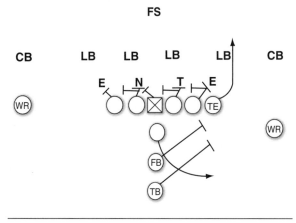

Figure 9.29 Fake passing play.

We prefer to use a combination of a passing tree with the complementary routes (routes run by inside receivers) built into the tree. If we want to vary the complementary route, we simply tag the inside receiver with the route we want him to execute. For example, if we call 81, the outside receiver (the number one receiver) executes a fade route while the inside receiver (the number two receiver) runs a seam route. If we want to vary the complementary route, we simply say 81 H flat. This would change the H-back's route to a flat instead of a seam. This system allows great flexibility in our communication and play selection. We certainly don't want to limit our play selection to a simple passing tree.

Three-Step Routes

Our three-step fade routes (figure 9.30) are used to stretch the defense deep. Using the three-step drop minimizes the risk of being sacked and gives us a chance for a big gainer against a one-on-one corner. We can also tag inside receivers with several alternative routes and simply use the outside fade route to clear out for other receivers in the area. We build into the 81-91 game the ability to convert the route to a hitch route in case the corner is playing a bail or loose technique.

81-91 quick route (three-step fade)

Formations: All.

Tags: Flat, hitch.

Frontside receiver 1: Fade.

Backside receiver 1: Fade.

Frontside receiver 2: Seam.

Backside receiver 2: Seam.

Frontside receiver 3: Shoulder.

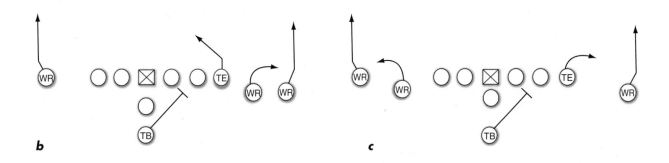

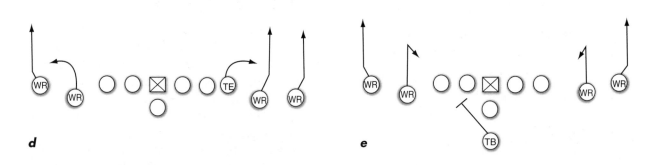

Figure 9.30   81-91 quick routes (three-step fade): *(a)* left 6 91; *(b)* right 6 81 H flat; *(c)* right 3 81 flat; *(d)* right 5 guy 81 flat; *(e)* shoot right 91 hitch.

83-93 quick route (three-step hitch)

The three-step hitch (figure 9.31) is a vital part of our quick game. A hitch is like a 5-yard running play only easier to execute. With practice, the hitch can become nearly automatic. It forces the corner to come up and play tighter, which can lead to bigger plays down the field. We have the ability to check to a fade route if the cornerback is in an up position playing press or squat coverage.

Formations: All.

Tag: Seam.

Frontside receiver 1: 6-yard hitch.

Backside receiver 1: 6-yard hitch.

Frontside receiver 2: 6-yard hitch.

Backside receiver 2: 6-yard hitch.

Frontside receiver 3: 6-yard hitch.

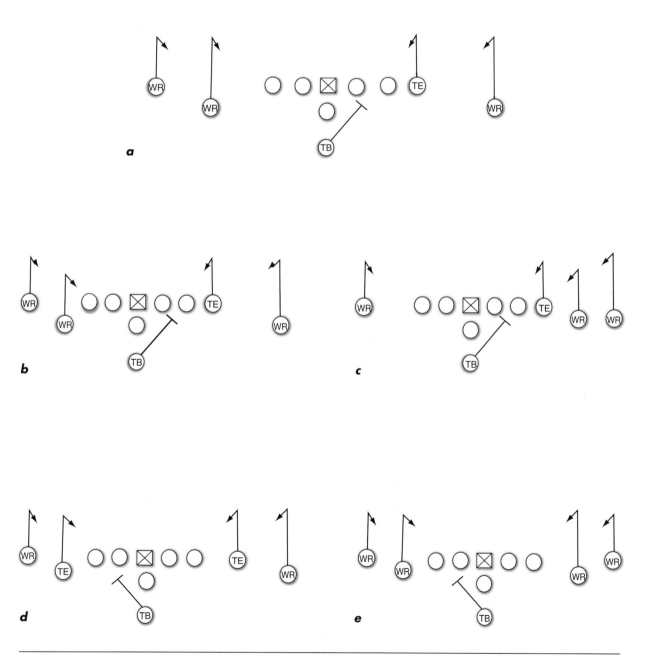

Figure 9.31 83-93 quick routes (three-step hitch): *(a)* right 5 83; *(b)* right 3 83; *(c)* right 6 83; *(d)* right flex 5 93; *(e)* shoot right 93.

84-94 quick route (speed out)

The 84-94 is our speed-out route (figure 9.32). We practice this route over and over, even to the point of timing the route with the number of steps the wide receivers take before breaking to the outside. This route is very difficult to stop when executed well and also sets up the out-and-up route for the big-play opportunity.

Formations: All.

Tags: Seam, hitch.

Frontside receiver 1: 5-yard out.

Backside receiver 1: 5-yard out.

Frontside receiver 2: 6-yard slant.

Backside receiver 2: 6-yard slant.

Frontside receiver 3: 6-yard slant.

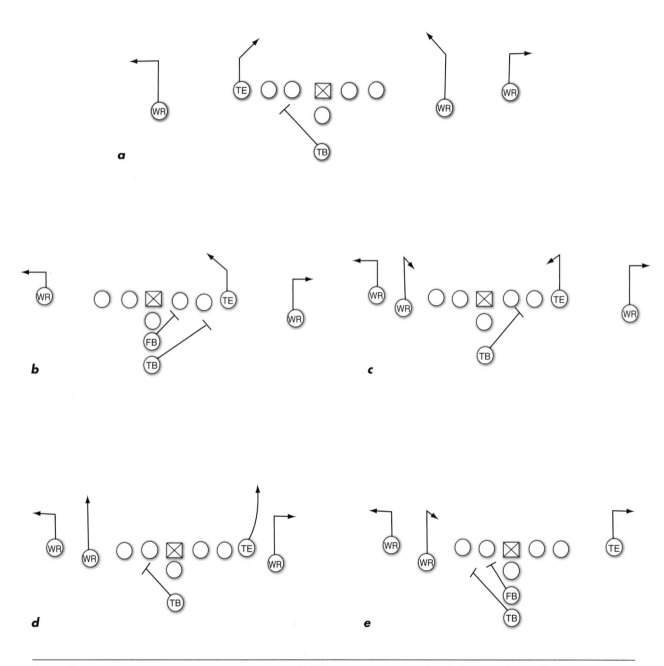

Figure 9.32 84-94 quick routes (speed out): (a) left 6 94; (b) right 84; (c) shoot right 84 hitch; (d) right 5 94 seam; (e) right flex shoot 94 hitch.

86-96 quick route (quick slant)

The quick slant (figure 9.33) is the staple of everyone's three-step passing game. Work a variety of moves and techniques that allow your receiver to get inside position against the defender and teach your quarterback to throw the ball on time. Make sure the quarterback throws the ball to the open area and doesn't lead the receiver into an underneath defender with the pass.

Formations: All.

Tags: Flat, hitch, bubble.

Frontside receiver 1: 6-yard slant.

Backside receiver 1: 6-yard slant.

Frontside receiver 2: 6-yard slant.

Backside receiver 2: 6-yard slant.

Frontside receiver 3: 6-yard slant.

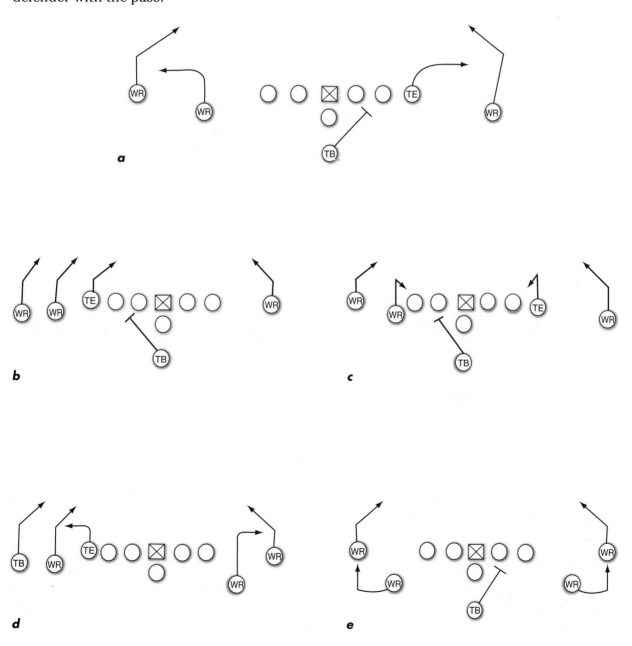

Figure 9.33 86-96 quick routes (quick slant): *(a)* right 5 86 flat; *(b)* left 5 96; *(c)* right 3 96 hitch; *(d)* left 6 hope 96 flat; *(e)* shoot right 86 bubble.

88-98 quick route (stick route)

The stick route (figure 9.34) is one of the most common routes used in football. The play has evolved, and now you see many versions of this great play. The play horizontally stretches any zone defense while allowing the receivers to beat a man-to-man scheme as well. Teach the receiver running the stick to feel the defense and find the open area in zone coverage.

Formations: All.

Tag: T swing.

Frontside receiver 1: Fade.

Backside receiver 1: 6-yard slant.

Frontside receiver 2: Arrow.

Backside receiver 2: 6-yard slant.

Frontside receiver 3: Stick (6 yards).

Backside TE: Normal position, always splits goal posts.

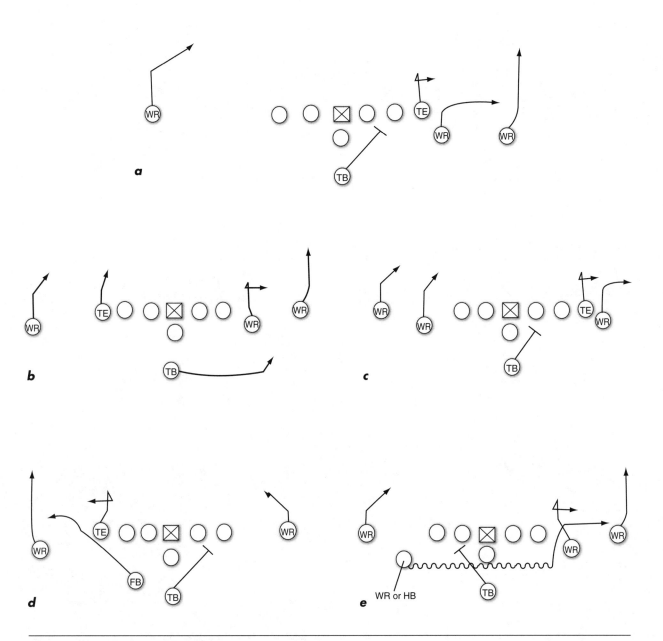

Figure 9.34 88-98 quick routes (stick route): *(a)* right 4 88 Y H flat; *(b)* left 6 88 H T swing; *(c)* right 4 slot 88 H flat; *(d)* left 1 88 Y H flood; *(e)* shoot right H6 88 Z H flat.

Five-Step Routes

Our five-step vertical passing game (figure 9.35) allows the quarterback and receivers to read the defensive secondary and take advantage of the coverage they are trying to incorporate. We simply tag the receiver we want to read, and, based on the alignment of the safeties, he converts his route. If the middle of the field is open, he bends his route to the middle. If the middle of the field is occupied, he continues his route down the seam. This is a great route against any two-deep alignment.

51-61 passing route (five-step vertical passing game)

Formations: All.

Frontside receiver 1: Fade.

Backside receiver 1: Fade.

Frontside receiver 2: Seam read.

Backside receiver 2: Seam.

Frontside receiver 3: Opposite seam.

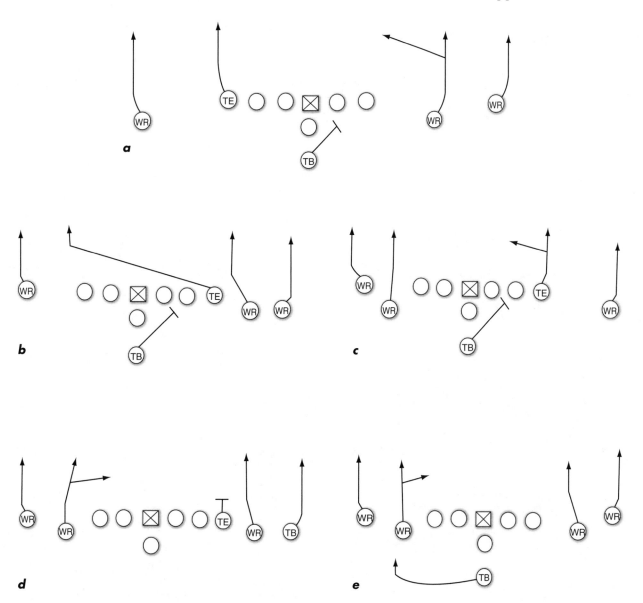

Figure 9.35 51-61 passing routes (five-step vertical passing game): *(a)* left 5 61; *(b)* right 6 61; *(c)* right 3 61 Y; *(d)* right 5 guy 51 stay; *(e)* shoot right 51 T swing.

53-63 passing route (curl/flat)

The 53-63 play (figure 9.36) is everyone's classic curl-to-flat concept play. The quarterback identifies the defender who is playing the curl and throws the ball off his coverage alignment. The wide receiver defeats man-to-man coverage with his route. We also use this curl/flat concept to attack a variety of different coverages by simply incorporating additional receivers into the route to manipulate defensive alignments and responsibilities.

Formations: All.

Frontside receiver 1: 12-yard curl.

Backside receiver 1: 12-yard curl.

Frontside receiver 2: Flat.

Backside receiver 2: Flat.

Frontside receiver 3: Spot (8 yards).

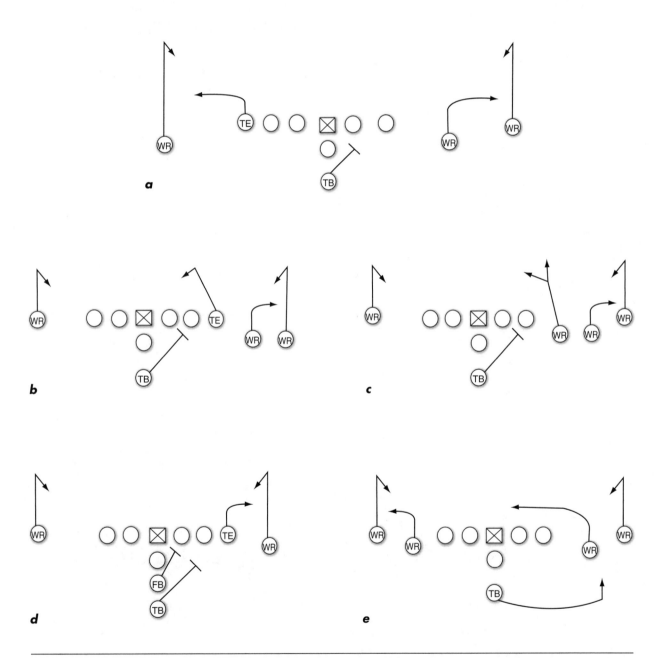

Figure 9.36 53-63 passing routes (curl/flat): *(a)* left 6 63; *(b)* right 6 63; *(c)* trips right 63 H seam; *(d)* right 63; *(e)* shoot right 63 Z drag T swing.

54-64 passing route (high/low against CB)

The 54-64 play is our high-to-low play against the cornerback (figure 9.37). The quarterback simply reads the corner to see if he plays the flag or the comeback and delivers the ball accordingly. The comeback is also a route that we expect to beat man-to-man coverage.

Formations: All.

Frontside receiver 1: 14-yard comeback.

Backside receiver 1: 14-yard comeback.

Frontside receiver 2: Flag.

Backside receiver 2: Flag.

Frontside receiver 3: Arrow.

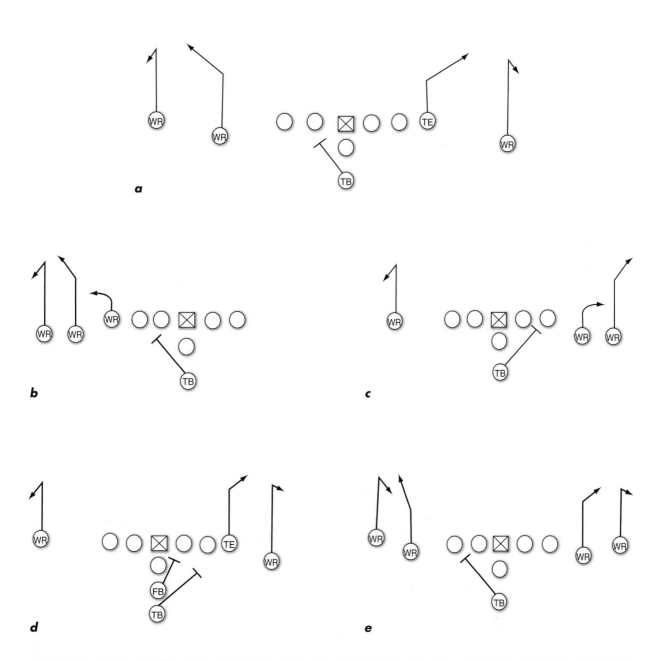

Figure 9.37 54-64 passing routes (high/low against CB): *(a)* right 5 54; *(b)* left 5 54; *(c)* trips right 64; *(d)* right 64; *(e)* shoot left 54.

55-65 passing route (mesh series)

The 55-65 passing routes (figure 9.38) make up what we call our mesh series. The combinations in this series are nearly endless and can be used to beat man or zone defenses by using a series of high-to-low crossing routes or meshes. All of our combinations in this series are run from three receiver groupings. We simply tag the different players and routes to change the assignments and appearance of the play.

Formations: 3×1.

Frontside receiver 1: High mesh.

Backside receiver 1: Dig.

Frontside receiver 2: Flag.

Frontside receiver 3: Flat.

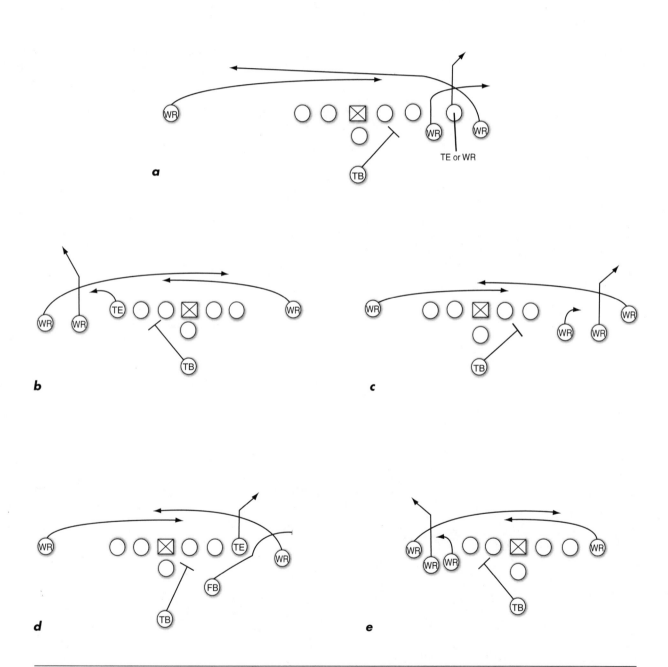

Figure 9.38 55-65 passing routes (mesh series): *(a)* right flex 6 crunch 65 X sneak; *(b)* left 5 55 X sneak; *(c)* trips right 65 X sneak; *(d)* right 2 65 H flood X sneak; *(e)* trips left bunch 55 X sneak.

56-66 passing route (post route)

The post route (figure 9.39) is one of our best plays because we can stretch the defensive secondary in a variety of ways. The threat of throwing the ball deep down the middle of the field is there, but add to that the ability of the number two receiver to run a variety of routes to threaten the other safety or corner and you have a whole passing game in itself.

No passing system is complete without the deep post play.

Formations: All.

Frontside receiver 1: Post.

Backside receiver 1: Comeback.

Frontside receiver 2: Dig.

Backside receiver 2: Low mesh.

Frontside receiver 3: Flat.

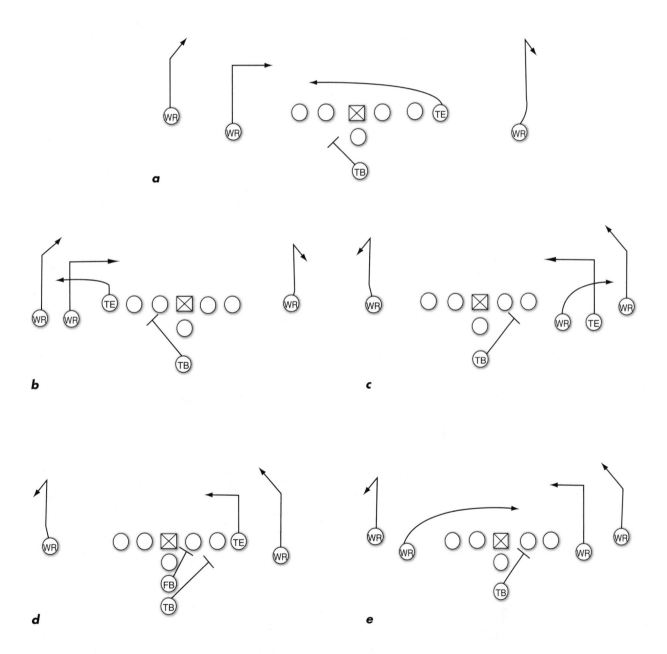

Figure 9.39 56-66 passing routes (post route): *(a)* right 5 56; *(b)* left 5 56; *(c)* trips right 66; *(d)* right 66; *(e)* shoot right 66.

57-67 passing route (shoot route)

The 57-67 (figure 9.40) is our basic cover-2 beater sometimes called the shoot route. The quarterback reads the cornerback and simply throws high or low based on the corners' alignments and techniques. We add a third receiver to the scenario if our opponent is good at disguising his coverage because this route is not nearly as effective against cover 3.

Formations: All.

Frontside receiver 1: Corner.

Backside receiver 1: Corner.

Frontside receiver 2: Flat.

Backside receiver 2: Flat.

Frontside receiver 3: Seam read.

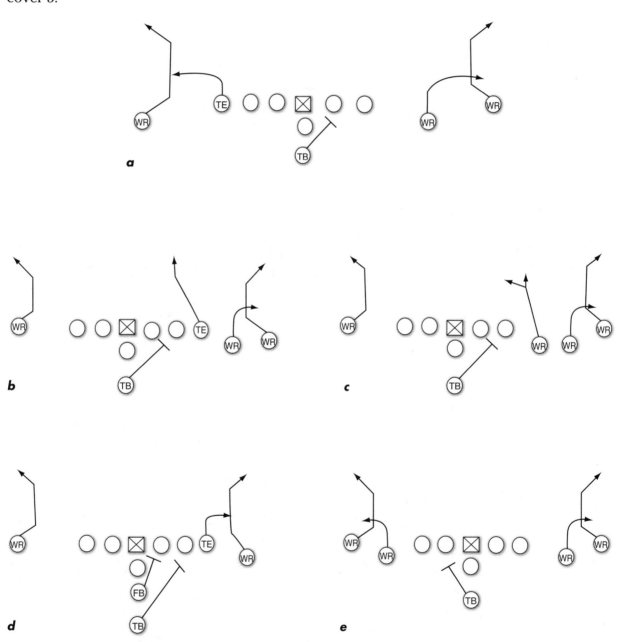

Figure 9.40 57-67 passing routes (shoot route): *(a)* left 6 67; *(b)* right 5 67; *(c)* trips right 67; *(d)* right 67; *(e)* shoot right 57.

58-68 passing route (fade-out series)

We use the fade-out series (figure 9.41) as the foundation for several passing plays. In the most basic and productive route, the number one receiver clears out with a fade route, the number two receiver runs a 10-yard out route, and the number three receiver runs a flat route. The quarterback simply reads the flat defender and throws high or low to number two or three based on the defenders' alignments and action. We add a variety of combination routes for the number two and three receivers as we progress with this passing play.

Formations: All.

Frontside receiver 1: Fade.

Backside receiver 1: Fade.

Frontside receiver 2: Out. Flat if three WR.

Backside receiver 2: Out.

Frontside receiver 3: Out.

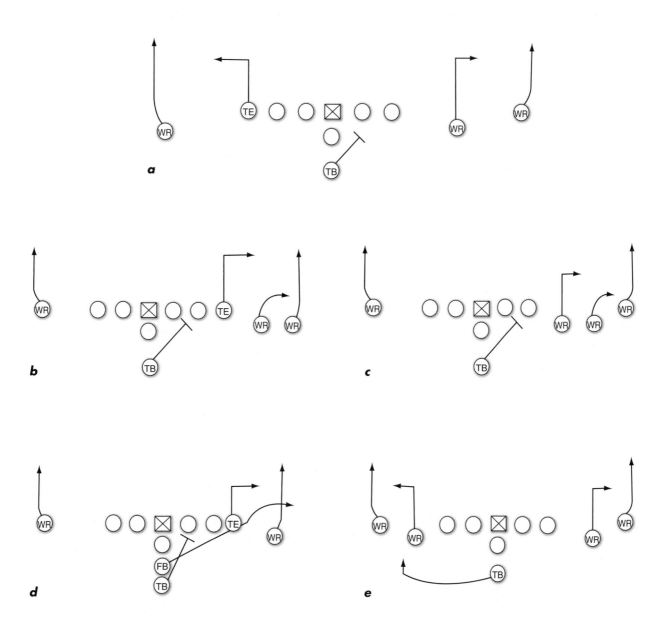

Figure 9.41   58-68 passing routes (fade-out series): *(a)* left 6 68; *(b)* right 6 68; *(c)* trips right 68; *(d)* right 68 H flood; *(e)* shoot right 58 T swing.

59-69 passing route (smash)

The 59-69 is our smash route (figure 9.42). We can throw it against almost any coverage with some simple sight adjustments made by the number two receiver and quarterback. If we get cover 3 and the corner bails to the deep third, we take the hitch and the quarterback releases the ball quickly. If we get cover 2, we read the corner to make sure he takes the hitch by number one and convert the inside route to a bench, or a flat flag, as we call it. The quarterback throws the ball to the sideline away from the safety and behind the cornerback. If we get cover 1, we still read the corner and adjust the inside route to a man-beater flag and throw the ball behind the corner and away from the safety. The smash has been a great play for us for a long time.

Formations: All.

Tag: Seam.

Frontside receiver 1: 6-yard hitch.

Backside receiver 1: 6-yard hitch.

Frontside receiver 2: Flag.

Backside receiver 2: Flag.

Frontside receiver 3: Seam read.

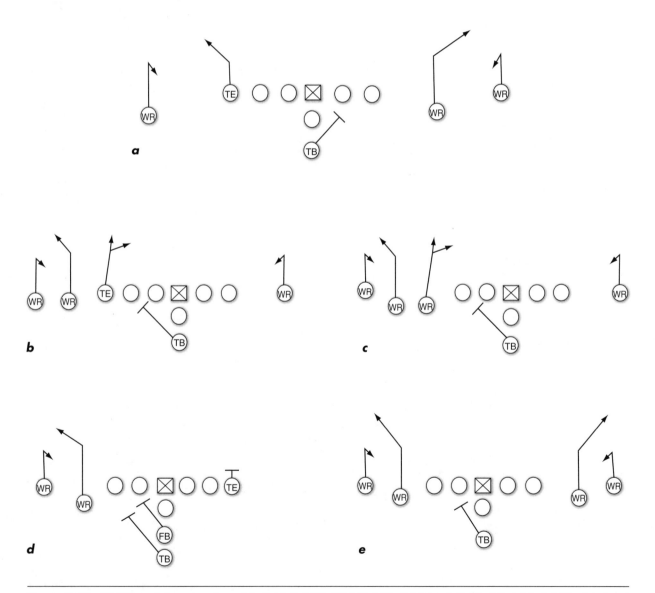

Figure 9.42 59-69 passing routes (smash): *(a)* left 6 69; *(b)* left 5 59; *(c)* trips left 59; *(d)* right slot 59; *(e)* shoot right 59.

Passing Formations

It is vital to an offensive system to be able to run and throw effectively from the same formation. Having formations that you can only run or only pass from gives the defense a definite advantage when trying to stop what you do.

We implement passes off of our favorite run fakes, and runs out of our favorite pass formations. Your imagination is your only limitation when developing a passing game. Set up your passing game with a strong running game and force your opponent to overload against the run. When the defense must overload (put more men in the running box), it creates great opportunities down the field for the passing game.

Consider your offensive philosophy as well as your offensive personnel when devising your passing formations. We prefer to run and pass from every formation we incorporate. This forces the defense to balance up and play it safe in most cases because they can't predict our offensive intentions.

If you are fortunate enough to have exceptional receivers whose speed and ability outmatch most defenses, place as many great athletes on the field as possible. Some of the greatest offensive teams use three, four, or even five wide receivers to capitalize on their abilities against certain defenses. If your philosophy is like ours and you want a powerful running attack, build some of your passing game from your most popular running formations and take advantage of running defenses.

Consider your quarterback's ability when selecting offensive formations. Does he throw well from the pocket, or is he better when he's on the run or after a play action fake? Does your quarterback read defenses well, or do you need to align the offensive formation so that it limits his responsibility in these areas? Devise your formations and passing attack around what your quarterback does best. Your quarterback must be able to execute the plays you choose or your offense will be ineffective.

Your offensive line must be able to protect the quarterback at all costs. No matter how great your triggerman may be, he will not help the team if he is on his back or is hit by the defensive pass rush. Select formations that allow you to predict the pressure points the defense will attack, and make sure you have a plan to take advantage of the defense's blitzing methods. To help your quarterback get the time he needs to deliver the ball, use screens and draws, sprint-outs, and play actions along with formations that allow you to predict the defense's intentions.

Tips for the Passing Game

As with everything in the game of football, you will be good at what you emphasize. A consistent passing game requires great attention to detail and tons of repetition. Work on the passing game under gamelike conditions. Offensive linemen, receivers, and quarterbacks must develop timing by practicing against tremendous defensive pressure. Throwing the ball around without pressure may help develop timing, but throwing out of a live pocket against a live rush polishes the passing game and makes it great.

Make sure your quarterback practices timing routes with the receivers he will throw to in a game. Often in practice the wrong receiver is in the huddle when you call a pass play. Make sure the receivers and quarterbacks practice routes together so that the timing will be solid.

Study defensive personnel carefully and find players who match up well in the passing game. Does your opponent have a big linebacker who is a great run player but is not athletic enough to cover your running back one on one? Does the defense have a safety who is very aggressive against the run and may bite on a good play action fake? Any way you can isolate your best players against the defense to win matchups will help your team execute the passing game and win ball games.

CHAPTER 10
DEFENSIVE POSITIONS AND ALIGNMENTS

Defense is the name of the game when it comes to winning championships. If the opponent can't score, they can't win—we take that slogan to heart at Jenks. Emphasizing great defensive play is vital when developing a championship-caliber program. Great defenses are given famous nicknames like the Steel Curtain or the Doomsday Defense. Our defensive teams do the same thing each season. Developing great pride and intensity on the defensive side of the football greatly increases your team's chances of winning big ball games.

In this chapter I discuss individual defensive positions and the attributes we look for in each position as well as basic defensive alignment characteristics to consider when developing a defensive system. Keep in mind that there are many, many ways to skin a cat. While developing your defensive system, make sure the system is versatile, multiple, teachable, and likeable. We use the KILL slogan—Keep it likeable and learnable.

DEFENSIVE ALIGNMENTS AND PERSONNEL

Because the rules in football do not limit the number of players the defensive team may place on the line of scrimmage, defensive alignments are virtually unlimited. Some defenses employ a four-man front with four defensive linemen; this alignment is usually called an *even* or *split front*. Defenses that use three defensive linemen are usually called an *odd front,* and they almost always have a lineman aligned over the center. Even and odd fronts are the most common alignments in football today, but all great defenses are flexible and can adjust to the strengths of any offensive system.

Great defenses play with a million watts of intensity and can stop the opponent's running game. If your opponent can consistently rush the football for first downs, your team will have a very difficult time winning regularly. Your defensive system should be gap sound, covering all the rushing gaps, while protecting against the passing game as well. The ability to disguise a defensive alignment is also important when trying to keep the opposing quarterback and offensive coordinator guessing at what your team is trying to accomplish.

Preventing big, game-changing plays is also important when designing a defensive system. It takes a lot of discipline and execution to win ball games with no rushing game and a short passing game, so make sure your defensive unit is sound against big plays. No matter what defensive alignment you choose or what defensive system you employ, remember the old saying, "It's not the Xs and the Os, it's the Jims and the Joes." Having great personnel always helps you play great defense. Later in this chapter I get into the attributes defensive players need at defensive end, lineman, linebacker, cornerback, and safety. Also I discuss actual defensive alignments. (See chapter 12 for more on defensive alignments.)

Coach's Keys

1. Defensive players can be divided into defensive ends, defensive tackles and nose guards, linebackers (both inside and outside), cornerbacks, and safeties. Be diligent when placing players in position to use their skills to the maximum in the defensive system.

2. Defensive ends must be versatile and able to rush the passer and play against the rush.

3. Defensive linemen and nose guards must be big and physical and force the offensive line to double-team them. This allows linebackers to make tackles.

4. Linebackers are the defensive warriors. They must be tough and great tacklers. They must also be intelligent enough to communicate defensive calls and adjustments to the rest of the defense.

5. Cornerbacks must have short memories. They play the toughest position on the field and must cover the fastest players on the field. Look for athleticism and confidence.

6. Safeties need to be hybrid players who have cornerback ability in the passing game and linebacker ability in the running game. Teach safeties to be interchangeable.

7. Research opponents thoroughly to understand what you need to do to defend their offensive systems. Choose defensive alignments that allow players to be successful against the given offense.

8. Make sure your system is likeable and learnable. In order for your defensive system to evolve and grow, you must be able to teach it, communicate it, and implement it against any alignment or formation.

Defensive End

No matter which defensive alignment you implement, you'll need great defensive ends. This defensive line position is critical to a team for several reasons. If your opponent can't run the football around the end, he must run the ball offtackle. If he can't run the ball offtackle, he must run the ball up the middle. If he can't run the ball up the middle, he must throw the ball. If your opponent can control your defensive ends, they will be able to successfully run and pass the football. A defensive end who can disrupt both the run and the pass is a tremendous weapon and can alter the offensive team's game plan. Defensive units that have solid defensive ends who can make plays against the run and the pass are usually very good defenses.

Defensive ends need the tenacity, speed, and athletic ability to rush the passer while working against players, usually tackles, who are much larger than they are. Defensive ends also must be physical and strong in order to fend off larger blockers in the running game.

Look for athleticism, strength, and power when placing defensive ends on your squad. In a perfect world, defensive ends would be 6 feet, 4 inches to 6 feet, 6 inches and 250 to 280 pounds with tremendous takeoff ability. But perfectly sized ends are rare and are usually playing on Sundays in the league.

A defensive system should allow for different types of defensive ends with different attributes. If you primarily use a four-man front, you will need great defensive ends who can make plays. If you use an odd front, you can get away with a little bigger, less-athletic player at end and put more responsibility on your outside linebackers.

Defensive Tackle and Nose Guard

Having a dominant defensive interior is vital to stopping an opponent's rushing attack. If you employ an even front, both interior defensive linemen are usually called tackles. If you run an odd defense, the man in the middle is the nose guard.

Either way, the guys in the middle of the defensive line must be big, strong, and physical and have the ability to win one-on-one blocking battles. Defensive tackles must be dominant enough to draw double-team blocks from the offensive line. The ability to penetrate the offensive backfield and draw double-team blocks keeps the offensive linemen from reaching the second level of the defense and blocking the linebackers, your best tacklers.

Defensive tackles and nose guards come in all shapes and sizes, but one thing is consistent. They show up to the game in a bad mood, and they play with great passion and tenacity. Look for big, strong players who are agile enough to penetrate and get upfield into the offensive backfield. Defensive line-

A strong defensive interior—nose guard and tackles—is key to stopping the opponent's running game.

men are mean and enjoy a good physical battle, so look for the most aggressive big players you have.

Linebacker

Linebackers are usually separated into two types—inside and outside. Inside linebackers are the hub of great defenses and, like defensive linemen, enjoy a good fight every now and then. The great inside linebackers are instinctive and have a natural feel for where the ball carrier is going. They are physical and have the tenacity and athletic ability to fend off fullbacks and linemen who are trying to block them. Linebackers also need to be intelligent because they communicate most of the defensive calls and adjustments that come from the defensive coordinator. Great linebackers must be tremendous tacklers and play with relentless effort on every snap. They are the gladiators of the modern day.

Outside linebackers need to have many of the same attributes as the inside linebackers, plus they need to have the speed and athleticism to cover running backs and receivers in the open field during passing plays. Outside linebackers also need to be good pass rushers because one of their defensive responsibilities is to blitz and put pressure on the quarterback in passing situations.

Cornerback

The secondary concepts you choose to implement may determine what type of corners you need to develop. Our defensive system requires corners to play a great deal of man-to-man coverage against the fastest players on the field, so we look for the best athletes with great speed to play cornerback. We will sacrifice size for speed if we have to in order to ensure enough ability to run with the offense's best receivers. Some defensive systems are predominantly zone defenses. These defenses require larger, more physical players at corner to match up with bigger, taller personnel and to assist the defense in the running game.

Corners have the hardest job on the field because they are normally isolated from the rest of the defense. They must perform well all of the time. The fans will be the first to know when a corner makes a mistake. Corners must have short memories; if a corner makes a mistake and gets beat, he must learn from the mistake, regroup, and go back and play great again. An athlete who cannot play under such pressure cannot play corner. Look for the most skilled and confident players you can find to play cornerback.

Safety

Safeties are hybrid players in today's game. They must have the pass coverage abilities of a cornerback and the tackling abilities of a linebacker. This combination makes great safeties hard to find; many players are good tacklers but not good pass coverers and vice versa.

Safeties must be able to break up pass plays like cornerbacks and tackle like linebackers.

Safeties should be cerebral players who can make adjustments on the run. They are the generals in the defensive backfield. Usually they make the secondary calls and adjustments during the game.

We prefer our safeties to be interchangeable, meaning they each understand the other's responsibilities and can execute safety duties at either free or strong safety. The safety's ability to be interchangeable is a great tool when adjusting to offenses that move and change strength a lot.

If you are not blessed with two safeties of equal ability, you may need to structure your defense with a true free safety, who is a great pass defender, and a true strong safety, who is a better run player. When choosing safeties, look for a hybrid-type player who is both physical and athletic. Intelligence is a great attribute as well.

DEFENSIVE FORMATIONS

The defensive system you choose should address your defensive philosophy and match up with your particular team personnel. Consider the league you play in as well. Is your conference a passing conference, a rushing conference, or a combination? Your defensive system should be structured around the teams you must beat in order to win championships.

Our district includes a variety of offenses. A couple of teams spread the field and use four and five receivers; other teams run the power-I and try to run the ball right over the top. I stress implementing a multiple defensive system that allows a variety of alignments and flexibility. If the opponent's offensive coordinator knows where your defense is going to line up, he will have a great play to defeat you. Make sure your defense is versatile. Here are a few of the most common defensive formations and my ideas about the strengths and weaknesses of each.

3-4 or 5-2

The pro 3-4 alignment (figure 10.1) is a commonly used defensive system for several reasons. This alignment is sometimes called a 5-2 when the outside linebackers are in the up position on the line of scrimmage because technically there are five defensive linemen.

The beauty of the 3-4 defense is the ability to disguise alignments and defensive responsibilities. Having four linebackers allows the defense to dominate the run and the pass from the same alignment, preventing the offense from adjusting until after the ball is snapped. The outside linebackers are the keys in this defense. They must be able to rush the passer and play man-to-man or zone coverage against the pass. Versatility at outside linebacker is vital in the 3-4 to use the system to the fullest. The defense

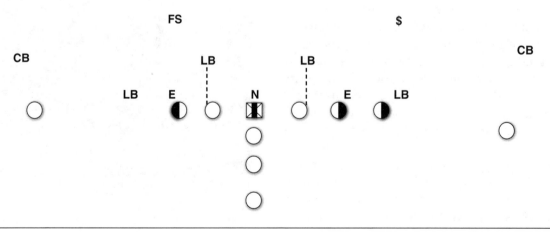

Figure 10.1 3-4 defensive formation.

also allows the secondary to employ either a two-deep concept or a three-deep concept from virtually the same presnap alignment, making the defense adaptable and versatile. Make sure you have a dominant nose guard and two great outside linebackers if you want to use this defense.

Finding the prototype outside linebackers who are big and physical enough to play on the end of the line against offensive tackles is usually not as much of a problem as finding a linebacker who also is fast and athletic enough to drop from the line of scrimmage to play man to man on a receiver or cover a curl to the flat zone. Not many linebackers can do both well.

4-4 or Split 6

The 4-4 or split-6 defensive formation (figure 10.2) employs four defensive linemen, two inside linebackers, two outside linebackers (sometimes called rovers or bandits), and three secondary players. The defense is very strong against running teams because in the basic alignment, eight players are near the line of scrimmage with the possibility of moving the free safety near the line of scrimmage as well.

The defense usually includes a wide variety of both run and pass blitzes and pressures to give running football teams a lot of trouble. The defense is easy to organize and adjustments are relatively simple, which can be

either good or bad. It's good because your defensive personnel can easily understand their assignments, but it's bad because the offensive team can sometimes easily understand your defensive adjustments. That is never good.

The defense is weak against teams that can execute well in the passing game because the free safety usually has to cover for the outside rusher's responsibility, tipping off the quarterback before the snap. A well-trained quarterback and offensive coordinator can take advantage of the three-deep secondary with wise use of fast personnel in the vertical passing game. The 4-4 defense usually has to change to the 4-3 defense against effective passing teams unless the defense is blessed with great hybrid run–pass players. Otherwise they will suffer the consequences of big pass plays down the field.

4-3

The basic 4-3 (figure 10.3) is the most popular defense for several reasons. The main reason is the defense's ability to adapt by sliding the four defensive linemen, sliding the three linebackers, or both. The 4-3 uses an even front with four defensive linemen, three linebackers, and four secondary players, making the defense versatile and multiple against any offense. The middle linebacker must be a great player, and the defensive ends must be playmakers for this defense to succeed.

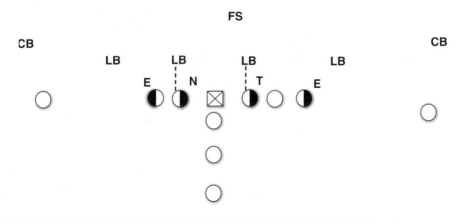

Figure 10.2 4-4 defensive formation.

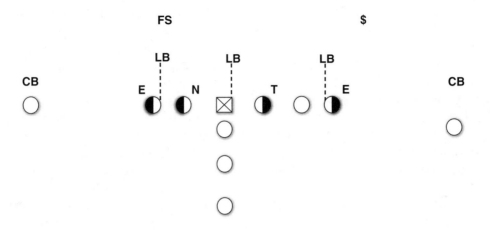

Figure 10.3 4-3 defensive formation.

Because there are only three linebackers in the defense, the two safeties must be great hybrid players, equally talented in defending both the rush and the pass. Outside linebackers must also be talented enough to cover receivers and running backs and physical enough to battle blockers against the run. This defense can be the basis for a sound and fruitful defensive system.

The versatility of the defense can also become the defense's weakness. The two outside linebackers and the two safeties must be versatile players with great athletic ability in order to use the defense to its full potential.

Jenks Trojan Defense

At Jenks, we package out of the 4-3 alignment but over the years have developed a versatile, multiple defensive system (figure 10.4). Our conference is very diverse offensively. If you can imagine it, you will probably see it on the offensive side of the ball in our league. From wing-T to five receivers, we have to be able to defend it in order to win ball games. Therefore, we set out to develop a defensive system that allows us to defend a variety of offensive systems and implement, teach, and communicate one system that can take on a variety of defensive looks. In other words,

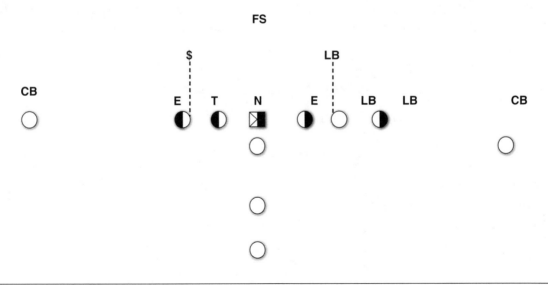

Figure 10.4 Jenks Trojan Bear defense.

our rules and teaching don't change from one alignment to the next.

From Basic to Bruising

Before I became head coach at Jenks in 1996, we had been a basic defensive football team. Our defenses had always executed well and played hard, but the simplicity of our defenses hurt us. Offenses would take advantage of knowing where we were going to line up and control our defense with formations and personnel groups. My new defensive coordinator, Matt Hennesy, and I vowed that we would never be controlled by an opponent's offense again and implemented our version of the Jenks Trojan multiple 4-3 defense.

At that time, almost everyone ran standard offensive formations with two backs in the backfield. When they spread out, they used three receivers and one running back. My college defensive line coach, Ronnie Jones, was working with Buddy Ryan at the time, so I called him and asked if coach Ryan would mind if we borrowed a few of his famous Chicago Bears "Bear" defenses. Coach Jones mailed me several of Coach Ryan's two- and one-back pressure packages, and we built them into our defensive system.

The Bear defense changed offensive football in our district forever. Our 1996 and 1997 defenses dominated offenses like few defenses had ever done. In fact, our 1997 varsity Legion of Doom defense didn't give up 100 total rushing yards during the entire season, playoffs included.

Since that time, offenses are a lot different, rarely lining up in two-back formations that would allow us to overload the running box. Football has progressed both offensively and defensively. Stay as current as possible to maintain an edge on your opponents. You never know when a little edge may win an important game or championship.

Against two-back running teams, I prefer the 5-2 defense with its ability to outnumber the offensive blockers in the running box. In our system of defense we accomplish this by sliding defensive linemen to the weak side, sliding linebackers to the strong side, and assigning run responsibility to a safety. We are a 4-3 defense that can line up in a 5-2 when we need to.

Against four- and five-wide passing teams, we like to be versatile enough to thoroughly cover all receivers or outnumber the pass blockers and put pressure on the quarterback with blitzes. We accomplish this by implementing a four-man front and sliding linebackers outside the box where they can assist in both the run game and the passing game. Another way to accomplish the same goal is to substitute additional defensive secondary players and align the same way. The rules of the system don't change, the personnel is just a little different. We create a 4-3 alignment with multiple coverages and blitzes so that the offense cannot dictate what we do against them.

Our defensive system has continued to evolve and develop from year to year as offenses keep adjusting to find ways to defeat the latest defensive concepts. Carefully research the latest strategies and ideas and stay as current as you can. If you can make your opponent adjust and change, you are in control.

CHAPTER 11 TEACHING DEFENSIVE SKILLS

Every defensive player on a team must develop position-specific techniques and skills to defeat the offensive player in front of him. The one constant that all defensive players must possess is the willingness and ability to play with relentless effort. Without effort, a defensive unit will never develop into the type of team that can compete for championships.

Great defense wins championships. Without a great defense, you simply cannot win at the highest level. Having been a defensive coordinator for several years, I understand the three main components of developing a championship defense. First on the list is attitude. The guys who play and coach on the defensive side of the ball must be fighters. They must be willing to fight until the end and never give up no matter what the circumstances may be. We say it all the time: "Defense is all an attitude." I want tough, aggressive guys on my defensive team.

The second component of championship defense is molding players into a unit. Defense is a total-team effort. Corners cover, ends rush, linebackers tackle—it all works together. The better we cover, the more sacks we get. The more pressure we get up front, the more interceptions we get. Everyone must play their assignments in order for the team to excel.

The third component of championship defense is skill or technique. Great athletes with great technique win games. Great athletes who do not play with great skill are average football players. In this chapter we discuss a few of the essential drills for developing defensive skills position by position.

DEFENSIVE END

Defensive ends are vital to any defensive unit. A great defensive end can actually change a good offensive game plan by being a threat to the quarterback or the running game.

For defensive end, we look for a player who has a great motor and great speed and is relentless in his effort to disrupt plays. He must be disciplined enough to contain the bootleg and the reverse, but intense enough to rush the passer and play the offtackle running plays. One thing I know, when our defense has great ends, we have a chance to have a great defense.

Stance and Takeoff

When teaching defensive end techniques, we start by teaching a stance that allows the defensive end to have tremendous takeoff when the ball is snapped. Ends assume a three-point stance with a lot of weight forward on their hands, like a sprinter in track (figure 11.1a). Ends always place the inside hand on the ground. The outside hand is up in the ready position. Ends concentrate on the football and use their peripheral vision.

Figure 11.1 Defensive end (*a*) stance and (*b*) takeoff.

The takeoff is a series of rapid steps upfield taken while attacking the offensive lineman in front (figure 11.1b). The first two steps in the takeoff should be rapid and relatively short to ensure that the defensive end has both feet firmly planted on the ground when contact is made with the offensive lineman. This ensures great power and leverage on contact.

Hand placement is also very important during the takeoff. The defensive end attacks the offensive player with both palms (thumbs up), delivering a vicious blow on each breastplate while grabbing the jersey for control. The goal of the punch and hand placement is to stymie and control the offensive lineman's attack.

Pressure, Escape, and Redirection

At this point, the defensive end feels or reads the pressure of the offensive lineman's block to determine the direction of the play. Is the offensive lineman trying to hook, base-block, or pass-block? This information is vital so that the end can initiate the correct escape move. Once the end knows the direction of the play, he redirects in the correct direction using a variety of escape moves to get away from the offensive lineman's hands.

During passing situations, ends set up the blockers with a variety of initial moves. The first move we teach all ends is to butt and press the blocker, meaning the end attacks the opponent with face and hands to separate himself from the blocker. Once in this press position with hand control, the end initiates one of the pass rush techniques.

Another initial setup we use is the juke. The defensive end makes a false attack move to force the offensive player to adjust his position and stance. For example, if the defensive player is aligned outside the offensive player, the defensive player might jab-step inside the offensive player to fake him out. This causes the offensive player to shift his weight and balance to the inside, creating a great opportunity to gain outside leverage and control. The juke-and-swim and butt-and-rip will be covered in more detail later in the section on pass rush.

Because holding by offensive linemen is legal in today's game, defensive ends need to learn methods of escaping the grasp of offensive linemen. The first escape technique we teach is the simple rip (figure 11.2a). The rip is executed once the end knows which side of the offensive lineman he wants to escape from to pursue the ball carrier. Once the direction is determined, the end pulls with the hand on the side he wants to escape to while throwing an uppercut or rip with the backside hand through the offensive lineman's playside armpit. Usually this technique will knock the offensive lineman's hands loose and allow the end to pursue the ball.

Another escape technique, the swim move (figure 11.2b), is similar to the rip technique except that the backside hand and arm swim over the top of the offensive lineman's playside shoulder. While using a swim move, the defensive end must pull hard on the lineman's jersey to get his shoulders turned away from the play and open up an escape path. After the swim move, the end clears the offensive lineman's hands and escapes.

Coach's Keys

1. Championship teams execute proper defensive technique. Teach position-specific techniques and have players practice over and over. Great athletes with poor technique are average football players; average athletes with great technique are good football players.

2. Defensive linemen must have great takeoff and must attack the line of scrimmage. Teach them to read blocks and to escape from offensive linemen.

3. Teach linebackers to read the flow of the offensive play. Attack angle is crucial when making plays against the run. Hold linebackers to a high standard and accept only their very best in practice and in games.

Figure 11.2 Defensive end techniques: *(a)* rip move; *(b)* swim move.

4. Place the most athletic and confident players at cornerback. It's the most difficult and high-pressure position on the field. Make sure they have short memories.

5. Safeties must play the run and the pass equally well. Teach safeties to recognize run versus pass.

6. Develop a great tackling defense by practicing position-specific tackling drills and techniques several times a week. If your defense can tackle, they have a chance to win.

Defensive End Drills

We use the following drills to develop defensive ends. The first key for a defensive end is to get off the ball—the takeoff. A defensive end must beat the offensive lineman off the ball and use his speed and agility against the much larger and slower offensive player. We practice takeoffs and block recognition every day. We work on reading base blocks, hook blocks, down blocks, and trap blocks every day. We want ends to simply react on game day and be disrupters. Defensive ends also drill tackling. All members of the defense should be great tacklers, so we often drill tackling. Normally, ends work on angle tackles and sideline tackles because these two situations are the most common for ends.

Takeoff Release

The objective of the takeoff drill is to develop an explosive release upfield on the snap. We work this drill in pairs with strong ends and weak ends together. We have a device called the snapper, a football on the end of a broom handle, that allows the coach to stand upright with the football in snapping position and call the cadence while watching the ends take off on the ball movement. The ends assume a great stance and concentrate on ball movement, not sound. The coach calls out the snap count and then moves the football, triggering the takeoff. We work this drill every day.

Read

The objective of the read drill is to teach defensive ends how to react to blocking schemes and offensive lineman techniques. Usually, this drill is run against five or six offensive linemen, depending on what type of offense we will see that week. Ends assume their stance and proper alignment. The offensive scout team executes various blocking techniques and play schemes against the ends. Start with the simple base block, hook block, and down block and then progress to double-team blocks, trap blocks, and backfield blocks.

Live Pass Rush

The live pass rush drill incorporates the escape methods discussed earlier as well as the takeoff drill and the various pass rushing techniques we teach. We take the escape drill one step further, teaching the butt-and-swim, butt-and-rip, juke-and-swim, juke-and-rip, and an inside countermove when the tackle runs the ends by the quarterback. When the pass blocker overcompensates by getting too far upfield, this leaves the door wide open for an inside countermove off one of the initial pass rush moves. We prefer to teach an inside-club move in which the pass rusher takes his inside forearm and literally clubs the blocker to the outside, creating an inside rush lane to the quarterback.

For some of our more athletic pass rushers, we teach an inside-spin move. Once the pass rusher gets upfield and actually passes the depth of the quarterback, the end throws on the brakes, reverse pivots, and spins back to the inside while stepping under the pass blocker to gain leverage to the quarterback. Both countermoves are effective and important for keeping the pass blocker honest and protecting his inside gap. We work pass rush every day with the offensive line.

DEFENSIVE TACKLE AND NOSE GUARD

Interior defensive linemen must be tough guys, preferably big and strong enough to require a double-team block when the offensive team wants to run the ball. Just like defensive ends, defensive tackles and nose guards must be quick off the ball (figure 11.3) and beat the offensive lineman to the punch.

Figure 11.3 Defensive tackle (*a*) stance and (*b*) takeoff.

We teach many of the same pass rush and redirection techniques to the inside linemen as we do to the ends. The main difference is that the likelihood of double-team blocks inside is much higher. We preach to inside players to draw double teams and to fight, claw, kick, or whatever it takes to penetrate the opponent's backfield and disrupt the play. When the offense has to double-team our linemen, our linebackers are free to roam and make plays. This is vital in any defensive system.

Six Fundamentals for the Front Seven

1. Hold shoulders square.
2. Make sure gapside arm and leg are free.
3. Keep pads out over toes.
4. Keep a base.
5. Cross face; don't run around blocks.
6. Hit with eyes, hands, and shoulders.

When incorporating a head-up nose guard, it is important to understand that he must be responsible for either A-gap whether on the frontside or backside. The head-up nose guard must aggressively attack the center and drive him deep into the backfield while trying to fight across his face toward pressure. If the center beats him across his face, the nose guard should go ahead and stay in the backside gap and chase the play from behind, keeping the center on the line of scrimmage so that he cannot effectively block the linebacker. If the center doesn't beat the nose guard across his face, the nose guard stays in the frontside gap and pursues the play. This technique makes life much simpler for the linebackers when they are trying to fill the correct gaps during a running play.

Defensive Tackle and Nose Guard Drills

The tackles use the same drills as the ends, especially emphasizing the double-team read because inside linemen are often double-teamed in run schemes.

Redirection

We work very hard to teach interior defensive linemen redirection skills. The drill starts with two defensive linemen lined up in front of two scout-team offensive linemen. The coach blows a whistle to begin the drill. The defensive linemen take off and get hand control of the offensive linemen. The defensive coach stands behind the offensive linemen and simulates the offensive ball carrier by running to the right or left after the linemen are engaged. The defensive linemen then work to escape and redirect flat down the line of scrimmage in pursuit of the ball carrier. This drill teaches defensive linemen to react as they should when they read running plays and teaches them the correct pursuit angle to tackle the ball carrier.

Nose Guard Head Up

The nose guard uses a special drill to learn his head-up technique on the center against the run. The nose guard lines up opposite three offensive linemen and even with the middle one. The coach stands behind him. The coach gives the desired blocking scheme to the offensive linemen and then issues the snap count for the play. When the nose guard is aligned head up, his technique requires him to attack and control the center and maintain the line of scrimmage during a double-team block. This drill teaches the nose guard body control and leverage, skills required to play the double-team block. Carefully control this drill to prevent injuries.

Tackling Drills for Defensive Ends and Linemen

All solid defenders must be good tacklers in order for a defensive unit to be successful. During drills we try to place defensive linemen in situations that are as close to the reality of game day as possible. Most tackles made by defensive linemen are at an angle or in the chase position and often are made after the tackle has escaped from an offensive blocker. With this in mind, we incorporate the following tackling drills into our daily practice routine.

Angle Tackling

Because most tackles made by defensive ends and linemen are made at an angle, we use a simple tackling drill to demonstrate this situation (figure 11.4). The defensive player is placed in a heads-up position 5 yards away from a scout-team running back. Cones are placed 4 yards on either side of the defensive player as landmarks for the running back. The defensive coach stands behind the defensive player and tells the running back which cone to run toward. The defensive player must attack at the proper angle, getting his head across the running back's body while wrapping his arms around the back and driving him backward away from the line of scrimmage.

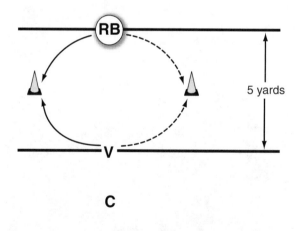

5 yards

Figure 11.4 Angle tackling drill.

Escape Tackling

This drill begins with the defensive lineman in attack position with hands inside as he engages an offensive lineman. The scout team running back is 5 yards behind the offensive

lineman. When the whistle blows, the defensive lineman must rip or swim and escape the blocker's hand and make a good form tackle on the running back. This is a realistic drill for the defensive linemen because they have to defeat blockers to make tackles on every play.

LINEBACKER

Linebackers are the hub of every defense. They communicate the calls from the sideline to the defensive unit, they make the adjustments during the play, and they are relentless in their pursuit of the football. Linebackers must be equally adept in playing the running game and covering pass receivers as well as blitzing and rushing the quarterback.

The best linebackers I have coached have had a couple of common attributes. They were all tough guys who played with tons of passion and had an intense love of the game. The great ones also studied their opponents and entered each game understanding their opponent's entire offensive personality. Linebackers are the heart and soul of every great defense.

Linebacker Drills

Training linebackers correctly is vital. If a linebacker misreads a play, doesn't understand his gap responsibility, or can't tackle in the open field, the entire defense will suffer.

We start by teaching linebackers the four types of flow they will see during a typical ball game (figure 11.5). Cylinder flow refers to any play that is run straight up the gut in the A-gaps. Hard flow is any play that is run off-tackle or at a hard angle relative to the inside linebackers. Fast flow is any play in which the backfield is running laterally or away from the linebackers. Counter flow is any play in which the members of the backfield split or go in opposite directions.

Once the linebacker understands flow, we continue his training by teaching him various escape techniques to use to make plays against the offense. Of course, every play

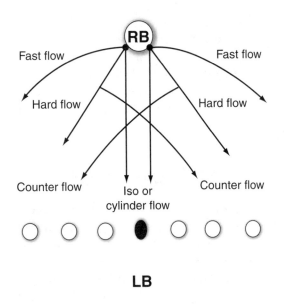

Figure 11.5 Linebacker flow keys.

on. The linebacker attacks the blocker with his face and hands and actually butts him while gaining separation from the defender by pressing him away with his hands. This technique is very effective for taking on an offensive blocker who is coming to block the linebacker above the waist.

The second escape technique is the rip (figure 11.7). The rip technique is used during hard or fast flow situations in which the blocker attacks at an angle. The linebacker dips his hips and shoulders and delivers a crossarm uppercut to the outside shoulder of the blocker, creating leverage and space in order to clear the block and continue pursuit of the ball.

Finally, we teach the linebacker to play the cut block or the block below the waist

begins with the linebacker lining up in the correct stance (figure 11.6).

Butt-and-press is the most common escape method used when taking on an offensive blocker who is attacking high and straight

Figure 11.6 Linebacker stance.

Figure 11.7 Rip escape technique.

Figure 11.8 Cut block.

(figure 11.8). When taking on a cut block, the linebacker must attack the defender with his hands by stymieing the defender's momentum and forcing him to the ground while at the same time getting one leg over the top of or around the cut block and on the ground. Getting a leg over or around the cut block allows the linebacker to continue his pursuit of the ball.

Flow

The flow drill teaches linebackers the proper pursuit and attack angles for running plays. Begin the drill with three linebackers lined up in proper position across from two running backs in I-formation. Agility bags are used to simulate offensive linemen. The linebackers coach stands behind the linebackers, gives directions to the scout-team running backs, and then calls the snap count. Linebackers are assigned responsibilities based on their alignment and the flow of the backfield.

Escape or String Out

The escape or string-out drill (figure 11.9) places linebackers in the three most common escape positions they face: straight-on attack,

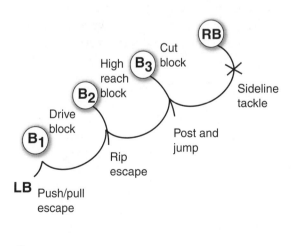

C

Figure 11.9 Linebacker string-out drill. Linebacker works downhill through the drill.

angle attack, and cut block. The drill begins with a linebacker face to face and engaged (hands inside) with a blocker. The linebacker executes an escape technique and then continues to pursue the play, taking on another blocker with a rip technique. After the linebacker executes the rip technique, the third, and final, blocker throws a cut block (sometimes we use a blocking dummy) and the linebacker executes a post technique—both hands force the blocker's head to the ground as the linebacker throws his feet back and away from the blocker—against the cut block. He then pursues and tackles the scout-team ball carrier. This is a great drill for simulating linebacker escape techniques and the downhill flow that linebackers need to accomplish when pursuing the ball carrier.

Tackling Drills for Linebackers

In addition to understanding flow and escape techniques, linebackers must also be great tacklers who have great footwork. We incorporate a variety of drills to help develop footwork and agility while reinforcing flow techniques.

Downhill Tackling

The downhill drill (figure 11.10) is one of my favorite tackling drills. Not only does it train good tackling technique, but it also teaches the downhill attack angle toward the line of scrimmage that great linebackers possess.

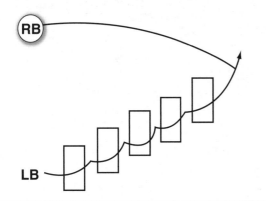

Figure 11.10 Linebacker downhill tackling drill. Linebacker gets his head across the running back and executes a good form tackle.

Align five or six agility dummies about 1 yard apart and staggered downhill toward the line of scrimmage. When the whistle blows, the linebacker must laterally flow through the bags and make a great form tackle on the scout-team running back. Make sure the linebacker gets his head across the ball carrier and wraps his arms completely around him while driving him back and away from the line of scrimmage.

In-and-Out Tackling

The in-and-out tackling drill (figure 11.11) is great for teaching linebackers to change direction, stay under control, and make solid tackles. Line up four agility bags parallel to each other and 1 yard apart. The linebacker aligns laterally next to the first agility bag with the running back 5 yards directly in front of him. The coach yells a number between one and four. The number represents the number of agility bags the linebacker must laterally cross and return before making a form tackle on the running back. This drill is a realistic teaching tool for inside linebackers.

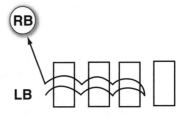

C

Figure 11.11 Linebacker in-and-out tackling drill. In this example, the coach yells, "Three." The linebacker must cross three bags, return, and execute a form tackle on the running back.

CORNERBACK

Having great corners who can cover is crucial. If every member of a defense does his job perfectly, but the corner is beaten deep on a pass, everyone fails. Solid corner play allows you to play aggressive defense and provides great flexibility because you can free up safeties to play the run or blitz. Average corners require safety help or must play loose technique, which takes away from your ability to be aggressive in your approach.

Cornerbacks must be great athletes who have a solid knowledge of body control and position because they spend the majority of their time covering the most athletic players on the field in one-on-one situations. They must also have short memories; they must learn quickly from their mistakes and forget about them. A corner who worries about getting beat is normally not a very good corner. We look for athleticism and boldness in corners.

Teaching and drill work should involve numerous close-quarters events. Corners drill bump-and-run, trade offs, and switches daily. Try diligently to create the speed and intensity of game day when you practice coverage drills. No one remembers who gets beat in practice; game-day performance is what counts. Put corners under pressure often and they will respond well when it counts.

Cornerback Drills

Corners play more man to man than they do zone, so we begin by teaching them jamming techniques to reroute the receiver's progress (figure 11.12). Once the corners have a good grasp of man techniques, we progress to teaching them the techniques they need to incorporate to play zone coverage (figure 11.13).

Figure 11.12 Corner (*a*) stance and (*b*) jamming technique.

Figure 11.13 As receivers come into their covered zones, the corners move to cover the receivers man to man.

Bump-and-Run

The bump-and-run is a simple one-on-one drill with a cornerback and a receiver. The corner assumes a narrow stance slightly inside of the receiver. He delivers a one-handed blow with his inside hand to the receiver's chest on his release. This inside hand jam naturally opens the corner's hips and puts them parallel to the receiver's hips as they run down the field. This is a very simple drill, but it helps teach corners the vital jamming technique they need.

In Phase, Out of Phase

Another one-on-one drill teaches cornerbacks about position and strategy as they play receivers in man-to-man situations. Because corners spend nearly 90 percent of their coverage time in one-on-one situations, develop their confidence and skills in this particular part of the game. By understanding which technique they must use based on their physical position with respect to the receiver, cornerbacks can become comfortable and confident while in one-on-one coverage.

Corners are considered in phase when they are running nearly hip to hip with the wide receiver. In other words, when in phase, the cornerback can easily reach out and touch his man. Out of phase means that the corner is beat or he is not in position to touch the opponent.

When corners are in phase, the technique they need involves turning to the inside just like the receiver and making a play on the ball as it comes from the quarterback. The out-of-phase technique is different but equally important. When a corner is out of phase, he needs to focus on the receiver's neck and sprint at maximum effort to try to regain proper position, providing an opportunity to break up the pass. Once the corner gains ground on the receiver, his focus shifts to the receiver's hands and eyes because the cornerback doesn't have time to turn to find the ball as it comes down toward the receiver. When the receiver's hands go up, the corner delivers an explosive stripping motion through the wide receiver's arms to deflect the ball or prevent the receiver from getting both hands on the ball at the same time.

We work this drill every day because our corners play man-to-man technique all of the time, and we want them to be comfortable in this situation.

Banjo or Trade

Cornerbacks who can work together are vital for man-to-man situations. This drill is used during sessions of two-on-two and three-on-three drills to allow players to get used to working together. Repetitions are crucial when developing a cornerback's ability to trade routes and switch responsibilities on the fly. We work the banjo drill every day so that trading routes becomes second nature to players.

When teams know you like to play a lot of man-to-man they often run passing routes where receivers cross or switch responsibilities. To counter this, we practice switching receivers in our man-to-man responsibilities. The term we use is *banjo*. I don't know where the term comes from, but we have always referred to a man-to-man switch as a banjo.

The banjo is called by the defensive back on the inside receiver. If the inside receiver releases outside toward the other corner, the inside defensive back yells, "Banjo!" He opens his hips and looks at the outside receiver to see if he is releasing inside to replace the other receiver. If the outside receiver releases inside, the defensive backs trade men and resume man-to-man responsibilities. The ability to switch men is important if you play a lot of man technique.

Tackling Drills for Cornerbacks

Corners are rarely point-of-attack tacklers. Usually they are support tacklers or over-the-top tacklers who clean up the play after the main tacklers have done their jobs defending the play. With this in mind, we work very hard with corners to develop their angle tackling as well as their ability to use the sidelines to force the ball carrier out of bounds. Corners are also taught pursuit angles and the importance of touchdown-saving tackles when the ball carrier breaks down the field and away from them. Another situation corners are often faced with is having to defeat stalk blocks by wide receivers. We address this

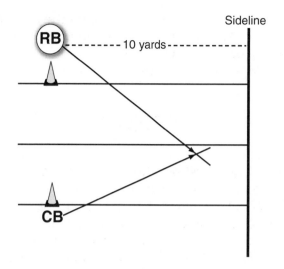

Figure 11.14 Sideline-tackling drill. Cornerback must stay inside out and use the sideline to contain the running back. Cornerback must not allow the running back to cut back to the inside.

situation through drills such as the escape drill used with defensive linemen, having the corner engage the blocker and defeat him while making a tackle on the ball carrier.

Sideline Tackling

The sideline-tackling drill (figure 11.14) teaches corners to use the sideline to force running backs or receivers out of bounds, preventing them from cutting back to the inside. Begin the drill with players approximately 10 yards apart. Use cones as landmarks with the sideline approximately 10 yards away. On the whistle, the running back can run anywhere he wants between the cones and the sideline. The objective is for the corner to maintain inside position on the running back and not allow a cutback toward the field. Remind players that the drill is about position and technique, not giving each other a concussion.

Escape Tackling

This drill is just like the escape tackling drill the defensive linemen use. The corner engages a scout-team wide receiver. The scout-team running back is 5 yards behind the wide receiver. When the whistle blows, the corner has to use one of the escape techniques to get away from the wide receiver and then tackle the running back in the open field.

SAFETY

Safeties are special players with special abilities. They must be athletic enough to man up on a solid number two receiver and yet be physical enough to step into the line of scrimmage and tackle a running back.

All our defensive secondary adjustments are made with safeties, so they must have the ability to learn the entire defensive system and be able to play strong or free safety on any given play. Safeties must be smart, fast, physical, and flexible.

The best safeties at Jenks have had an uncanny ability to feel whether the play was a run or a pass long before the play actually developed. We teach safeties to read uncovered linemen and tight ends to determine the offensive team's intentions. When they read run, they react and get to the point of attack in great position to tackle the ball carrier (stack, hide, and fit; figure 11.15). Safeties execute open-field tackling drills to develop as run defenders. When they read pass or see high hats along the line of scrimmage, they understand exactly what progression to follow to defeat the play. We incorporate the high-hat, low-hat drill each week to develop each safety's ability to read run or pass.

Safeties must be solid man-to-man players and yet be able to play zone coverage as well. Often safeties are called on to play curl-to-flat or a deep half-field zone and we drill these concepts every day. For a safety to be able to switch gears from man-to-man coverage to zone coverage is vital. Zone coverage means

Figure 11.15 Stack, hide, fit: *(a)* safety reads run and reacts; *(b)* safety runs to point of attack.

covering a receiver who enters a certain area of the field that the safety is responsible for covering. In short, safeties cover an area of the field until a receiver enters the area. Once the receiver enters the zone, the safety covers him man to man.

The ability to disguise their intentions is another valuable characteristic of safeties. We want the offense to think man-to-man while we are in zone and vice versa. A strong knowledge of responsibilities and hours of drill work can make this happen, so practice disguise every day.

Safeties are the generals of the secondary. They make the calls and adjustments for everyone in the secondary. When they have all these characteristics, we can run every page of our playbook and be an effective defensive unit.

Six Fundamentals for the Secondary

1. Communicate.
2. Don't give up the bomb.
3. Keep the ball inside and in front.
4. Build a fence around the ball.
5. Play the ball. The ball will always take you to the receiver. The receiver will not always take you to the ball.
6. Maintain cushion and leverage.

Safety Drills

Safeties must be hybrid players, both great tacklers and great coverage players. Safeties use the same drills as the corners plus additional linebacker-related drills.

Rob Drill

Because safeties are involved in stopping the running game, we incorporate a technique that gives us the best of both worlds for safeties. The rob drill serves as the basis for our defensive secondary. This drill greatly enhances the safety's ability to be in great position to tackle the ball carrier.

For the drill, the safety lines up 8 to 10 yards deep and 1 yard outside the tight end. The safety reads the tight end for a high hat or a low hat (run block or pass release). If the tight end run-blocks, the safety executes a technique we call a stack, hide, and fit. He attacks downhill toward the line of scrimmage, stacks behind the linebacker on his side, hides behind the defensive linemen to make sure he doesn't get caught up in trash, and then finally fits in the gap that the running back chooses to run through.

If the tight end releases downfield vertically, the safety reads pass and plays man to man on the tight end. If the tight end releases for a pass and runs a drag across the middle or a quick out toward the flat, the safety's eyes immediately focus on the next receiver outside. He and the cornerback double-team the outside receiver, turning tight end coverage responsibilities over to the outside linebackers.

Zone Drop

We occasionally play zone coverage, so we teach safeties and corners to play a part of the field instead of a man. To accomplish this, we run a couple of field-zone drills. These drills teach safeties to read the quarterback and take great angles to make a play on the throw.

To teach safeties cover 3, we put a receiver on each hash mark and align the safety 10 yards deep directly in the middle of the field. The receivers release and run down the hash marks while the safety backpedals for depth, reading the quarterback's shoulders. When the quarterback turns to throw the ball, the safety breaks on the release and makes a play on the ball.

To teach cover 2, or halves coverage, we run the same drill, only we place one receiver on the hash and the other receiver on the bottom of the numbers with the safety aligned 10 to 12 yards deep and approximately 1 yard outside the hash mark. When the receivers release downfield, the safety backpedals for depth and width while reading the quarterback's shoulders for the release of the ball. When the ball is released, the safety breaks on the throw and makes a play on the ball.

Tackling Drills for Safeties

The following are the most common drills we use with safeties to help them develop. Safeties execute open-field tackling nearly every day as well as escape and tackle, just like linebackers and linemen.

Open-Field Tackling

During a game, safeties make mostly open-field tackles. For the open-field tackling drill (figure 11.16), the safety begins 10 yards away from a scout-team running back. Cones define the perimeter of the drill. When the coach blows the whistle, the running back can run anywhere between the cones he wants. The safety sprints downhill toward the line of scrimmage and cuts off the distance between himself and the running back. After cutting the distance, the safety must break down in a good football position to make a sure tackle on the running back in the open field. This is a

great drill for teaching safeties the stack-hide-and-fit technique used at their position.

Safeties also engage scout-team wide receivers. The safety must use one of the escape techniques to get away from the wide receiver and then tackle the running back in the open field. The drill is just like the escape tackling drill used by defensive linemen.

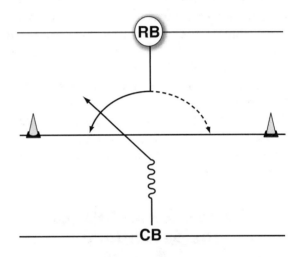

Figure 11.16 Open-field tackling drill. Safety must sprint to the line and cut off distance, then stack, hide, and fit. The safety must make a sure open-field tackle.

CHAPTER 12 TEACHING TEAM DEFENSE

Solid defensive play always gives a team a chance to win. In fact, great team defense wins more consistently than great team offense. If your opponent doesn't score, your team will never lose even if your own offense doesn't score much.

Great defense is the product of creating a close-knit group of players who completely understand not only their own responsibilities but also the duties of the players they play with, then coordinating them in the best possible position to be successful against an opponent. Great defensive teams can stop the run and the pass under any circumstances and can stop them consistently.

In this chapter we look at some of the thinking that goes into developing a defensive system. Different alignments and schemes allow a defense to be simple yet deceptive to the offense, making it difficult for the offense to get a bead on how the defense is trying to defeat them. I share with you virtually our entire defensive system and how we adjust to certain offensive formations and strategies. Remember, offense sells tickets, but defense wins championships. It's the truth.

Coach's Keys

1. Great defenses win championships. Emphasize the importance of team play and each player's vital role.

2. Your defensive system should match your personality, philosophy, personnel, and your opponent's tendencies and strategies.

3. Your defense should be versatile enough to complement your offense.

4. Research your opponent's offensive tendencies carefully, and develop your defense around what you need to defend. This method will reduce unnecessary risks and make you a more consistent defensive squad.

5. Understand your system like the back of your hand and be a great teacher. Make players extensions of their defensive coaches. They will be confident and play with great effort.

6. Stop the run and make your opponent one-dimensional. If you stop

what they do best, your opponent will struggle to execute something good enough to defeat you.

7. Keep your defensive system likeable, learnable, hostile, and versatile.

DEFENSIVE APPROACH

Great defense is all an attitude. Players must take the field ready for battle and believe that the defensive system in which they play gives them the best possible opportunity to stuff the opponent. We stress four defensive goals to players:

1. We will play harder than our opponent.

2. We will stop the run.

3. We will win third down.

4. We will not give up the big play.

To get the most out of any defensive system, the system must match your philosophy and personality, and you and your coaches must be able to understand it and teach it thoroughly. Keep your system likeable, learnable, versatile, and hostile.

Your defensive system must be consistent with your defensive philosophy. Your defense must fit your inner beliefs and personality. Do you take an aggressive approach and play a risk–reward type of pressure defensive football? Do you play it safe and implement a bend-but-don't-break philosophy? Both philosophies have their advantages, but consider several other variables when researching and developing a defensive system.

We have always taken a sound but aggressive approach to our defensive philosophy. We want to constantly stress the offensive team in a variety of ways and yet be sound and make our opponent earn everything they get. Make offenses execute to beat you; don't let them have an easy one. I've heard some defensive coaches say, "We'll give them the hitch." But, you won't hear one of my defensive coaches say that. We don't want to give the offense anything. Granted, it takes a lot of hitch routes to win a game, but we still want

to make the quarterback and receiver execute to be successful.

Another variable to consider is your style and ability on the offensive side of the ball. Does your offense score a lot of points, or is field position critical? If your offense is a scoring machine, then possession is important, and you may want to be aggressive on defense. If your offense is a little more conservative, you may want to try to play for field position and make the game as short as possible by running the football on offense and playing a little bend-but-don't-break on defense.

Whatever your defensive philosophy, consider all the variables and put your team in the best possible position to be successful. My choice is to assemble a defensive package that allows aggressiveness when required but can be bent when necessary and does not give up the big play.

There is no better way to control the tempo and outcome of a football game than to rush the ball for first downs. An offensive team that can run the ball consistently can win consistently. Make sure the structure of your defensive design enables your team to defeat the running game of any offense. Forcing the offense to be one-sided is a huge advantage for the defense. If the defense knows that the next play is a pass, it can tee off and play very aggressively and confidently. Structure your defensive schemes with the running game in mind, maintaining the ability to outnumber the run blockers at the point of attack.

Carefully study the opponents on your schedule and the opponents you know you are likely to face during postseason play. Gain a complete understanding of what types of offenses you will be up against. Some teams on your schedule won't be able to beat you no matter what defensive system you use, but for others you must have a great plan and a great scheme in order to be victorious. With this research in mind, begin assembling your defensive package. Like Dr. Stephen Covey says, "Begin with the end in mind."

Also consider the type of offensive system you use when developing your defensive system. Your defense must be versatile enough to complement your offense. If your offense is a "3 yards and a cloud of dust, grind it out" type of system, then your defense will need to provide great field position. You will need a pressure-type system to mesh with the offense. If your offense is a more progressive, wide-open system capable of producing field position and plenty of points, the bend-but-don't-break mentality may fit a little better.

When matching my defensive system with my offensive system, I make sure the defense is capable of adjusting from week to week in case the offense is sputtering and can't produce. Again, develop a defense that allows you to dictate what you want to accomplish, when you want to accomplish it.

By thoroughly breaking down an opponent on the scouting report, you can adjust your defensive system to meet the challenges your opponent's offense may throw at you. For example, if the opponent is a high-percentage first-down rushing team, you want to align the defense with enough players near the line of scrimmage to stop the running game. Second down and long makes calling defenses a little easier than second down and four when the offense can run any play in the playbook.

Another aspect to research is your opponent's offensive personality when they have the ball in different parts of the field. Are they aggressive when coming out from their own end? Do they take a conservative approach and run the ball and punt? Understanding field-zone tendencies allows you to adjust your defensive mentality to meet the challenges and tendencies of the offense.

Stop what the opponent does best. I like our odds of winning if the defense can force our opponent's offense to try to beat us with plays they are not used to running. Our defensive game plan educates coaches and players on our opponent's top five or six offensive plays, the plays they run with the most efficiency. The defensive coaches then use our system of schemes to stop their best plays. Think about it—if you can stop your opponent's top three or four plays, they will have a hard time executing something else to beat you. Make sure your defensive system allows you

to have multiple solutions to stopping your opponent's best plays.

Players must perform together consistently in order for the defense to be great. Constantly emphasize to players that they need each other to be successful. The by-product of great team play is success for everyone.

Here is an example of solid team defense. Imagine your opponent lines up with an All-American wide receiver who is awesomely talented. You know the corner will have a difficult time matching up with the wide receiver in pass coverage. Team defense provides many combinations for defending this great receiver. In one combination you might allow the corner to line up directly over the receiver and physically assault him on his release from the ball while playing the safety over the top to assist the corner with any ball down the field. The corner has the assurance of knowing he can give every ounce of energy he has to disrupt the receiver's release because his teammate is covering for him if he misses. Another strategy might be to align the defense in a basic man-to-man look, then on the snap, skate a defensive end into the flat for underneath help on the receiver while blitzing a safety from the backside. This underneath coverage by the end allows the corner to loosen his alignment and play with confidence while the added pressure of the safety blitz forces the quarterback to deliver the ball sooner than he wants to. Defensive systems should be versatile to ensure that players have the best opportunity to be successful.

Stress to defensive players that everyone on the field has an assignment. If each person does his job effectively, the team will be successful. Great coverage can be nullified by a lack of pass rush, and great pass rush can be nullified by a lack of secondary coverage. Everything works together on defense, and when it does, it's a beautiful thing.

Nothing hurts defensive performance more than confusion or indecision. Players must be able to simply react and play with great confidence at the snap of the ball. If they are wondering where to line up or what their responsibility is, they will be ineffective. Therefore, you and your coaches must understand the defensive system thoroughly and develop the ability to teach alignment, technique, and responsibilities to each defensive player. Leave nothing to chance. Don't expect players to learn how to play defense without being taught the intricate details of each position's responsibilities. The goal of great defensive coaches is to make players extensions of themselves on the playing field. When defensive players understand their responsibilities and the concepts of the defense called, they can turn it loose and play with fanatical effort and confidence. That's when you know you have a chance to dominate your opponent.

The average football play is about five seconds long. We ask defensive players to provide five seconds of wild-eyed, frenzied, 110 percent effort, execution, and explosion. A five-second explosion by every defensive player on every play will make us a great defensive team. If you went back and reviewed every football game ever played, 90 percent of them would have a different winner if you removed just five key plays from the game. During a game, no one knows which five plays might be the decision makers, so we ask defensive players to treat every play as if it were one of the five. Win with a continuous series of five-second explosions.

DEFENSIVE ALIGNMENTS

Some coaches say they are a 5-2 team or a 4-3 team or a 4-4 team. Most of them are lying. What I mean is, all defensive coordinators are employed to keep their opponents from scoring points. Defensive coordinators will do whatever it takes to stop the opponent.

I like certain defenses against certain offenses. And certainly we don't like some defenses against certain offenses. In this section of the chapter, I share our versatile defensive package and show you some of the formations and situations in which we implement different parts of our package.

You will notice that in our defensive system, run defenses are gap sound, meaning we have a defensive player assigned to every available running gap. Defenses also are zone or man sound, meaning we have players assigned to every available receiver or field zone almost without exception. Make sure the system you employ is always run-gap and pass-zone or man sound.

Huddle, Gaps, and Techniques

The defense begins with the huddle (figure 12.1). The tackle calls and sets the huddle. Rock (R) says, "Eyes," and the defense responds by saying, "Team." Buck (B) tells the situation. R gets the call from the coach on the sidelines and calls the defense in the huddle. After the calls are communicated, B says, "Wolf," and the team responds, "Pack," to break the huddle. The defense aligns according to the calls made by the linebackers. At the line of scrimmage, B recognizes the formation, R calls the defense, and Free (F) calls the coverage.

CB $ D   F   CB

E   N   T   V

R   B

Figure 12.1 Defensive huddle.

Figure 12.2 shows the gap responsibilities and the techniques that will be used. We use this system to make communication easier.

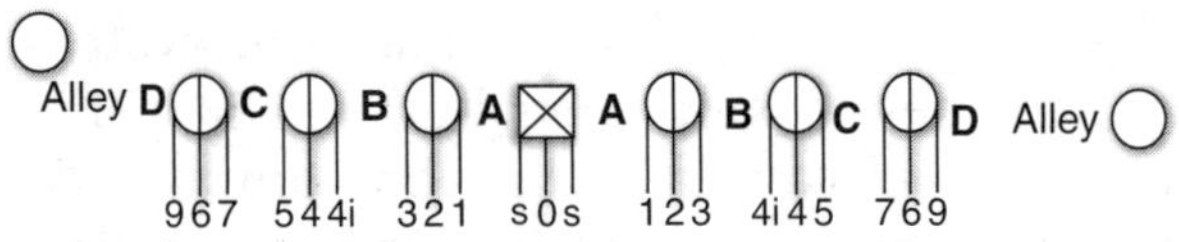

Figure 12.2 Gaps and techniques.

For example, when a coach asks his linebacker which gap he was playing, it's easier to respond, "B-gap" than to say the gap between the guard and tackle. The same is true for the number system for techniques. The defensive line coach can easily move his tackle from the outside shoulder of the guard to the outside shoulder of the tackle by simply saying, "Play a 5 technique instead of a 3 technique." Letters and numbers make communicating alignments quick and precise, which is important in the heat of the battle. At linebacker depth, a 0 is added to the technique. For example, head-up on the guard would be 20.

Personnel groupings are shown in table 12.1. We sort players into personnel groups; each has a specific name. For example, during the game the defensive coordinator might call, "Dime!" When the coach calls, "Dime," a specific group of 11 players takes the field. We gain an advantage by being able to rapidly deploy various defensive units during a game, so we spend quality practice time going over these groupings.

Linebackers have various calls for their individual alignments. We can add a great deal of stress to the offensive team with simple linebacker alignment changes. These adjustments are accomplished through simple, one-syllable words that communicate the following to each linebacker:

Up: Both linebackers walk up in gap.
Mug: All three linebackers walk up in gap.
Hug: Buck walks up in gap.
Show: Rock walks up in gap.
Fool: Show blitz. Do opposite of what is called.

Table 12.1 Defensive Personnel Groupings

	Linemen	Linebackers	Defensive backs
Regular	4	3	4
Nickel	4	2	5
Dime	4	1	6
30	3	3	5
25	3	2	6
Read	4	3	4
Boz	4	4	3
Goal line	5	3	3
Victory	3	1	7

Tight Defense, Five-Man Front

The tight defense (figure 12.3) is one of our favorites, especially against two-back running teams. We have seven players in the running box and could add two more with the safeties. This defense is very strong against a running game to the tight end side. It allows us to shift easily into the bear defense.

Some of the adjustments we make out of the tight defensive alignment are shown in figure 12.4. The loose adjustment (figure 12.4a) is used versus two tight end alignments or in situations in which there might be a threat to our weak side. This alignment also loosens the viper's alignment and allows him a good pass rush angle against the tackle.

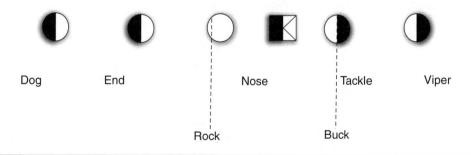

Figure 12.3 Tight defense, five-man front alignment.

The over adjustment (figure 12.4b) simply moves the nose guard over to a 1 technique or an inside shade of the guard. We use this adjustment against offensive teams that like to run to the tight end side and pull the guard. The over alignment makes it extremely difficult for the center to reach the nose guard or for the frontside guard to pull without disruption.

Tight out (figure 12.4c) is the adjustment we make against a tight wing set to the tight end side. *Out* tells the nose guard to move over, the end to move out to a 7 technique, and the dog linebacker to align on the wingback. This defensive shift gives us leverage against offtackle runs as well as the strongside sweep game teams like to run from the wing formation.

The following sections outline the defenses we use and a few adjustments and blitzes that go with those defenses. Table 12.2 lists the defenses and blitzes we use.

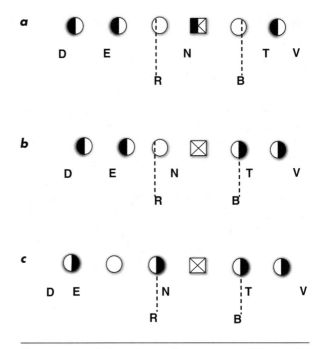

Figure 12.4 Tight defense adjustments and blitzes: *(a)* loose; *(b)* over; *(c)* out.

Table 12.2 Blitzes

Tight blitz	Bear blitz	Split blitz	Nickel blitz	Stack blitz
Stack strong	Nue	Stack strong	Griz	Redskin/flip
Stack weak	Nut	Stack weak	Griz/buck	Ice/flip
Stack pinch	Eun	Stack pinch		Lightning/flip
Stack flare	Tun	Stack flare	Rock	Rain/flip
Middle X	Due	Mid X	Buck	Rock deuce/flip
Strong X	Dur	Weak X	Double backer	Dog deuce/flip
Weak X	Nue/dur	Strong X	Rock X	Dog/flip
	Strong		Buck X	Rock/flip
Rock	Weak	Rock	Double backer X	
Buck	Weak X	Buck	Redskin	Rain/cut
Double backer	Eun/dur	Double backer	Ice	Lightning/fire
Rock X		Rock X		Flip/rain/cut
Buck X	Wish	Buck X	Cowboy	Flip/lightning/fire
Double backer X	Wash	Double backer X	Stud	Pirate
	Buck	Dog	Ram	Buccaneer
Fire	Buck/due	Cat	Fire	Double backer/cut/fire/dev
Blaze	Weak/dog/buck	Fire	Blaze	
Smoke	Strong/fire	Blaze	Smoke	Dime/cut/fire
		Smoke	Cut	Dime/redskin/razor/smoke
Crash			Razor	Dime/double backer/cut/fire
Crush			Blade	Dime/double backer X/cut/fire
			Fish	Dime/double backer
				Dime/double backer X
			Tiger	
			Cobra	
			Wolf	
			Buick	
			Chevy	
			Bingo	

Bear Defense, Six- to Eight-Man Front

The bear defense (figure 12.5) that we use comes directly from Buddy Ryan's playbook when he was the defensive coordinator for the Chicago Bears. The defense incorporates a strong-side reduction by the end, nose guard, and dog linebacker along with an overshift of the linebackers to the strong side. In a nutshell, this defense gives every defensive player a one-on-one opportunity against his offensive opponent. This defense allows us to get four strong or four weak pressure or at least threaten it on every snap, causing the offense to constantly adjust its protection schemes or risk having the quarterback hit. We love bear defense against two-back running teams and pocket throwing quarterbacks.

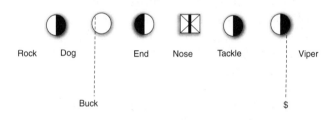

Figure 12.5 Bear defense, six- to eight-man front alignment.

The term *go* is tagged with any bear defensive call to alert all pass rushers to go all out in their pursuit of the quarterback and completely disregard the running game (figure 12.6a). We tell players to go all out with their best pass rush moves on the snap of the ball. If the play turns out to be a running play, players adjust on the move.

The majority of our bear blitzes are named with an acronym created by using the first letter of each player's position in order of their blitz responsibility. *Nue* (figure 12.6b) stands for *nose under end* or a simple line twist in which the nose guard and end switch gap responsibilities. The nose guard hits the move first because his letter comes first in the acronym. *Nut* (figure 12.6c) is another line twist in which the nose goes under the tackle. Again, this is simple but informative communication.

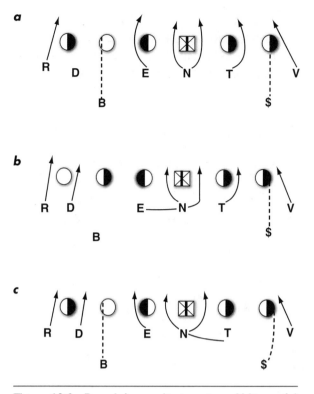

Figure 12.6 Bear defense adjustments and blitzes: *(a)* go; *(b)* nue; *(c)* nut.

30 Defense, Three-Man Front

The 30 package (figure 12.7) is used mainly against teams that are predominately throwing teams or when we can take advantage of an odd look on defense. This personnel package allows us to put at least five defensive backs on the field and makes us a fast, athletic, and diverse defense. We use a variety of blitzes, coverages, and alignments while in 30 defense. We research the opponent carefully and then decide the best way to defend him with our 30 personnel because we can assume a perceived 3-4 alignment or a perceived four-man front depending on our adjustments.

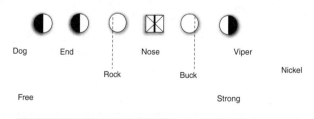

Figure 12.7 30 defense, three-man front alignment.

We use numbers to control the alignment of the end and nose guard. The first digit, 3, tells everyone we are in 30 personnel. The second number tells the end which technique alignment to take. The 35 call (figure 12.8a) means 30 defense with the end in a 5 technique; 34 (figure 12.8b) and 33 (figure 12.8c) are just minor adjustments we use for blitzing against the run or pass with the end aligning in the second number technique call and the nose adjusting to the backside A-gap.

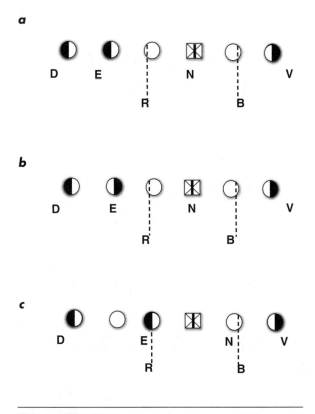

Quarter Defense, Three-Man Front

Quarter defense (figure 12.9) takes another linebacker out of the 30 defensive package and adds an additional defensive back. The running box is normally controlled by assigning one of the safeties to a gap using a spy call or by controlling gaps by blitzing linebackers and forcing the ball to the perimeter. This is a very versatile defensive grouping both in coverages and pressures.

Just like all linebacker blitzes in any personnel group, if the linebacker hears his name called, he blitzes through his gap responsibility. *Rock* (figure 12.10a) sends the rock linebacker through his gap, while *rock X* (figure 12.10b) tells rock to blitz through the opposite A-gap while the nose guard rushes through the frontside A-gap. *Rock X buck* (figure 12.10c) is the same blitz with rock and the nose while buck blitzes through his B-gap. As you can see, this defense can attack with a variety of pressures and stunts.

Figure 12.8 30 defense adjustments and blitzes: *(a)* 35; *(b)* 34; *(c)* 33.

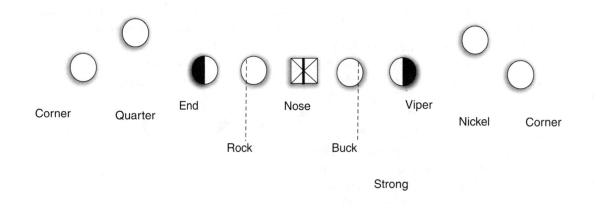

Figure 12.9 Quarter defense, three-man front alignment.

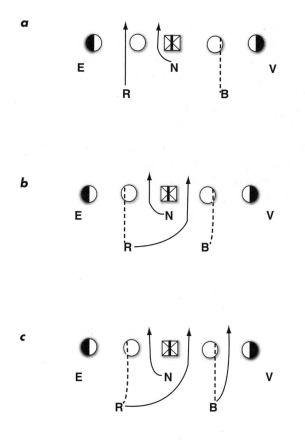

Figure 12.10 Quarter defense adjustments and blitzes: *(a)* rock; *(b)* rock X; and *(c)* rock X buck.

Split Defense, Four-Man Front

The split defense (figure 12.11) is our most common alignment and the defense we would choose if we had to play just one look. The strength of our defense is called away from the tight end, and we assume a four-man front alignment. Notice that the linebackers have the same gap responsibilities and alignments they had in the tight defense. The only exception is that the dog linebacker is now off the line of scrimmage. This defense is very flexible; we can run every secondary coverage in the playbook while in this defensive alignment.

The loose adjustment in split (figure 12.12a) is exactly the same as the loose adjustment in the tight defense. The backside tackle and viper loosen their alignments to gain leverage back to the tight end side. The tackle plays a 4 technique while the viper plays a head-up 6 technique.

Easy (figure 12.12b) is an adjustment in which the defensive tackle widens his alignment to a 4 technique while the viper aligns outside the tight end in a 9 technique. Wide (figure 12.12c) tells the viper to align outside the tight end in a 9 technique and contain the rush while the tackle and nose guard play their normal split alignments. The beauty of flipping linemen is that loose means the same thing to the tackle whether he is in tight or split defense.

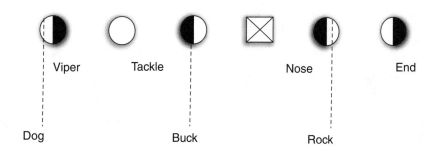

Figure 12.11 Split defense, four-man front alignment.

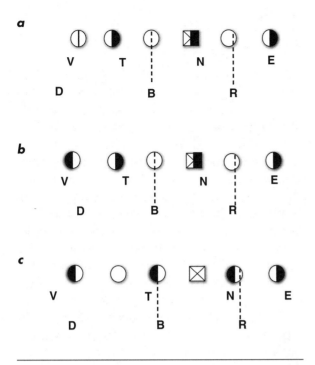

Figure 12.12 Split defense adjustments and blitzes: *(a)* loose; *(b)* easy; *(c)* wide.

Grizzly Defense, Six- to Eight-Man Front

Grizzly, or griz, as we call it, is our bear defense from a four-man front defensive approach (figure 12.13). Some coaches refer to it as the pro bear because Coach Ryan was unique in his approach to bear defense by placing all three linebackers on the same side of the formation. We get the same one-on-one matchups as our bear front, except that the rock linebacker is now the edge rusher on the weak side with the viper now rushing off the tight end side. This alignment allows more

flexibility in coverage because linebackers are all relatively close to their normal split alignments. We like to shift from the split defense to griz and vice versa because it can give the offense a lot of things to think about before the ball is snapped.

We use many of the same terms in the griz defense (figure 12.14) that we use in the bear defense. Notice that some are now spelled in the opposite direction because the defensive linemen are on opposite sides; for example, *nue,* nose under end, becomes *eun,* end under nose.

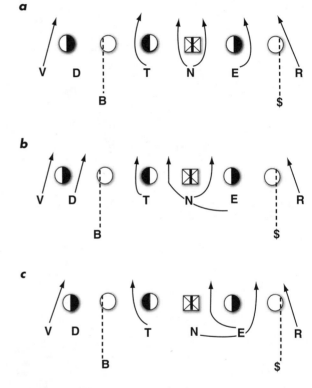

Figure 12.14 Grizzly defense adjustments and blitzes: *(a)* go; *(b)* nue; *(c)* eun.

Figure 12.13 Grizzly defense, six- to eight-man front alignment.

Nickel Defense, Four-Man Front

Nickel (figure 12.15) is a simple personnel change that replaces the linebacker who has the poorest pass coverage skills with a defensive back who matches up better with the opponent's tight end or wide receiver. This is a valuable package for us, and we use it often against teams that have a running game we believe our defensive front six can consistently stop. We also play a lot of cover 1 (to be explained later) and use the free safety in the running game.

We like to man up and pressure the running box or the passing pocket in our nickel package. Figures 12.16a and 12.16b demonstrate our normal griz defense using our nickel personnel. *Go* is pass rush freedom for the rushers, and *buck* tells the buck backer to blitz through his gap responsibility or, in this case, assign the nose guard A-gap and take the other one. Figure 12.16c shows an adjustment when we are facing two tight ends.

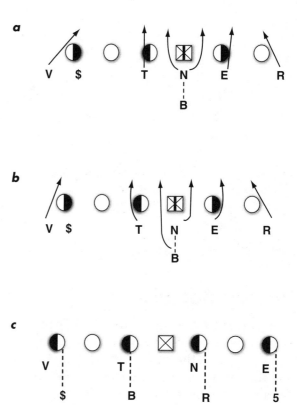

Figure 12.16 Nickel defense adjustments and blitzes: (*a*) griz go 1; (*b*) griz buck 1; (*c*) two–tight end adjustment.

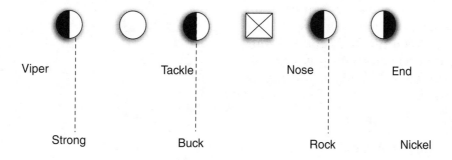

Figure 12.15 Nickel defense, four-man front alignment.

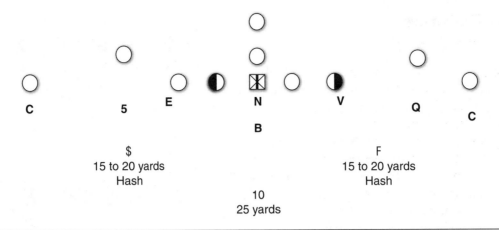

Figure 12.17 Victory defense.

Victory Defense

The victory defense (figure 12.17) places at least seven defensive secondary players on the field at the same time. Normally, we use this grouping as a bend-but-don't-break defense when the offense has a long way to go and a short time to get there. We also deploy this personnel group against heavy passing teams and play many of our man and zone combinations.

Goal Line Defenses

We put an extra defensive lineman in the game when we are in short-yardage situations and we feel the offense will run the football. The 60 stack alignment (figure 12.18) is a balanced 6-2 defense that uses man-to-man coverage and a very aggressive mentality. We believe the offense will run the ball, and we must stop them. Linebackers will give the two techniques directional slant calls based on scouting reports.

60 stack

Viper: 9 alignment. Attack blocker. Create new line of scrimmage. Contain.

End: 5 alignment. Attack blocker. Create new line of scrimmage. C-gap.

Tackle: 5 alignment. Attack blocker. Create new line of scrimmage. C-gap.

Nose: 2 alignment. Attack blocker. Create new line of scrimmage. Make a play.

X-man: 2 alignment. Attack blocker. Create new line of scrimmage. Make a play.

Rock: 20 alignment. B-gap to, A-gap away. First back out.

Buck: 20 alignment. B-gap to, A-gap away. First back out.

Dog: 9 alignment. Attack blocker. Create new line of scrimmage. Contain.

Strong safety: 60 or 2 alignment. Force strong, cutback weak. Man on TE.

Tight C: 60 or 1 alignment. Force weak, cutback strong. Man on TE.

Open C: 1 alignment. Man on 1. Second contain.

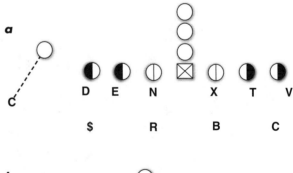

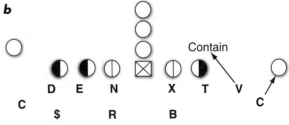

Figure 12.18 (a) 60 stack goal line defense; (b) two-receiver adjustment.

We use a variety of 60 defenses depending on how we believe the opponent will attack us (see figures 12.19, 12.20, and 12.21). We can align defensive linemen in virtually any gap or technique position based on scouting information or down and distance.

60 goal line (figure 12.19)

Viper: 9 alignment. Attack blocker. Create new line of scrimmage. Contain.

End: 5 alignment. Attack blocker. Create new line of scrimmage. C-gap.

Tackle: 5 alignment. Attack blocker. Create new line of scrimmage. C-gap.

Nose: 1 alignment. Attack blocker. Create new line of scrimmage. A-gap.

X-man: 3 alignment. Attack blocker. Create new line of scrimmage. B-gap.

Rock: 20 alignment. B-gap to, A-gap away. First back out.

Buck: 20 alignment. B-gap to, A-gap away. First back out.

Dog: 9 alignment. Attack blocker. Create new line of scrimmage. Contain.

Strong safety: 60 or 2 alignment. Force strong, cutback weak. Man on TE.

Tight C: 60 or 1 alignment. Force weak, cutback strong. Man on TE.

Open C: 1 alignment. Man on 1. Second contain.

60 gap (figure 12.20)

Viper: 9 alignment. Attack blocker. Create new line of scrimmage. Contain.

End: 5 alignment. Attack blocker. Create new line of scrimmage. C-gap.

Tackle: 5 alignment. Attack blocker. Create new line of scrimmage. C-gap.

Nose: Gap alignment. Attack gap low. Make a play.

X-man: Gap alignment. Attack gap low. Make a play.

Rock: 20 alignment. B-gap to, A-gap away. First back out.

Buck: 20 alignment. B-gap to, A-gap away. First back out.

Dog: 9 alignment. Attack blocker. Create new line of scrimmage. Contain.

Strong safety: 60 or 2 alignment. Force strong, cutback weak. Man on TE.

Tight C: 60 or 1 alignment. Force weak, cutback strong. Man on TE.

Open C: 1 alignment. Man on 1. Second contain.

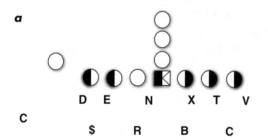

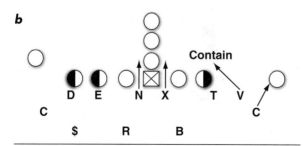

Figure 12.19 *(a)* 60 goal line; *(b)* two-receiver adjustment.

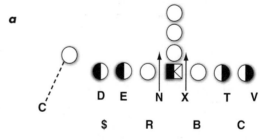

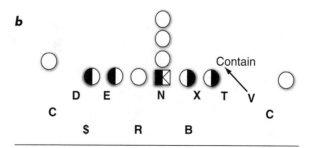

Figure 12.20 *(a)* 60 gap goal line defense; *(b)* two-receiver adjustment.

60 'noles, inside the 5 (figure 12.21)

Viper: 6 alignment. Attack blocker. Create new line of scrimmage. Don't let TE release.

End: 6 alignment. Attack blocker. Create new line of scrimmage. Don't let TE release.

Tackle: 4i alignment. Attack blocker. Create new line of scrimmage. Make a play.

Nose: 4i alignment. Attack blocker. Create new line of scrimmage. Make a play.

X-man: 0 alignment. Attack blocker. Create new line of scrimmage. Play behind block.

Rock: 50 alignment. Force strong, cutback weak. Man back on inside release.

Buck: 00 alignment. Fill A. Pursuit inside out.

Dog: 50 alignment. Force weak, cutback strong. Man back on inside release.

Strong safety: 8 or 2 alignment. Contain strong. Man back on outside release.

Tight C: 8 or 1 alignment. Contain weak. Man back on outside release.

Open C: 1 alignment. Man on 1. Second contain.

Dime Defense, Four-Man Front

The dime personnel package leaves only one true linebacker on the field with our four best defensive linemen (figure 12.22). Our four best secondary players join the nickel and dime backs to create a very athletic personnel group with the ability to cover or blitz. This package is versatile and fast, so we play it against four- and five-receiver sets mainly on passing downs.

We use buzzwords to alert the extra defensive backs (nickel in this case) to their blitz gap responsibility. *Cut* (figure 12.23a) is the buzzword for C-gap. *Blade* (figure 12.23b) is the buzzword for B-gap. *Razor* (figure 12.23c) is the buzzword for A-gap. These words also alert other members of the coverage team that they must be in position to cover the blitzer's man after he releases to run at the quarterback.

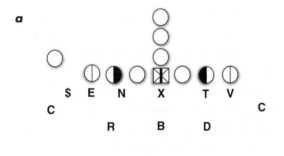

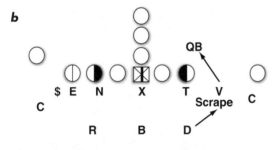

Figure 12.21 (a) 60 'noles, inside the 5; (b) two-receiver adjustment.

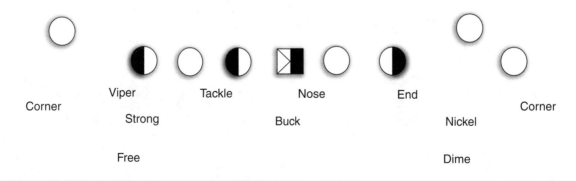

Figure 12.22 Dime defense, four-man front alignment.

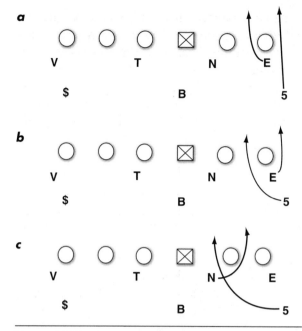

Figure 12.23 Dime defense adjustments and blitzes: *(a)* cut; *(b)* blade; *(c)* razor.

Coverages

Cover 1 (figure 12.24) is a man-under, one-deep coverage concept. The dog linebacker mans up on the tight end, the corners match up on the wide receivers, and the inside linebackers sort the backs on their release and man up on the running back who releases to his side. The strong safety plays man to man on any back who releases outside or vertical to his side. This coverage concept assigns eight defenders near the ball with the free safety available to support the run or double team a vertical pass down the middle of the field. This is a tremendous pressure-style defensive concept that overloads the running box and allows the free safety to prevent the home-run ball.

Cover 1

Position	Alignment	Versus pass	Versus run	Notes
Dog	90	Man on TE	Contain pitch	Funnel TE inside
Buck	20	Man on first back to your side	A-gap to, cutback away	
Rock	30	Man on first back to your side	B-gap to, A-gap away	
Corner	Inside #1, 3-4 yards	Man on #1, funnel him outside	Support late	Against trips, weak C comes over and plays man on #3 If #2 is wide, wheel alert
Strong safety	Inside #2, 4 yards	Man on #2	Primary contain; pitch	Against motion, two spoke Reroute #2 inside If #2 is wide, wheel alert
Free safety	Middle, 6-10 yards	Free	Primary contain; alley	Against motion, two spoke If #2 is wide, wheel alert

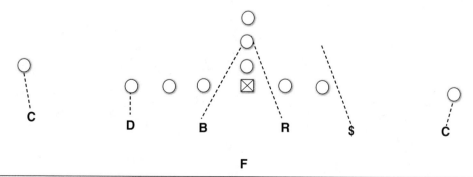

Figure 12.24 Cover 1.

Cover 2 (figure 12.25) is a tremendous zone pass defense that has five defenders playing underneath zones and two deep safeties playing half-field zones. The underneath passing game can be difficult to execute with five defenders all looking at the quarterback, and this coverage forces the quarterback to throw the football with great velocity and usually down the field to be successful. The safeties are deep and read the quarterback while watching the routes progress in front of them. This technique normally leads to interception or big-hit opportunities for the safeties. One weakness of the coverage is that both safeties are deep and a long way from run support position.

Cover 2

Position	Alignment	Zone	Versus run	Versus pass	Versus boot	Notes
Dog	90	Hook/ curl	Contain pitch	Curl drop 12 yards Read #2, carry vertical Between #2 and #3	To, jump flat Away, check screen and get back in hole	Don't let #2 inside #2 inside release, yell, "Drag," find #3
Buck	20	Wall/ middle	A-gap to, cutback away	Straight hook drop Key #3 to #2 #3 vertical carry	Roll back and get under crosser	
Rock	30	Flats/ curl	B-gap to, A-gap away	Same as SLB	Same as SLB	#2 vertical reroute and carry to 15, stay inside #1
Corner	Outside #1, 4-5 yards	Flats	Primary run support Force from outside in	Force receiver inside Read #2 32 out: cushion post/C break up on ball 2 in or vertical, sink with #1	Run to 1/3	Leverage #3 If #2 is wide, wheel alert Run with wheel
Safety	On hash, 10 yards	Deep 1/2	Late help; fit off C	Read #2 to #1 #2 vertical, stay between hash and 3 yards outside 2 blocks or out, work to #1 Always aware of #3		Against motion, two spoke Reroute #2 inside If #2 wide, wheel alert

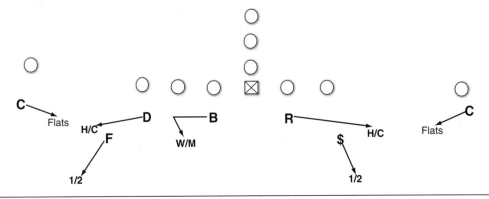

Figure 12.25 Cover 2.

Cover 3 (figure 12.26) is probably the most commonly used zone defense in football. Cover 3 is a four-under, three-deep zone coverage that uses two curl-to-flat players and two hook-to-curl players underneath and three deep-zone players, each playing thirds of the field. This defense has the ability to place eight defenders near the running box while covering the deep part of the field as well. The coverage is a little more vulnerable in the underneath zones than cover 2, but when executed properly it can be a solid pass-and-run defense.

Cover 3

Position	Alignment	Zone	Versus run	Versus pass	Versus boot	Notes
Dog	90	Flats	Contain pitch	Flat/curl drop Read #2 Between #2 and #3	To, jump flat Away, check screen and get back in hole	Don't let #2 inside #2 inside release, yell, "Drag," find #3
Buck	20	Wall/curl	A-gap to, cutback away	Straight hook drop Key #3 to #2 #3 vertical carry	Roll back and get under crosser	
Rock	30	Flats/curl	B-gap to, A-gap away	Same as SLB	Help on crosser	#2 vertical reroute and carry to 15; stay inside #1
Corner	Inside #1, 4-5 yards	Outer 1/3	Late run support Force from outside in	Think man on #1 unless #2 threat No quick underneath help FS help in middle	Run to 1/3	Maintain depth Tackle the hitch If #2 is wide, wheel alert Run with wheel
Strong safety	Away from TE, 4 × 4	Flats	Contain pitch	Same as SLB	Same as SLB	If 2 receivers on your side, run with #2 vertically
Free safety	Middle 12 yards deep; cheat to #2 receiver	Middle 1/3	Late alley support	Read #2 Maintain depth	Run to middle 1/3	#4 vertical, jump TE

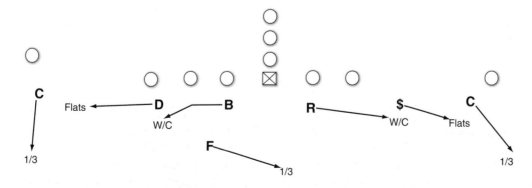

Figure 12.26 Cover 3.

Cover 5 (figure 12.27) combines man-under coverage with two-deep zone coverage. The beauty of this coverage is the aggressive approach the underneath defenders can take because they have safeties standing behind them if they miss a jam or get burned. This coverage also frees up the two deep safeties to rob pass routes, play the run game, or undertake any of a variety of assignments deemed important by the coordinator. Cover 5 is a must-have for every defense.

Cover 5

Position	Alignment	Versus pass	Versus run	Notes
Dog	90	Man on TE	Contain pitch	Reroute TE outside
				Against trey, man on #2
Buck	20	Man on first back to your side	A-gap to, cutback away	Against trey, man on TE
Rock	30	Man on first back to your side	B-gap to, A-gap away	Man on #2 weak
				Reroute outside
Corner	Outside #1, 3-4 yards	Man on #1; funnel him inside	Support late	Against trips, weak C comes over and plays man on #3
				If #2 is wide, wheel alert
Strong safety	Hash, 6-10 yards	1/2	Alley, primary support	Read #2 to #1
				If #2 is wide, wheel alert
Free safety	Hash, 6-10 yards	1/2	Alley, primary support	Read #2 to #1
				If #2 is wide, wheel alert

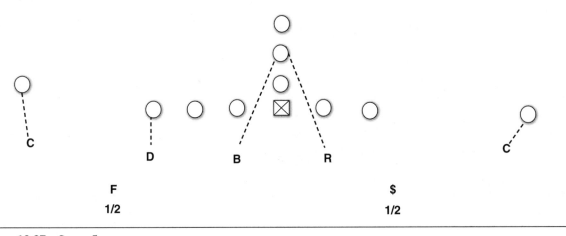

Figure 12.27 Cover 5.

Cover 8 (figure 12.28) is the first coverage we teach players. Technically, cover 8 is a quarter-field zone coverage, but with its aggressive approach at the safety position, it could also be classified as a man–zone combination coverage. Cornerbacks are responsible for the deep outside-quarter of the field, while safeties read the number two receivers on their respective sides for their route progressions. If the number two receiver runs vertically down the field, the safety plays him man to man. If the number two receiver releases to the outside or drags across the middle, the safety immediately turns his eyes to the number one receiver and double-teams the post, curl, or seam route with the cornerback. In a nutshell, if there are four receivers vertical, the secondary will be in pure man-to-man coverage. If the inside receivers are not vertical, there will be natural double teams on the outside receivers while the outside linebackers cover the flat or drag routes. Cover 8 is a tremendous coverage for freeing up safeties to play the run or give corners assistance in the passing game.

Cover 8

Position	Alignment	Zone	Versus run	Versus pass	Versus boot	Notes
Dog	90	Flats/curl	Contain pitch	Curl drop 12 yards Read #2 Between #2 and #3	To, jump flat Away, check screen and get back in hole	TE removes, be alert for banjo
Buck	20	Middle	A-gap to cut-back away	Straight hook drop Key #3 to #2 #3 vertical carry	Roll back and get under crosser	
Rock	30	Flats/curl	B-gap to, A-gap away	Same as SLB	Same as SLB	#2 in back-field, be alert to run with #2 on wheel
Corner	Inside #1, 7-8 yards	Outside 1/4	Support late	Protect post Key #1 You are man on #1 on everything except shallow crossing route	Run to 1/3	If #2 is wide, wheel alert
Safety	Outside TE, 10 yards	Inside 1/4	To, stack 3-4 yards Behind contain, fill where needed Away, up and in Stay backside	Key #2 Vertical (10 yards), play him Out-rob #1 under post or curl Cross, look for #3 or help on #1	To, sit and find crosser, help flats late Away, run to 1/3	If #2 is wide, wheel alert

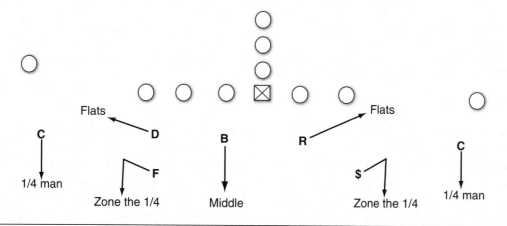

Figure 12.28 Cover 8.

The standard bootleg has proven effective against cover 8 because of its aggressiveness. Because of this weakness we have developed a boot rule (figure 12.29) or bootleg coverage that we incorporate after the defense determines the play. When the defense is playing cover 8 and the offense runs a bootleg play, we automatically rotate to cover 3. Cover 3 gives every defensive player a great chance to be successful against the bootleg. The player who normally has the greatest difficulty with the bootleg rotation is the playside linebacker. He must determine the bootleg and then burst to the playside flat to cover the fullback in the route. This technique can be developed through many repetitions and great scouting. The boot rule is essential to all cover 8 teams.

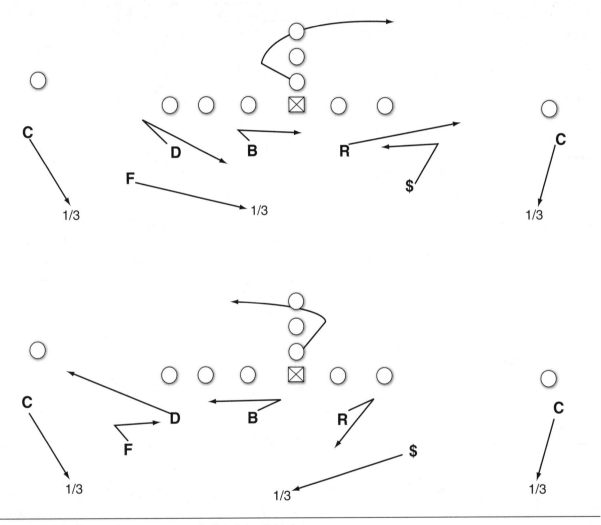

Figure 12.29 Boot rule versus cover 8: (*a*) right; (*b*) left.

Cover 9 (figure 12.30) is a man–zone combination coverage for trips formations. We also use cover 9 against two-back passing teams that like to overload one side of the field with additional receivers from the backfield or by dragging them across the field. Some coaches refer to this alignment as quarter, quarter half.

Cover 9 is really a condensed cover 3 on the trips side and a form of cover 2 on the one-receiver side. The dog linebacker mans up on the tight end in cover 9. This allows the defensive backs to play three-on-two zone to the remaining receivers on the trips side.

Cover 9

Position	Alignment	Zone	Versus run	Versus pass	Versus boot	Notes
Dog	90	Flats	Contain pitch	Man on TE Zone call: Jam TE, look for B in flats	To, jump flat Away, check screen and get back in hole	Listen for zone call #2 inside release, yell, "Drag," check flats
Buck	20	Wall/ middle	A-gap to, cutback away	Wall TE Stay between #2 and #3	Roll back and get under crosser	
Rock	30	Hook/ curl	B-gap to, A-gap away	Stay between #2 and #3	Help on crosser	
1/4 corner	Inside #1, 6-8 yards	Outer 1/4	Late run support	Read #1 If #1 goes in, look for wheel	Run to 1/3	Maintain depth Tackle the hitch If #2 is wide, wheel alert Run with wheel
1/2 corner	Inside #1, 4 yards	Outer 1/2	Alley	Read #3 receiver Play your 1/2	Run to 1/3	Maintain depth Rob #3 vs. trips
Strong safety	Inside #2, 4 yards	Flats	Contain pitch	Reroute #2 Play flats	Same as SLB	Be aware for wheel alert
Free safety	Middle 12 yards deep; cheat to hash	Inner 1/3	Late alley support	Read #2 Maintain depth	Run to middle 1/3	Wheel alert 4 vertical jump #2

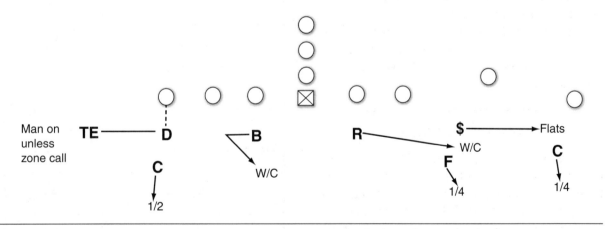

Figure 12.30 Cover 9.

We use a variety of techniques for the backside corner when he is isolated to the single-receiver side. The linebacker walks out in space to help with the curl and the slant, or we make a buzz call, and the linebacker bursts to the flat when he reads pass.

Another important coaching point regarding cover 9 is that the corner on the tight end side against conventional trips will cross-key the number three receiver across the formation to protect against four vertical passing routes.

TEAM DEFENSIVE DRILLS

It is extremely important to develop great work habits, team effort, and enthusiasm in every practice. One of the drills we use daily to accomplish each of these characteristics is the team pursuit drill. We praise great effort and great angles and punish poor effort and poor angles by making the team repeat the drill until it meets our expectations.

We also teach and preach the importance of creating turnovers on defense. We use a variety of turnover drills to establish this mindset with defensive players. The Oskie drill uses our entire defense during the pursuit period. A defensive coach intentionally throws an interception to a player, and the rest of the team must turn into an offensive return team and give maximum effort to lead the player with the ball into the end zone. This drill develops unity and pride in scoring while on defense. We also use the scoop-and-score drill in which the ball is intentionally fumbled and must be picked up by a defensive player and carried into the end zone with the rest of the defense going full speed to assist him.

Use team drills to develop attitude, effort, and the overall mindset of a successful defense. Team drills are a great way to begin defensive practice.

Team Pursuit

The team pursuit drill (figure 12.31) teaches the defensive unit several valuable characteristics of team defense. First, it teaches every member of the defense to pursue the football with tremendous effort. The drill doesn't end until all 11 players give maximum effort. Second, the pursuit drill teaches each member of the defensive unit the proper angle to cut off the ball carrier. Great effort without the proper angle is worthless and will result in a defensive breakdown. We begin every defensive practice with this drill to establish tempo and intensity.

Each defensive player is assigned a yard marker as a landmark for his pursuit path. The drill begins with the defense in perfect huddle alignment as the defensive alignment is called. The team breaks the huddle with enthusiasm and aligns in the proper formation, focusing on the ball before it is snapped. When the ball is snapped, the coach throws it to one of the receivers; the receivers are aligned on each number. When the defense reads the direction of the throw, players sprint with maximum effort to get to their established landmarks as quickly as possible. Loafing or running with poor angles means doing the drill over again.

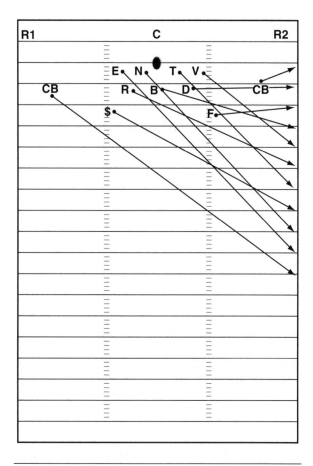

Figure 12.31 Pursuit drill.

Oskie Drill

The Oskie drill instills a scoring mentality into the minds of defensive players. The drill begins just like the pursuit drill, only the quarterback throws the ball down the field. The pass is intercepted by one of the linebackers or safeties. When the ball is intercepted, the player with the ball yells, "Oskie," turning the defensive team into an offensive team with blocking responsibilities. The player with the ball sprints to the nearest sideline and picks up the convoy of defensive players who run interference and block the first offensive players they come in contact with. We always send two inside linebackers directly to the quarterback to make sure he's blocked thoroughly and understands that when he throws an interception, he will get smashed.

Team Adjustment

Every Thursday we script a minimum of 15 offensive plays, formations, motions, shifts, tendencies, personnel groupings, and any other potential situation we feel our defense may have to defend on game day. These plays involve every position on the field and place each defensive player under pressure to perform in a gamelike environment. Some plays involve only the secondary, some only linebackers, and others involve the entire front seven, any situation our team may have to adjust to on game day.

Make sure each position coach is completely aware of each adjustment and is available to coach his players on the run during this period. Hopefully, if you have done a great job preparing your squad, this drill goes smoothly and you can get a little sleep the night before the game. This is a great drill for teaching players focus and concentration.

CHAPTER 13 TEACHING THE KICKING GAME

The kicking game is on the same plane of importance as the offense and defense. Well-executed special teams plays can win close ball games faster than any other phase of the game. I believe this philosophy completely, and I also believe that poor special teams execution can lose ball games faster than good special teams can win ball games.

The key elements to great special teams are developing an attitude and an atmosphere of ownership for special teams players, finding the athletes that best fit your special teams philosophy and mentality, and teaching players the techniques of being great special teams members. In this chapter we discuss these issues and thoroughly cover each phase of special teams.

SPECIAL TEAMS ATTITUDE

To emphasize the importance of special teams, I am personally involved in every phase of the kicking game. I am present in the game-planning phase and an integral part of each special team segment during practice. I want each coach and player to understand why we call this phase of the game "special" teams. The special teams coordinator and I evaluate special teams practice and game video daily to ensure special teams players are performing at a championship level and constantly progressing and evolving.

We emphasize to special teams units that our philosophy is based completely on effort and execution. Every special teams member will give full effort on every play. Special teams will be used as a weapon. We take an aggressive approach to game planning to ensure that opponents must work extremely hard in this area or risk the consequences of losing the special teams portion of the game.

It is important to develop multiple special teams alignments, coverages, formations, and plays. Keeping the opponent guessing and on their heels is advantageous for special teams units because it limits the opponent's ability to use its entire package to try to defend our system.

We practice special teams at game tempo. Certainly we want to minimize the risk of injury to players, but gamelike intensity is important when developing the special teams mindset. When it comes to reps, we emphasize quality over quantity. We want gamelike intensity, focus, and mentality during every special teams drill.

Special teams players must have several traits in order to excel in this critical phase of the game. Select the most athletic, aggressive players on the team to be members of the special teams. Everyone on our roster is fair game for our special teams units, although we do weigh the costs of each player on the field. Unless a player is someone we cannot afford to replace, an All-American quarterback for example, if he can make our special teams units better he's going to be on the field.

Example at Oklahoma

In 2000, when the University of Oklahoma won the national championship, Roy Williams (Jim Thorpe Award winner) and Rocky Calmus (Butkus Award winner), arguably the two best players in America at their positions two years running, were on Oklahoma's special teams. Their participation on special teams said it all. If the two best players in the nation think it's important to be on special teams, then special teams must be vital for a team's success. Their willingness to participate on Oklahoma's special teams demonstrates the attitude every team needs. This attitude made the University of Oklahoma the best college football team in 2000.

A couple of issues need to be addressed. Aggression and athleticism without good judgment and control can be detrimental to a special teams unit. There is a fine line between someone who is completely out of control and selfish and someone who plays recklessly but with great focus and judgment. Penalties on special teams can hurt your team in two critical ways. First, penalties take away field position, and no matter how you slice it, field position is the name of the game in special teams football. Second, penalties also take away the momentum gained by good special teams play. Nothing is worse than running back a punt or a kickoff and then receiving a 40- or 50-yard penalty because someone used poor judgment during the kick return.

SPECIAL TEAMS INSTRUCTION AND PRACTICE

We teach special teams using the same methods and techniques we use to teach the offensive system or the defensive system. We start by breaking down each particular special teams unit into individual components. Breaking each team into parts allows more individualized, effective instruction and more repetitions than could be achieved trying to practice and coach 11 players at the same time.

For example, the kickoff return team is broken into three parts. The front five—center, guards, and tackles—practice their responsibilities and techniques together. Second-level players—fullbacks and tight ends—work on their roles together. The deep return men work on their responsibilities. Once each kick return group can execute proficiently, they come together as a team and put the whole project together. After each player learns and masters his individual responsibilities, players begin to learn team concepts of the kickoff return and intricate ideas behind each kickoff return we practice. Great results will be achieved when players master their positions, become familiar with their teammates' responsibilities, and understand the philosophy of the overall system.

I prefer to cover every special teams area during Monday's practice. We practice kickoff, kickoff return, punt, punt return, and field goal execution every Monday. On Monday, we put in our special teams game plan, brush up on technique, and correct mistakes made during the previous ball game. Normally, on Monday we spend 10 minutes on each phase of the kicking game in addition to a film session with the specialists before practice.

On Tuesday, we practice punt protection during prepractice and then again during the special teams phase of practice. If there is one area in the kicking game that needs to be flawless, it's punt protection and coverage. Kickoff return is also practiced during the special teams segment on Tuesdays.

Wednesday's prepractice is dedicated to defensive drills. We work on field goals and extra points after the two-minute segment of offensive practice. The kickoff coverage team also works on Wednesdays.

Thursday is pregame preparation day, so we incorporate every phase of the kicking game using a gamelike script. We include special areas of the special teams such as kicking after a safety, onside kickoff, emergency field goal, and free-kick opportunity. Table 13.1 summarizes the schedule we use for special teams practice.

Table 13.1 Special Teams Weekly Overview

Monday		Tuesday	
Areas of concentration	**Notes**	**Areas of concentration**	**Notes**
Kickoff coverage General kickoff defense	20 min, 2 teams No huddle alignment Focus: Left hash kickoff, lanes, ball placement Drills: Take the line, cover Prepractice: John with kickers, holders, snappers; Brad with return	Kickoff return Kickoff onside defense	20 min, 2 teams plus sophomore kickoff team Focus: 5 min double wedge vs. air; 10 min sideline right (Rudy); Brad has back 3, JJ has 4, John K. has 4, Trim has scout; 5 min live returns Prepractice: John with punters, punting out of end zone (bad snap, etc.), returners with Brad working on fair catch

Wednesday		Thursday	
Areas of concentration	**Notes**	**Areas of concentration**	**Notes**
Punt security Punt coverage Punting out of end zone Eliminating touchbacks Punt return Punt holdup Punt block General punt defense	20 min, 2 teams plus sophomore punter 5 min protection/release bullets working on eliminating touchback 5 min right and middle hash, cover down inside 10 (timed) Punt returners: 5 min 4-line Mary drill with snappers and punters; 5 min punt block/return Prepractice: Punters eliminating touchback	PAT and field goal security PAT and field goal execution Field goal coverage PAT defense Basic field block	10 min 5 min alignment, protection, practice snaps and holds (timed) 5 min live 5 × extra points, 5 × 25 right hash, 5 × 25 left hash Prepractice: Kickers, holders, snappers working on PAT/field goals

1. Great teams have great special teams. Place the same emphasis on special teams as you do on offense and defense.

2. Evaluate special teams just like you do the offense and defense.

3. Choose great athletes who take pride and use good judgment.

4. Be aggressive and use special teams to change the momentum of the game.

5. Be diverse and force your opponent to prepare thoroughly or risk defeat.

6. Study, watch film, and develop a solid special teams game plan each week.

KICKOFF COVERAGE

The kickoff team establishes the tempo and the attitude of the game. We hope the coin toss allows us to defer our choice of possession to the second half so that we can begin the game with our coverage team.

During the opening kickoff, the players and coaches are near their peak of emotion, so discipline and control must be used at all times. Nothing establishes momentum like pinning the opponent inside their 20-yard line and putting your defensive unit in great position to be successful. Nothing takes away momentum like allowing an opponent a big return and great field position on a kickoff return.

Kickoff coverage players need to remember what they are on the field to accomplish—tackle the man with the ball. It doesn't do our team any good for a player to sprint down the field and drill the first player he sees if the guy with the ball is still on his feet and running.

Personnel and Alignments

Successful kickoff coverage begins with a great kicker. In staying consistent with our philosophy of being aggressive and versatile, we use a variety of kicking techniques and careful ball placement to allow our coverage team to hone in on the return man. If the kicker can create a touchback by kicking the ball out of the end zone, we want to take advantage of his leg. Sometimes weather or field conditions make it nearly impossible to achieve a touchback. During these situations, kick placement and hang time are very important. A well-placed kick with great hang time makes it nearly impossible for a team to return the ball with much consistency or success. Our kicker lines up in a variety of positions to keep the return team guessing where he will kick the ball and where the strength of our coverage team is headed.

The kickoff coverage unit uses five basic aiming points: deep left, deep right, pooch left, deep pooch left, and squib. Deep left and deep right are just what they sound like—the kicker aims the ball at the call side numbers and kicks the ball as high and deep as he can. The coverage team leverages the ball in its lanes and hopefully executes a tackle inside the 20-yard line.

The majority of our kickers at Jenks have been right-handed, so we kick pooch kicks to the left. Most right-handed kickers prefer to control kick to the left. Work with your kickers to discover which direction they are most comfortable with. The pooch-left kick is designed to take advantage of the opponent's personnel if we are playing against someone who is not used to fielding a kickoff. Many of our opponents place fullbacks, tight ends, or small linemen in the up position near the 35-yard line. We want to force them to field the ball and return it. We have forced many turnovers using this technique.

We also like to take advantage of a deep pooch kick, and we spend time during practice perfecting this kicking play. The kicker places the ball on the right hash and establishes his aiming point where the 15-yard line and the left sideline meet. This aiming point allows him to attack the ball with maximum power, concentrating on getting as much height and hang time as possible on the kick. Our coverage team knows exactly where the ball will land and can tee off and be aggressive in their coverage lanes. The key to an effective deep pooch kick is hang time. The ball needs to be in the air for at least five seconds to allow the coverage team to get nearly 50 yards downfield before the ball is fielded. The deep pooch kick is particularly effective when kicking into a head wind, and the kicker can get some height on the kick.

Usually the squib kick is used at the close of a half or game when there is little time left on the clock, and we want to disrupt the kickoff return to take time off the clock. The kicker addresses the ball and purposely line-drives the ball through the first two levels of the return team, preferably skipping the ball across the ground quickly and erratically. This kind of kick is difficult to field and disrupts an organized return, using additional clock time during the return.

The coverage unit is numbered 1 through 10 from left to right for communication and assignment responsibilities (figure 13.1). Normally, 1 and 10 are contain men or safeties. The 2, 3, 8, and 9 players are bullets or gunners, depending on the scheme we are incorporating. The 4, 5, 6, and 7 players are bigger and more physical players such as linebackers or safeties because their responsibilities sometimes involve breaking through an opponent's wedge return team.

Using numbers to communicate alignment and assignment makes adjustments during the game very easy. Athletes understand their individual responsibilities by their number position and the kickoff coverage called in the huddle by the kicker.

Placing the ball on a hash (figure 13.2) allows the kicker to kick accurately to different areas of the field. We spend time with the kickers establishing different ball placement areas in which they feel comfortable when kicking off. Different alignments give you the advantage of predetermining your coverage zone and coverage lanes. When your coverage team knows that the ball will land on the deep left hash, they know exactly where their landmarks are and where they should leverage the ball. Another advantage of moving the ball around on the kickoff is that the return team cannot detect where you will land the ball. If a return team is a wedge team and you can place the kickoff in the deep right or left corner of the field, it will be extremely difficult for the wedge team to establish an effective wedge in this area of the field, especially if they have to guess which way the ball will be kicked.

Against return teams that use numbering assignments for blocking responsibilities, we incorporate covey coverage pods (figure

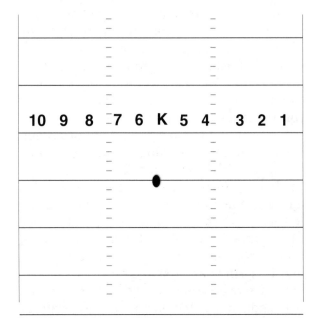

Figure 13.1 Kickoff team's standard alignment and position numbers.

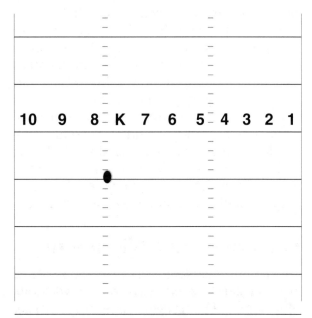

Figure 13.2 Kickoff alignment, ball on hash mark.

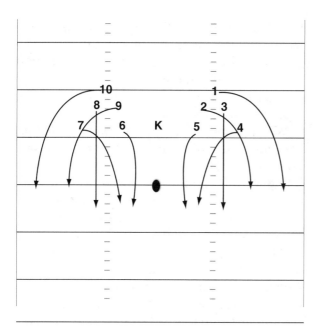

Figure 13.3 Covey kickoff alignment.

13.3). The covey is nothing fancy, just a way for our coverage personnel to cross each other as they approach their coverage lanes. This crossing action confuses the opponent's numbering system and gives our defenders an advantage during coverage. Practice a couple of different release patterns and thoroughly practice the takeoff timing with the kicker.

The bottom line in all kickoff plays is to make sure the kicker is comfortable with what you ask him to do and to make sure coverage personnel can consistently execute their assignments.

Three Phases of Kickoff Coverage

We break the football field into three phases for the kickoff coverage team. The first phase is the avoidance phase. As the coverage unit times the takeoff with the kicker, they accelerate to full speed, getting their eyes on the first blocking threat. The coverage team must completely avoid the first-level kickoff return players if at all possible. If a blocker attempts to engage a kickoff coverage player in this first phase, he uses a rip, swim, or club technique to avoid the first blocking threat, constantly trying to maintain acceleration and speed down the field.

The second phase of the field is the free-run area or the speed phase. Once the coverage player avoids or defeats the first-level blocker on the return team, he turns on the jets to cover ground. We emphasize the importance of reducing the space between the coverage team and the ball as quickly as possible. The coverage team scans the return team constantly to adjust to the blocking schemes being used by the return team and adjusts their paths as they converge on the ball carrier.

Next comes the fit phase or the breakdown and tackle part of kickoff coverage. This phase must be practiced over and over to teach the coverage team how to fit the different return schemes they will be defending. We teach a butt-and-press technique in the final phase. Players need to have great awareness of what the return team is trying to accomplish with their blocking schemes while we are in the speed phase of coverage. At the point of attack, we want two gap players to engage the return team. In other words, we don't want to take a side and allow the blocker to beat us. Defenders learn to directly attack the blocker and press him off the chest with the hands, getting the eyes up and shedding the blocker to make the tackle.

Onside Kickoff

There are two basic types of onside kicking situations: first, when your team is behind and you do not have enough time to win the ball game unless you get the ball back immediately and second, when you want to change the momentum of the game by taking the return team by surprise with a special onside kick attempt.

Statistics say that when the kicking team lines up to attempt an onside kick in desperation and the opponent knows it is coming, the kicking team will recover the kick less than 25 percent of the time. When the kicking team uses a surprise onside kick and the return team is unaware of the onside kick, the kicking team will recover the kick more than 50 percent of the time. This is a huge difference statistically.

Our desperation onside kick is completely different than our surprise onside kick. For the desperation onside kick, the front five players (the bullets) align approximately 7 yards from the line of scrimmage and number the return team from the outside in. Bullet number one will attack and block the number one return-team member from the outside in, bullet number two will block the number two return-team member, and so on to the inside. Second-level players are our best athletes; they are assigned simply to recover the ball if at all possible or attack the recovery team so that someone else can recover the ball. The kicker strikes the ball very high to create top-spin and hopefully a very high skip over and above the receiving team's head so that the bullets can create a path for one of our players to recover the ball as it is coming down. The safety, who is standing near the kicker, has two responsibilities: first, to start everyone in motion and second, to loop over the top to make sure the receiving team doesn't get loose on an errant kick.

Our surprise onside kick can be executed from any standard kickoff alignment. Because most kickoff return teams place five players on the front line, we develop blocking rules based on this standard alignment principle. We always double-team the frontline player closest to the kicker. We single-block the remaining four frontline players from the inside out. Our outermost players loop back inside as safeties as the kicker onside-kicks the ball to himself and recovers it. The kicker has to place the ball exactly between two defenders so that the assigned blockers can take the best angles to their blocking assignments. (Remind players that there is no blocking below the waist on a free kick.)

KICKOFF RETURN

The kickoff return team is an integral part of the special teams unit. Unfortunately, most kickoff returns take place immediately following an opponent's score, so the momentum is usually in the opponent's favor. What better time to swing the momentum to your team's favor by busting a huge return for a touchdown or favorable field position for the offense? When executed correctly, the kickoff return can get the entire crowd on their feet in excitement and completely change the momentum of the game.

We approach this special teams area just like our other systems. We break the return team into parts and teach each area before bringing all 11 members together for the execution phase of practice.

The front five players are physical and athletic, usually linebackers, fullbacks, tight ends, or very athletic linemen. The front five always practice together, whether setting a wedge return or a man-to-man scheme. The front five are referred to as center, left and right guard, and left and right tackle. The two outside players are left tight end and right tight end; the inside players are the left and right fullbacks.

The second-level players are preferably big receivers and safeties with great skill and toughness. Our four second-level players are usually involved in assigned blocking schemes and reverses, and sometimes they set a secondary wedge. They must be versatile.

The two deep returners are the most explosive athletes on the team. They must have explosive speed and the courage to run in traffic. These are the guys who make the crowd stand up with anticipation and beg for more. A great returner is the key to a consistent return scheme.

Two kickoff return schemes that have worked well for many seasons are the wedge and alley. Notice that the depth of engagement for each return-team player is important for the timing of the returns. We also incorporate automatic transition returns in case the ball placement does not allow us to execute the return we called on the field.

In our alley return (figure 13.4), the returner must field the ball and initiate the return toward the middle of the field to encourage and invite the coverage team to converge in the middle of the field. This initial move establishes outside leverage for the blockers as the return man cuts to the alley and accelerates with everything he has. The initial upfield

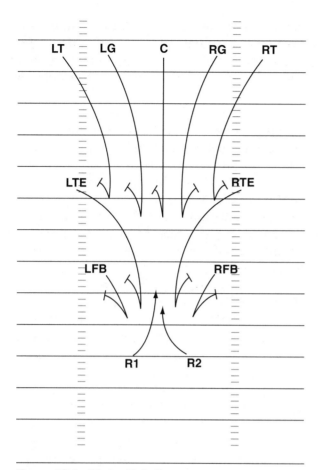

Figure 13.4 Wedge kickoff return.

move also sets up the timing of the play by giving our blockers time to set up and get in position to attack defenders.

We like to incorporate a moving-wedge return against teams who do a good job changing their kicking coverages or cross their coverage people to make it difficult to number off our assignments. The wedge setter always sets the wedge 10 yards directly in front of the return man, and the secondary wedge aligns 10 yards directly in front of the primary wedge (see figure 13.4). During the wedge return, the returner must field the ball cleanly and drive upfield in the direction of the first wedge as the wedge builder is moving the wedge toward the returner. Once the primary wedge is established, the ball carrier must use great vision to find a seam in the wedge and burst through the crease created by the wedge men who are blocking their men to the outside. Returners must have sprinter speed and running back vision to be great.

Because the double wedge is our catchall and conversion return, we practice it every day as a complete unit. The primary wedge is made up of the back four players, and the secondary wedge is made up of the front five linemen. The primary wedge sets up 10 yards in front of the kick returner, and the secondary wedge sets up 10 yards in front of the primary wedge. When the returner catches the ball, he yells, "Go!" and members of each wedge attack upfield, engaging and blocking the first defender who enters their field of vision, maintaining contact and driving them upfield and outside to create running lanes. The returner uses his vision and speed to explode through the creases created by the blockers.

We practice our alley return (figure 13.5) in groups. Our two double-team pairs work together with a coach and our five players with numbered blocking assignments work together with their individual coaches. The two returners work together to coordinate who catches the ball and who becomes the

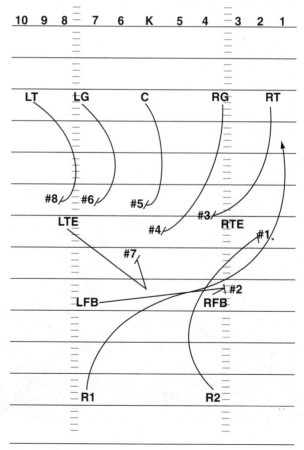

Figure 13.5 Alley kickoff return.

lead blocker. The double-team blockers need great acceleration and angles to their landmarks. They must be able to work together to ensure a solid double-team block. The numbered blockers need acceleration at good angles to get to the proper depth to execute their blocks. They need to be patient and allow the coverage team to run into position to be blocked legally. (No clipping.)

POINT AFTER TOUCHDOWN AND FIELD GOAL

From a fan's perspective, this phase of football looks easy and automatic. From a coaching and preparation standpoint, however, a coach knows it takes hundreds of repetitions to develop the timing needed to develop a first-rate point after touchdown (PAT) and field goal unit. I have won and lost football games many times in this particular area of the game. We spend a great deal of time practicing this part of the game to ensure the consistency needed to win games.

Holder, Deep Snapper, and Kicker

The holder is the leader of the field goal squad. His many responsibilities include making sure the team has all 11 members on the field, communicating instructions to the team, fielding the deep snap from the center, and holding the ball correctly on the kicker's mark.

The holder stands 7 yards from the ball and kneels on one knee. He always aligns on the side of the kicker's kicking leg. He places the hand closest to the kicker on the ground to establish the spot. The hand closest to the center is extended to give the center a target for the snap (figure 13.6a). The holder asks the kicker if he is ready to kick then makes the proper cadence call to alert the protection team and center. When the ball is snapped, the holder catches the ball with both hands (figure 13.6b), arms extended, and quickly places the ball on the established spot (figure 13.6c), spinning the ball to turn the laces away from the kicker's foot (figure 13.6d). The entire process from snap to kick must take place in less than one and a half seconds to keep the opposing team from blocking the kick.

The center, or deep snapper, is a specialized position. Teams with great deep snappers have a chance to have great special teams. Teams without a consistent center usually don't have good special teams. Deep snappers spend every extra moment of practice perfecting their skills with the ball. They must have great touch and accuracy because the

Figure 13.6 Holder's techniques: *(a)* the holder extends a hand to give the snapper a target; *(b)* he catches the ball with both hands; *(c)* he places the ball on the spot or tee; *(d)* the holder turns the ball so the laces point away from the kicker's foot.

holder is only 7 yards from the ball. Timing and ball placement are everything on a field goal attempt.

The center assumes a wide stance over the ball so that he can throw the ball between his legs to the holder. He looks through his legs and waits for instructions and the cadence from the holder (figure 13.7a). His stance also sets the alignment for the rest of the protection team.

We teach a two-handed snapping technique with the dominant, or bottom hand, used for power and speed and the top hand used for guidance, stability, and added spin for a tight spiral and smooth ball flight (figure 13.7b). The center snaps the ball directly at the holder's extended hand (figure 13.7c). The hand is his focus and target.

In the protection scheme, the center is asked first to make a great snap. The snap is

Figure 13.7 Snapper's technique: (a) the snapper assumes a wide stance and looks through his legs to the holder; (b) the bottom hand generates speed and power and the top hand provides guidance, stability, and spin; (c) the snapper follows through after snapping the ball to the holder.

his number one responsibility. Second, after delivering the ball, the snapper gets big in the hole. He tries to get his arms and elbows out quickly to help the guards as much as possible for the hard push up the middle by the blocking team. Guards are fully aware that the center's main job is to deliver the football, so they work very hard to step inside with a lot of power to protect the center as much as possible.

The field goal kicker dedicates all his practice time to enhancing his kicking skills. The kicking coach gives him an itemized checklist of things to accomplish each day during practice, including flexibility and strength exercises, ball-contact repetitions, onside kick technique, pooch kicks, squib kicks, pop-up drills, and field goal kicks from every conceivable angle and distance. The kicker is truly a specialist. Most of the successful kickers in today's game have strong soccer ties and have adapted those skills into kicking a football.

Each kicker I have coached has been completely unique in his technique. Some kickers plant the foot and mark off steps at an angle (figure 13.8). Some mark off steps while walking straight back and straight across at a right angle. Some take three steps and are very aggressive, while others take five steps and are very calculated in the approach. I have learned over the years to be very cautious when instructing kickers. Most are wound up tight and, in some cases, asking them to change one small piece of their routine will make them change a dozen other things, leading to confusion or inconsistency. It's always best to be positive and subtle when working with kickers. Each has his own personality and technique. My experience has been that when things are good, leave them alone, and when things are not good, make subtle tweaks and constantly let them know you believe in them.

Some must-haves with kickers are consistency in timing and takeoff toward the ball. We want the ball airborne the same way and for the same time every time. We time extra points and field goals every day to develop consistency. A good kicker should also practice cutting the ball (hitting it low) to get immediate altitude on extra points and shorter field goals so that the opponent's middle blockers cannot reach the ball as it flies over the line of scrimmage. All kickers are different, but all kickers can develop manageable consistency through strong practice habits.

Developing timing between the center, holder, and kicker is the most important aspect of building a consistent extra point and field goal team. The center, holder, and kicker practice the snap, hold, and kick several times each day to ensure an automatic feeling of confidence. The kicker's points of emphasis are:

1. Establish your plant spot and mark off your approach steps consistently.

2. Establish a comfortable stance and focus on the spot.

3. Begin your approach when the ball reaches the holder's hands. Many variables exist in the approach phase, including the speed of the snap, the quickness of the holder, and the number of steps taken by the kicker.

4. Drive through the ball with your head down, focusing on the ball, and follow through after contact.

Basic Protection and Alignment

We use the standard double–tight end, double-wing alignment for field goals (figure 13.9). This alignment is the most consistent for protection and for developing fake-kick situations. Many teams employ unbalanced formations; research which philosophy works best for your team.

Offensive linemen and tight ends take four- to six-inch splits with their inside hands down and inside feet back. We use a zone protection scheme for all field goal and extra point attempts. Each offensive lineman focuses on the snap for takeoff. When the ball is snapped, offensive linemen step to the inside with their inside feet, protecting their inside gaps. We stress the importance of keeping the outside

Figure 13.8 Kicker's technique: *(a)* the kicker begins by aligning with the holder; *(b)* the kicker marks off steps at an angle to the spot; *(c)* the kicker stands, ready for the snap; *(d)* the kicker makes the kick and follows through.

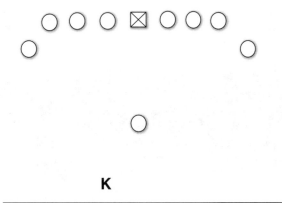

Figure 13.9 Basic field goal and PAT formation: double tight end, double wing.

foot planted firmly and not giving any ground or allowing penetration. The inside foot is back and inside for additional leverage and power.

Each wing man aligns one foot outside the tight end on his side and one foot behind the tight end's outside foot. Their responsibility is the same as everyone else's in the protection scheme—protect the inside gap. They align with their outside feet back and at a 45-degree angle to the tight end's stance.

Fakes

In staying consistent with our special teams philosophy, we use special teams as a weapon to change the momentum of a game. Each week we work a fake PAT or field goal into our game plan, based on the blocking team's personnel and alignment. We practice this fake several times during the week so that the kicking team will feel excited and confident when we decide to use the play. The element of surprise is very important when running a fake kick, but having your team prepared to execute the play is more important. Figure 13.10 illustrates a couple of our favorite fake field goals. Use your imagination and creativity to develop your own game-changing fake kicks.

For simplicity and disguise, we use colors to call our fake field goal plays. The holder is the quarterback, and he initiates each kick by calling a series of two colors and then "ready" to tell the center to snap the football when ready. The first color of the series tells the team whether we will kick or fake. The second color tells the kicking team which direction to

execute the fake—red for right, blue for left. The dummy, or normal, call is "green–green, blue–blue." Green tells everyone on the field goal team to execute the normal kicking routine; blue is simply a dummy call. If we want to run a fake, the holder calls, "Red–red," to alert everyone to the fake we want to use. The next color, either red or blue, tells everyone which direction to execute the fake. Through scouting and practice, we have taught the holder which direction we want to attack the block team.

In figure 13.10a, the kicking team draws the coverage of the cornerback and safety by running drag routes directly through their paths. After fielding the snap, the holder rolls out to draw the defense farther out of position. He then throws the ball back to the kicker who has quietly leaked out of the backfield.

Figure 13.10b shows a very simple fake that is run to the side of the block. After fielding the snap, the holder draws the defense inside

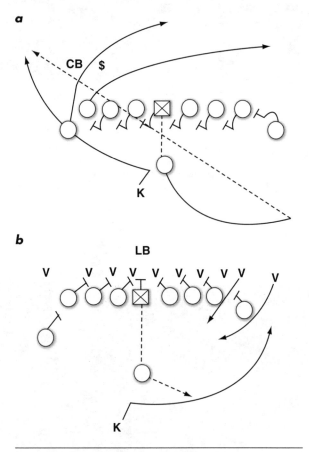

Figure 13.10 Fake field goal and PAT plays: *(a)* holder rolls out to draw defense then throws to kicker; *(b)* holder blindly tosses ball over his shoulder to kicker.

by placing the ball on the tee. He then tosses the ball blindly over his shoulder to the kicker who is running around the end.

PUNT

The punt team is a vital tool in a football team's success. The punt could be construed as negative because it means the offense wasn't able to advance the ball to get a first down. When used as a weapon, however, the punt can help a football team win the all-important field position battle. We pay special attention to punt protection and coverage because errors in this phase of special teams can cost the team the game or momentum.

Personnel

The deep snapper's responsibility during a punt is much the same as his duties during a field goal with the exception of his protection rules. The punter aligns 14 yards from the ball so that the deep snap is exactly twice as long as the field goal snap. The snapper can whip the ball back on the punt and not have to worry as much about touch. The punter is far enough back to handle a fast pass. Probably the most important coaching point on the deep snap is to put a lot of spin on the ball so that it will fly smoothly with

high velocity. Another coaching point is to never, never, never snap the ball high. If the ball is snapped high, the punter doesn't have a chance to field the ball. If the ball is low, he at least has a chance. The center focuses on the punter's hands and plays catch with him by throwing the ball through his legs.

The punter is a special player. He needs above-average athletic ability in order to field the center's snap and punt the football with correct timing (figure 13.11). The punter also needs to be a football-smart player in order to deal with emergency situations that arise from time to time in the punting game. The center's snap may not always be easily managed, and the protection team may not do a flawless job; therefore, the punter must perform under extreme pressure.

The punter must directionally punt the football. Proper direction and height of every punt is important for effective punt coverage. A 70-yard punt, although impressive, may be detrimental to members of the punt coverage unit if they don't have the speed to cover a punt that deep. Or if the punt coverage is called into the boundary and the punter punts the ball to the field, the coverage team will be out of position to defend the return.

To produce a winning play, the punter must follow this sequence:

1. Assume an athletic stance 14 yards directly behind the center.

Figure 13.11 Punter's techniques: *(a)* the punter catches the ball from the snapper; *(b)* he steps into the kick and extends the ball for the drop; *(c)* the punter drops the ball and swings his kicking leg back; *(d)* the punter kicks the ball and follows through.

2. Listen to the personal protector for the protection call or special communications on the play.

3. Present or extend your hands toward the center when you are ready to receive the deep snap.

4. Field the ball.

5. Punt the ball with proper timing.

6. Call out the direction of the kick.

7. Assume your coverage responsibility.

Although some of the punter's responsibilities sound simple, all are important and must be performed flawlessly in order for the punt team to be successful.

The personal protector is the quarterback of the punt team. His responsibilities include taking a head count to make sure all 11 members of the protection team are in position, assigning the center his gap responsibility, and placing the protection team in the ready position to begin the play. He must be ready at all times to call and execute fake punts for special plays that may have been prepared for the punt team.

The bullets are a special group of players who have several important traits. First, they must be great-effort players and give their best effort on every punt attempt. The bullets must be outstanding athletes with speed and the ability to escape from blockers and make open-field tackles against the opponent's best return men. All effective punt coverage teams have bullets who make great plays. We recognize these players in every drill and in every film session for being unselfish and vital to our team's success.

Punt Protection

I have studied many different punt protection schemes, but the one that has proven itself over time and at every level of football is the basic zone protection system (figure 13.12). The zone scheme is sound and versatile and easy to teach. For the protection team, we emphasize working together as a sound coverage unit.

We use the spread punt alignment with a

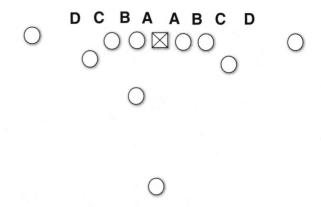

Figure 13.12 Basic spread punt alignment with gap names.

center, two guards, two tackles, two wingbacks, a personal protector, and two wide outs referred to as bullets. We incorporate six-inch splits between the center and the guards. This small distance puts the guards in position to assist the center with protection responsibilities. Guards and tackles have one-foot splits between each other. Wingbacks align one foot outside and one foot behind the tackle's outside foot. The personal protector is aligned 5 yards from the ball and directly behind either guard.

From the basic spread punt alignment, we use a zone protection scheme. Each member of the protection team, except the punter and the bullets, is responsible for protecting a gap. Center–guard gaps are A-gaps, guard–tackle gaps are B-gaps, tackle–wingback gaps are C-gaps, and the gaps outside the wingbacks are D-gaps. The rules are very simple. The center and personal protector are responsible for their respective A-gaps, the guards are responsible for their respective B-gaps, the tackles are responsible for their respective C-gaps, and the wings are responsible for their D-gaps. No matter where the punt block team aligns, the protection is sound and the responsibilities of each protection member are consistent. With each member of the punt protection squad working out through their outside gaps, a natural pocket is formed for the punter to step into and deliver the ball.

But what if two players attack or rush through the same gap? The technique we employ with the protection team has two parts: first, to punch with the inside hand to slow the rusher in the inside gap, thus helping the protection player to the inside; second, to kick-slide with the outside foot while punching with the inside hand. We emphasize the importance of punching with the inside hand and getting the eyes or vision outside into the gap responsibility. We practice this protection technique every day until it becomes automatic. This two-part technique allows each player to work out through his gap to widen the rushers. The outside rusher will be slowed by the player's protection partner to the outside. Two rushers through the same gap are rarely successful if we use proper technique.

Another question to deal with is which way to send the center in protection and what factors to use to determine that decision. Remember, the center's main responsibility is to deliver a great snap. Then we ask him to do his best to help in the protection scheme. With this in mind, the personal protector always assigns the center the A-gap not occupied by a rusher. If both A-gaps are occupied, the personal protector sends the center to the A-gap occupied by the rusher closest to the center so that the center doesn't have to cover as much distance.

Punt Coverage

Punt coverage responsibilities are relatively simple and based on where the football is fielded (figure 13.13). The center and two bullets go directly to the ball carrier to make the first contact or tackle. The two guards work to keep the ball carrier on their inside shoulders and converge on the ball as they get closer to the return man. Tackles run tracks similar to the guards, only they take wider paths—approximately 5 yards outside the

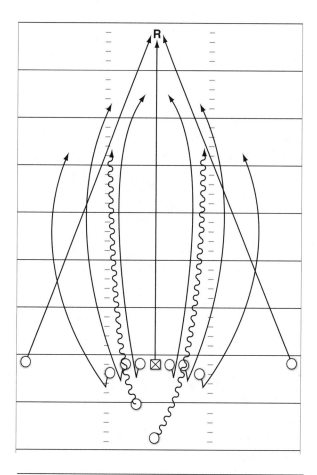

Figure 13.13 Punt coverage responsibilities and lanes.

ball carrier—and converge on the ball as they approach the return man. Wingbacks are outside contain players. They are responsible for plays that take the ball outside the coverage scheme or special plays such as reverses or wall return schemes. They are aggressive but constantly cautious about perimeter threats to the coverage. Both the punter and personal protector are used as safeties in our coverage scheme. They aggressively trail the action and place themselves in position to make a touchdown-saving tackle should the return beat the initial coverage team.

PART IV   PERFORMANCE

CHAPTER 14 PREPARING FOR GAMES

The preparation segment of coaching is one of my favorite areas. It all boils down to the head coach's ability to direct his coaching staff and team in a manner that allows them to be successful. Every member of the organization must channel his efforts in the same direction in order to accomplish the goal of playing at a highly consistent level. Many variables are involved in preparing for a game.

Make sure your team is physically prepared. Let your team get a realistic look at the opponent's speed and power during practice, but be sure they will be fresh and uninjured so that they can perform at their highest level. A team's mental frame of mind is developed from hard physical practice as well. Tough, physical, intense practice develops a proud confidence or swagger in players. This confidence is vital on game day.

Scouting preparation is also a key component of game-day success. The hope is that our team will simply have to line up and play like we practiced all week. The better prepared we are, the more time we spend playing in our comfort zone, lining up and playing with confidence and intensity. Superior game-day performance is taught and coached each week during practice; poor game-day performance is allowed each week during practice. There is no in between.

After we complete our postgame responsibilities, the coaching staff enjoys unwinding together. We go to a late dinner or get together at someone's home to rehash the game and discuss the good and the bad. It's an important time for the coaches to reflect and gather their thoughts on the successful things the team and coaching staff accomplished and what could have been done better. Everything is fresh in our minds. The time we spend discussing the game adds a lot of value to next week's game plan.

Coaches grade player effort and performance directly off the game video. We go over every play by position in order to communicate what is expected in every situation during the game. This process is completed and put behind us the day after the game. Coaches and athletes must learn from their mistakes and successes, then put the emotions and thoughts of the previous game behind them as soon as possible. In the words of the great Paul "Bear" Bryant, "Identify your mistakes, learn from your mistakes, and forget your mistakes." Win or lose, a team must be totally focused on the next opponent as soon as possible.

TRAINING ROOM

Athletes have to be healthy to perform at their highest level. Football is a violent game. Pain and injury are inevitable for every player. I have been fortunate to work with some of the best medical and training staff. I have a staff that keeps the team's best interest in mind and that gives every ounce of energy to maintain and rehabilitate players and keep them on the field.

We take a long-term approach with athletes. We understand that the team must be at full strength at the end of the season when the playoffs begin. Our staff makes its decisions based on this perspective at all times.

We incorporate mandatory training room time for athletes during the season. The training room opens at 7:00 every morning. Treatment is available before classes, between classes, at lunch, before practice, and after practice. Counting preseason, we hope the team will play for 16 consecutive weeks. With this in mind, we remind players how important it is to maintain a high level of health by managing small injuries before they become big problems that could affect the whole team. Whether the injury is a major problem or a minor issue, players must be responsible for their long-term health management.

Coach's Keys

Performing consistently at a high level is a by-product of several components. Preparing the offense, defense, and special teams to meet the demands of the opponent are paramount. Consider the following preparation components when developing your plan:

1. Thoroughly understand your team's strengths, weaknesses, and tendencies.

2. Believe in your system and make small adjustments, not major changes.

3. Make sure your team understands your opponent's game personality.

4. Make sure your team is well grounded in the fundamentals of football. Always outexecute your opponent.

5. Be thoroughly prepared, but don't waste time defending ghosts.

6. Organization breeds confidence and performance. Trivia breeds inconsistency and demise.

7. Study film.

YOUR TENDENCIES AND GAME PERSONALITY

Thoroughly understanding your team's tendencies is an important part of game preparation. The coaching staff needs to have a strong understanding of the team's game personality. Do you throw the ball or run the ball on first down? What is your third-down efficiency on offense and defense? Do you have a special player who only touches the ball on certain plays or in certain areas of the field? Does your defense gamble on first down to try to put the offense in a hole? Does your punt block team align in the same position every time? Many more questions of this type could be asked. Understand your team's personality. Remember, your opponent is asking the same questions about your team while developing their game plan against you. The opponent is building a game plan directly off the information they have assembled from breaking down your team's game films.

It is important to have tendencies because this means your team is executing parts of the game at a high level. However, we develop and implement tendency breakers for each game plan. Tendency breakers are ways to take advantage of the opponent's strategy to stop what your team executes well. For example, if your team likes to run the football on first down, the offensive coordinator may want to implement an action pass off the same

What are your tendencies on offense, defense, and special teams? What is your team's personality?

running play the team had been using successfully in previous games. Your opponent will have the defensive unit ready to stop the running play on first down, and your offense can take advantage of the defense's aggressiveness by throwing a pass off a great run play fake.

OPPONENT'S TENDENCIES AND GAME PERSONALITY

Gain a thorough understanding of your opponent's tendencies when developing your game plan and weekly practice routine. The

coaching staff needs to gather as much data as time permits in order to teach players as much about the opponent as possible before the game.

Players need to have a complete understanding of the opponent's game personality before taking the field for the game. Each day of practice is a building process for players to learn to think and react in a proper way to defeat the opponent. Our job as coaches is to make sure the team has a complete understanding of the opponent's game personality before they take the field to play.

Almost all the data we use to develop scouting reports and game plans is gained from breaking down our opponent's game video. Every conference has rules about film trade to preserve the integrity and quality of the video for every team. Our conference trades the previous three game videos; some conferences trade an entire season. I would love to have one of my assistant coaches actually watch the opponent in person to get a sense of how physical the team is and what type of team speed they possess, but manpower and distance to certain games make us rely almost exclusively on game video.

I divide the staff into specialized groups to break down the opponent's video. Each offensive coach is assigned a particular area of video research on the opponent's defense. Each member of the defensive staff has a special area of video to break down on the opponent's offense. The special teams coordinator and I handle the video breakdown for all special teams situations.

Offensive line coaches are responsible for breaking down and gathering data on all defensive fronts, alignments, slants, and blitzes as well as personnel matchups in the front seven. The receivers coach works hand in hand with the quarterbacks coach to break down and gather information about the opponent's secondary and coverage alignments. These areas include alignment and down-and-distance tendencies as well as personnel matchups.

Once all the video is broken down and entered into the computer for analysis, the offensive staff meets to start piecing together a game plan and practice schedule. Every phase of our offensive team is discussed in detail including pass protection, blitz automatics, the running game we want to use against certain alignments, and personnel matchups. Once the planning is complete, we develop a game plan and weekly practice schedule based on the data and analysis information. We then assemble a scouting report book for each offensive player to study throughout the week of preparation.

Defensive line coaches are responsible for breaking down and gathering data on each offensive running play and scheme. They look at personnel matchups, special formations, personnel groupings, and red-zone runs. The linebackers coach handles all play action passes including bootlegs, waggles, and sprint-out passes. Because linebackers are in charge of making all the front seven adjustments and calls, the linebackers coach also creates a call sheet that includes all our automatics and special checks for the week. The coaches in charge of the secondary compile all passing-game data, including field zone, down-and-distance tendencies, and personnel tendencies and groupings.

After entering all the data into the computer for analysis, the defensive staff members puts their part of the scouting report in a book for every player to study during the week. The weekly practice schedules are then compiled based on the scouting report data revealed by the computer breakdown.

As with the offensive and defensive phases of the game, the special teams coaches thoroughly break down the opponent's special teams piece by piece. Attention to every detail is vital if our team is to win the all-important special teams battle. Finding every weakness to take advantage of or an alignment that would give us an advantage is diligently researched. We include personnel matchups and all alignments and tendencies in our special teams scouting booklet.

GAME PLAN

All game preparation is based on our system of offense and defense. Time is so limited between games that major changes in any system would lead directly to a decrease in execution. We want to use what we do well and never let an opponent's system dictate what we choose to do. Our offensive and defensive systems provide the flexibility we need to take advantage of almost any opponent's system. We believe in our system's ability to defeat the opponent if we execute at a high level.

The goal of any game plan should be to place players in position to be successful. The only way we should lose a game is if our opponent is more athletically talented and outexecutes us. Athletic ability is important, but execution is the key to consistency.

Put players in position to be successful.

To help us build a mental picture and formulate our game plan, the staff considers the following questions in all three major areas of football—offense, defense, and special teams:

1. What phases of our offense, defense, and special teams are we executing at a very high level? What do we do well?

2. Where are our strengths and weaknesses in personnel matchups with our opponent?

3. How will we stop what our opponent does best? How will we stop our opponent's best player?

4. Does our opponent have glaring weaknesses we can take advantage of?

5. How can we win the special teams battle and make game-changing plays?

6. Are we sound against their blitz schemes? What would we automatic in those situations?

7. Have we educated our players thoroughly on our opponent's personality?

AUTOMATICS AND CATCHALLS

It is impossible to expose a team to every possible game scenario. Opponents will attempt plays or formations that you have not seen on video and therefore have not prepared for. We try not to waste valuable preparation time chasing and defending ghosts. We structured our systems so that players have automatic calls to ensure a sound alignment or play that gives them a chance to be successful. For example, if a linebacker sees a confusing formation or situation, he simply automatics one of the base-alignment calls that the defense has played hundreds of times. This gives our team a chance to play the down with confidence.

The offense can call automatics as well. If the quarterback sees a strange defensive alignment or blitz, he has the authority and ability to change the play to one of our reliable and executable plays. If all else fails, our field leaders have the power at any time to call time-out to prevent a big-play situation for our opponent. Consistency increases when trivia decreases.

PRACTICE SCHEDULE

Game planning is a process that takes place over an entire week. We have never walked into a Monday practice completely prepared and confident in our game plan for the next weekend. The process begins on Monday and evolves through a series of organized events into a finalized game plan on Friday.

Monday is a busy day. We organize and present information to the team. The defensive coaches and players meet at 6:00 a.m. to review the scouting report and watch video of our next opponent. The entire team arrives after classes. I present my overview of the week along with the offensive coordinator's scouting report and the special teams scouting report.

All phases of special teams are covered during Monday's practice including the correction of the previous week's mistakes and the preliminary game plan for the next opponent. The offensive and defensive lines spend the majority of their time in individual stations correcting last week's mistakes and implementing the current game plan. Skill players work on different passing-game situations and are introduced to any new plays or adjustments off of old ones. The final phase of Monday's practice is a team period. In this period, we concentrate on our opponent's formations and alignments and the adjustments and automatics we will implement in those situations. We finish the day with conditioning drills and then offensive meetings and film study.

Tuesday is our offensive-priority day. The offense will practice 60 minutes, and the defense will practice 45 minutes. Tuesday's prepractice emphasizes punt protection schemes. After the team stretch, the punting team practices for 10 minutes followed by the kickoff return team.

Because Tuesday is an offensive-priority day, we begin with an individual offensive period, concentrating on basic progressions at each position and graduating into current game-planning needs. For example, receivers begin by working on stance, alignment, and releases. We work on this every day because all receivers must excel at these skills to be competitive at their position. We then graduate to receiving drills and route progressions, all relevant to the day's practice schedule. Individual periods are crucial for continuing to develop position skills.

After the individual period, we move into a seven-on-seven passing period with quarterbacks, receivers, and half of the tight ends and running backs. The other half of the tight ends and running backs stay with the offensive line while they implement and polish their offensive running plays. Seven-on-seven is where we concentrate on passing plays of many varieties. Plays are scripted by down-and-distance situations as well as hash mark and the suspected defensive alignment we will see. Generally, we script enough plays to go through the list twice during the allotted periods. Halfway through the drill, we switch the tight ends and running backs so that each group receives instruction in both passing and running situations.

After the seven-on-seven drills, we progress to five-on-five inside runs. During this time, receivers and quarterbacks go into one-on-one and two-on-two passing situations to work on timing and special passing situations. The five-on-five period is dedicated to developing the running game with down-and-distance, hash mark, and defensive personnel groups taken into consideration. Quarterbacks and running backs switch halfway through the running drills so that they can practice both running and passing phases.

After all 20 periods of offensive practice, we go directly to defensive practice. Because we are on an offensive-emphasis day, the defense will have a five-on-five run defense period for 15 minutes while defensive backs work on man-to-man coverage and other areas of pass defense. When five on five concludes, defensive backs begin seven-on-seven pass defense while defensive linemen are in individual drills or pass rush. After seven on seven, we close out practice with team defense and field goal block.

Tuesday is the first day we expose our game plan to what we feel our opponent will try to do to counter us. Every phase of practice is videoed so that we can evaluate our strategy for Wednesday's practice. We will see things we like, and we'll see things we don't like. We make adjustments for Wednesday's practice, making every attempt to refine and tweak each part of the game plan so that practice on Wednesday will be similar to what we think we'll see during the game.

We conclude Tuesday's practice with a couple of team offensive periods. We script a list of plays that include first and 10, third and long, red zone, and everything in between. We are teaching our offense what to expect on game day. We close Tuesday practice with our field goal team and with film watching with our offensive groups.

Wednesday is our defensive-priority day. The defensive squad practices 60 minutes, while the offensive team practices 45 minutes. Wednesday's prepractice includes a 10-minute team defensive walk-through of all blitzes and special situations we believe we will see on

game day plus any adjustments we made after Tuesday's film evaluation.

After the team stretch, Wednesday's practice becomes almost an exact replica of Tuesday's workout. Special teams include kickoff coverage and punt returns—three periods each. After the special teams period, the defense works on individual drills—seven on seven, five on five. Then we have a couple of team periods and close with field goal defense. After defense finishes, we begin three stations of offense including five on five, seven on seven, and team. We close Wednesday's practice with a two-minute offense on the field then the emergency field goal team. The conditioning coach works the team through 10 minutes of speed and flexibility drills before we watch practice film.

Thursday is the day for game preparation. Thursday's practice is our game dress rehearsal. I expect gamelike mental intensity and total focus from players and staff. We use a game-day script format for Thursday's practice. The script includes nearly every situation our team and coaches will see on game day. Every coach has a copy of the script and understands the situations we will put the team in throughout practice. Players are responsible for performing flawlessly and setting the tone for game day.

I am always demanding of players and expect them to give their best in every situation, but during Thursday's walk-through, I am a bear. Mental busts are not acceptable, and the coaches and players know it. The entire practice takes one hour and 10 minutes to complete if every player and coach executes his individual responsibilities. I will make the entire team begin practice over if the team does not perform at a championship level for the whole practice. It's my way of emphasizing the importance of team concentration and execution. Executing Thursday's walk-through makes game night a breeze, and a great Thursday practice helps me sleep better as well.

CHAPTER 15 HANDLING GAME SITUATIONS

I have been blessed to be a part of the greatest sport on Earth, a sport that teaches players and coaches about life and is the epitome of team play. Game time is the most exciting part of my job. At game time, all the hours of hard work and dedication come to fruition.

We enter every game believing we will be victorious. I always feel that we can win if we execute at a high level. The tradition of our program has led to a level of confidence in our coaches, players, and system that allows us to believe we will win every time we tee it up. Winning seven championships out of eight has led to high expectations for our football program. I believe this tradition of excellence is on our side every time we take the field.

As head coach, I want to place every member of the organization in a position to be successful on game day. I'm the one who has to make the difficult calls—when to go for it on fourth down, when to call the fake punt, when to use time-outs—but I've prepared for those moments. I know exactly how I want to manage a game based not only on my personal preparation but also on how the momentum of the game is unfolding. Most of the pressure comes from my feelings toward staff and players, my hope and desire for them to perform to the best of their ability. How can I, as the head coach, assist them in this task? I constantly write notes during the game and remind my assistants of situations I feel we can take advantage of or need to change. Because each member of the staff and team has game responsibilities, I try my best to assist them in their tasks while maintaining my own responsibilities. My game-day focus is nearly the same focus I used to have as a player. The ability to perform under fire can happen only if you are mentally prepared and focused. In this chapter I discuss important areas of execution on game day.

Coach's Keys

1. Develop a game-day routine that works for your program and stick with it.

2. Take care of what you have control over: equipment, clothing, cleats, nutrition, and hydration.

3. Channel emotion into focus and performance.

4. Play at a high level and let the emotion of the big game take care of itself.

5. Use scripting and diversity early in the game.

6. Refocus at halftime and reestablish the momentum early.

7. Be focused, intense, and confident. Coach 'em up. Players feed off the head coach.

8. Win, lose, or draw, always have character, class, and dignity.

9. Never, never, never give up.

PREGAME ROUTINE

I'm a big routine guy. If a system works consistently, stick with it. At the Thursday night team dinner, I distribute a game-day itinerary. When developing a plan for the game-day routine, it is best to begin with kickoff time and work backward. Having planned a few game days in my career, it comes naturally and easy for me. Put a lot of thought and creativity into your itinerary.

The reason I keep referring to the word *routine* is that I want game day to be just like any other day for players. Consistency is important. I want my squad to perform at a high level every time they take the field, no matter who the opponent may be. If players are accustomed to a routine on the day of the game, they can focus on their responsibilities and everything else (training room, FCA, pregame speech, and so on) takes care of itself.

I remind players about these game-day responsibilities each week:

- Check all equipment, buckles, snaps, strings, and cleats. We don't want a player to miss plays because of an equipment problem that could have been fixed in advance.

- Be prepared for the weather and field conditions. Have the proper cleats installed for the given field conditions and make sure you have options. Clothing should fit the conditions. Have clothes and socks to change into at halftime if the weather is wet.

- Eat a proper pregame meal three to four hours before kickoff.

- Stay properly hydrated. (Game day is too late.)

- Stick with your personal game-day routine (provided you are achieving solid results) and be mentally and physically prepared.

Home Games

Generally speaking, players are taped and dressed in their football pants and cleats two and a half hours before kickoff. We have five separate meeting times before the game. We include a voluntary Fellowship of Christian Athletes (FCA) segment in which we bring in a local youth minister who gives an inspirational message from the Bible to all team members who enjoy working on their number one priority. The other four meetings are for offense, defense, and special teams, and a varsity team meeting with me. These meetings always take place at the same time and the same place at every home game.

I prefer a quiet, orderly locker room before the game where coaches and players can focus in on their game responsibilities and build a strong visual picture of what they want to accomplish during the game. I assign two coaches to monitor the varsity locker room to make sure it's quiet and focused. All players get charged for the game in their own way. Some prefer to listen to loud music, which is fine with me as long as no one else has to listen to it. We encourage music listeners to bring headsets and listen to their music on their own without bothering other players.

I love playing at home in front of our fans. Jenks people come out in droves to support their football program. They understand the importance of making noise at just the right time to disrupt the opponent's offense. Playing at home is just that: it's home. The home environment enhances our team's pride and tradition.

Road Games

Travel is a part of every football season and careful planning is necessary to ensure team focus on the ball game. Nothing can take a team out of focus faster than a poorly organized road trip.

I'm big into routine when it comes to making travel plans. I prefer to arrive the same time for every road trip and use the same itinerary every time (see figure 15.1 for a sample travel itinerary). Simply start with the kickoff time and work backward through the itinerary. This ensures that every road game has the same schedule and the kids know when and where they should be at all times. The more planning and effort you put into your travel itinerary, the more consistency your team will develop on the road.

Whether you are on a bus for 20 minutes or 6 hours, have a travel plan. Be sure to confirm the number of buses and bus drivers and the departure and arrival times. Nothing is worse than arriving late to a visiting stadium and having to change every plan for the evening because of a preventable scheduling error.

I have had bad experiences with drivers who were unfamiliar with our travel concepts, so I require my assistant coaches to drive activity buses unless we charter private buses for longer trips. My coaches understand our travel philosophy and the importance of departing and arriving on time and maintaining a focused environment on the bus at all times.

We have a seating plan for every road trip. We travel in three buses with the varsity two-deep offensive players on the first bus, varsity two-deep defensive players on the second

bus, and all junior varsity players on the third bus. There are a couple of reasons for this configuration. First, players are grouped with the teammates they will play with so that it is easy for assistant coaches to have game-planning conversations with players on the way to the game if there are last-minute adjustments or questions. Second, by traveling with only varsity-level players on the first two buses, the players are comfortable and not cramped for room, making the trip as easy as possible on the players who will see the most action.

I prefer a quiet bus ride to all games. I want every player to mentally focus on the game, and all players do this in their own way. If players like to listen to loud music, they bring personal music players and headsets. If players like to study the game plan, they have a quiet environment in which to read and reflect on the task at hand. A quiet, controlled bus ride allows each player to focus in his own way. I have little tolerance for loud or unfocused behavior on the way to a game.

Postgame return trips are different. If our team was victorious, players will be happy and upbeat and want to celebrate. I am much more flexible on the trip home after a victory. As long as players maintain a safe, controlled environment, I don't care if they listen to music or have loud conversations. Return trips after losses are a little different. The sting of a loss will be on the mind of every member of our program, and thoughts on the way home will be directed toward areas of individual improvement. I'm not a very happy loser, so the bus ride home is usually a quiet, composed one.

We rarely travel far enough or play early enough to merit an overnight stay in a hotel. But when we do, the most important component of an overnight stay is a good itinerary and plan. Make the travel itinerary available to all parents and administrators so that player location is always known and contact is constantly available. Make sure all members of your football program are aware of your expectations for the road trip. My expectations on the road are strictly business at all times. Arrival and departure times as well as room checks and meal times are not approximations, they are deadlines. Failure to adhere

Thursday, Sept. 30	5:30 pm	Team dinner at Crossroads Baptist
Friday, Oct. 1	1:40 pm	Team meeting in team room
		Check all gear
		Pack and be prepared
	3:00 pm	Eat a good meal at home
	4:15 pm	Load buses for Owasso
	4:20 pm	Buses leave for Owasso
	4:55 pm	Training room open for taping
		Energy bars available in locker room
	5:00 pm	Silence in locker room (Carl and Loren)
	5:10 pm	Coaches and players free time, FCA
	5:20 pm	All players taped and pants on
	5:25 pm	Special teams meeting (sophomore locker room)
	5:35 pm	Two-deep defensive meetings (locker room)
	5:45 pm	Two-deep offensive meetings (locker room)
	5:55 pm	Specialty wave take field (Carl, Keith, John T.)
	6:15 pm	Special teams wave returns to locker room
	6:22 pm	Team stretch and form run (all coaches)
		Team breakdown at midfield
	6:37 pm	Individual stations
	6:47 pm	Punt team on 35, pin 'em deep; team on 50
	6:49 pm	Team D pursuit; team on 40
	6:52 pm	Team O polish; team on 30
	6:55 pm	Extra point; team to locker room
	7:00 pm	Offensive, defensive, special teams starters in locker room (coaches)
		All other players in sophomore locker room
	7:15 pm	Trimble with team; coaches to press box
		All players in locker room pregame
	7:24 pm	Captains leave for coin toss
		Captains join team at run-through after toss
		Team leaves for run-through
		National anthem
	7:27 pm	Team takes the field
	7:30 pm	Get a Ram
Saturday, Oct. 2	8:00 am	Treatments
	TBA	Running and lifting
Sunday, Oct. 3	Off	
Monday, Oct. 4	1:50 pm	Team meeting in team room

Figure 15.1 Sample itinerary for a road game.

to the travel itinerary results in disciplinary action or suspension.

Contact the hotel well in advance of your trip to confirm the bed count, meal count, and other special meeting rooms you may need while staying overnight. I assign assistant coaches to check rooms at the appropriate time and to make periodic hallway inspections throughout the night. I take seriously the duty of being responsible for other people's children and work hard to make sure they are not only ready to play football but also are safe.

Game-day routine is important even on road trips. No matter where we play, we live by our pregame preparation. We always eat three to four hours before game time. Players are taped and dressed two and a half hours before game time.

It is important to be flexible and adjust to your opponent's facilities if you are visiting a team for the first time. Sometimes facilities are small and require players to dress in waves or the younger JV players to dress in alternative areas to allow meetings to progress with the varsity players.

We try hard to make road games just like home games as much as possible. However, from time to time problems arise that are out of your control. Transportation delays and difficulties are unfortunate and can lead to challenging schedule changes. When confronted with delays, make sure you don't compromise your pregame itinerary if at all possible. Players should have the same pregame warm-up without exception. Adjust your meeting times, have your meals sent to the locker room, or make other adjustments, but don't change the pregame routine. When problems occur, keep the best interests of the team in mind and do your best to put players in position to succeed.

Pep Talk and Prayer

I want my team to play at a very high level always. When it's time for the pregame pep talk, players are only moments away from taking the field. Emotions are running very high. I rarely give a big fire-up speech to players. I remind them to channel their emotions into high-quality performance. It does no good

for them to go out on the field out of their minds and play hard but not well. There is a big difference.

Don't Forget to Box

I read an article once about a big boxing match challenge between a professional boxer and an NFL offensive lineman. A promoter offered the winner of the match $100,000 and plenty of publicity. Even though the boxer was a heavyweight, the football player physically outmatched the boxer in every important category except one. The football player was favored in height, weight, reach, strength, and power, but the boxer was highly trained in his profession. He had practiced his techniques over and over until he could execute them in his sleep. The boxer was a machine when it came to boxing.

In prematch interviews, the boxer was very humble. He told reporters he would have to box his very best to withstand the bigger, stronger opponent and be successful. He was respectful and focused. When asked how he was going box his opponent, the football player responded in a huge emotional tirade: "Box him? I'm not gonna box him! I'm gonna whip his butt all over that ring!" He was fired up and juiced to the max for the big event.

The bell rang to begin the first round. In an emotional fury, the NFL player charged the boxer to "whip his butt." The big problem was he charged directly into the boxer's straight right hand. The boxer delivered the blow with tremendous power and accuracy to the football player's chin. The boxing match took 16 seconds, and 10 seconds of that was the time it took the referee to count the football player out.

The moral of the story is to remember what you're going into the ring to do. All of the emotion, intensity, and training in the world will do you no good unless you do what you are supposed to do. Don't get into the boxing ring and forget to box, and don't walk out on the football field and forget to play football!

If an opponent is not as talented as we are, we will still play at a higher level, outexecute them, and beat them without being emotionally charged. When the opponent is of equal or better talent, a natural emotion arises through the challenge on the playing field. A speech is usually not needed to raise the team's emotion when we are playing another excellent team. My experience with teams who come out of the locker room running on emotion is about the same as the football player's was with the boxer. As soon as the ball is kicked off, you have to go play the game and execute.

I am blessed to work for a group of administrators and board members who believe in the importance of developing one's faith. I always lead our team in prayer right before we leave for the run-through. I gather my thoughts before entering the locker room and pray to God from my heart. I never pray for victory, but I always pray that we will play and coach in a way that would be pleasing to God and that we will never lose sight of the blessings that God gives us every day by allowing us to be a part of a great community, school, and football program. I pray for courage and confidence and other relevant issues that are on my heart. God has truly blessed our football program in countless ways.

COACHING STYLE ON GAME DAY

Everyone's game-day coaching style is different and usually reflects their personality. I am by nature a very emotional person; I was when I played as an undersized defensive lineman in college. I have learned over the years that my team will be a reflection of me during a game, and thus, I am aware of my approach. I coach with intensity and concentrate on exuding confidence in my players at all times. I want my players to go out and play with focus and resolve no matter what the score is or how much time is left on the clock. Coordinators handle the offense, defense, and special teams during the game. It's up to me to handle the players and their emotional ups and downs.

I also handle the officials throughout the game so that my coaches can coach and my players can play.

We teach and preach to players the importance of playing every play like it will make the difference in the ball game. We remind them to focus on their assignments and effort because they are the only two things that players can control. Players and coaches have no control over officials or fans and little control over the clock or what the opponent is going to do.

Here is a great example of being focused. A few years ago, we found ourselves in a real dogfight during a championship ball game. The game against our archrival, Union, kept swinging back and forth. The lead had changed several times during the game, and it was getting late. We were behind by a touchdown, and I was pleading with the defense to make a big play and get the offense back on the field. Sure enough, in championship fashion, our great strong safety Bobby Klink made a tremendous interception deep in our territory to kill a drive that could have put the game out of reach for us. Long story short, we drove down the field and scored the game-winning touchdown a couple of minutes later to win our fourth consecutive championship.

I gave Bobby our "Big Play" award at the team dinner for making a game-changing play with just three minutes to go in the game. Bobby accepted the award and replied, "I didn't know we were down by six." Everyone burst into laughter. I left the dinner that night knowing what kind of team we had because we had players doing what we told them to do, players who were focused on making plays and not on the clock or the score.

We try very hard to find great plays during the game and celebrate with our players. We constantly build them up and teach them during the game. There will always be mistakes and busts, but during the game it is vital to teach, adjust, and build up. If players feel you have lost confidence in them, they will not perform at a high level. Even when things are rough, coach players up and make them believe they can accomplish great things if they keep playing hard.

EARLY GAME

We script the first 15 to 20 plays on offense and defense for a couple of reasons. Offensively, we want to see where our opponent is going to line up against our personnel and formations. From this information, we develop another list of preferred plays against given alignments. We conduct research, then develop game scripts based on where we believe the opponent will line up against our personnel and formation. Our coach in the press box notes each defensive alignment early in the game as we go down our play list. This greatly helps the offensive coordinator develop and hone his preferred-play list as the game develops.

Defensively, we prefer to be diverse early in the game to make it more difficult for the opponent's offense to get a bead on what we are trying to do. Once we get our bearings and develop our plan of action, we like to stick with what gives us success until our opponent forces us to adjust. All offensive coordinators have a great play to beat any defense you might use, so the key is to keep the offense guessing and scrambling as long as possible. We accomplish this by scripting defenses to ensure that we give opponents multiple looks and at the same time can see how our preliminary adjustments work. Once we have success with some of our looks, we can come back to them at opportune times for big plays.

Our offensive philosophy has always been to take what the defense gives us. In other words, if the defense does a great job and takes away some of the game plan, we won't be stubborn and place our team at a disadvantage just for the sake of running a play. We will find something in our system that will allow the team to be successful against the opponent. Don't let turnovers or momentum change the thought process or your game plan. Stick with what you have practiced.

Defensively, we feel it is important to get a feel for the game. Are you getting four-man pressure or does the quarterback have all day? What blitzes are successful and what plays have hurt you? If you can knock a hole in their boat early, do your best to sink it.

Make their offense execute a bunch of plays to beat you, and no matter what, don't give up a big play for a score.

HALFTIME ADJUSTMENTS

I meet with the whole staff immediately after we return to the locker room from the field. This meeting allows assistant coaches to gather information and formulate their second-half game plan while the players are getting their halftime nutrition bars and drinks. This meeting allows me to get a feel for first-half performance directly from my coaches and gather my thoughts for my first meeting with the players. During the first half, the coaches record every play and personnel situation. They know what has worked and what hasn't. After the brief meeting with the staff, I talk to the team as a whole to get them to focus on their halftime mentality. They have to focus on absorbing information from their coaches and learn what to do to be even more successful during the second half. I am careful to mention both the good and the bad from my perspective on the first half. If our performance has been substandard, I point out mistakes and what needs to be corrected. Generally, I discuss penalties, mental errors, and effort with the whole team and then allow coordinators and position coaches to make the actual X-and-O adjustments.

After I meet with the players, we break up into offensive and defensive groups and make adjustments. Coordinators gather feedback from assistant coaches and players to finalize halftime adjustments. Subtle adjustments to offensive and defensive plays are made; sometimes simply changing a formation or alignment will give us the advantage we need to be successful. Other times we may need to completely change a defensive personnel group to stop one of our opponent's plays.

The dynamics of a normal halftime can be complex. Perhaps we have lost a player or two to injury and we must make offensive and defensive adjustments to give the backup players a chance to be successful. Maybe our

Our first 15 to 20 offensive plays are scripted. This allows us to gather information on our opponent's defensive tendencies and adjust our offensive plan accordingly.

team was a little flat in the first half and did not execute well. Halftime adjustments are less about work on the chalkboard and more about challenging the character, effort, and fortitude of players. Maybe our team pitched a gem, and we totally dominated the opponent during the first half. I praise the team and applaud their efforts, then prepare to play junior varsity personnel to reduce the risk of injury to starters. We never play to not lose, we always play to win. I challenge the starters who are going to play the second half to go out and finish the game so that the younger players can gain valuable experience in a varsity environment.

After the halftime dust clears, we meet again as a team to reinforce adjustments made, refocus, and take the field again, ready to win the second half. I remind players and coaches how important it is to establish and maintain momentum early in the second half

and then finish the game, playing well down the stretch.

When the officials return to the locker room to take us back to the field, I call the team together one last time. I challenge them to establish the momentum of the game early and finish the ball game. I suppose my favorite line is, "No one remembers who won the first half," meaning we have to finish the game to ensure the victory.

SECOND HALF

In staying consistent with our philosophy, "We will play with great effort and compete as long as there is time left on the clock," we remind players of the importance of certain situations during the closing minutes of a game. The difference between winning and losing a game can boil down to just a couple of plays.

Knowing how and when to finish a game is a trait of every championship-caliber team. The offense converting a first down late in the game so that our team can run out the clock or the defense making a big fourth-down stop to end a drive can mean the difference in finishing the game or not. Often special teams can make the difference—a last-second field goal or a great punt to pin the opponent deep in their own territory.

Finishing the game takes on a different meaning when a team has a comfortable lead and the younger players come into the game to get valuable playing time. We expect the same intensity and concentration out of young players that we expect from our varsity squad. I want to evaluate our younger lions to see if they have the intensity and toughness to be great players in the future.

Finishing the game when your team is behind, though uncomfortable, is probably the situation that shows the most about your character. When your team is behind and the cards are stacked against you, it is vital to reach down and play with great pride and effort. It is a sign of pure character to play your heart out in a losing cause. Fortunately, we haven't been subjected to this situation very often, but tough times were made for tough people, and champions will lace up their work boots and go back to work to make sure that they don't have to be in that situation again.

Never Give Up

In 1999 we were ranked number one in the state and archrival, Union, was ranked number two. We met in the second game of the season. Because it was early in the season, we didn't have all of our packages installed. Still, we felt like we had enough to have a chance to win the game if we played well. A crowd of nearly 40,000 turned out for what would be not only the most exciting game of my career but also a game that taught me to never lose heart, no matter what.

Our first two punts were blocked, and we missed our only field goal attempt of the first half. Because I play a big role in special teams, I was furious. In fact, I was more than furious. We executed poorly on offense, mustering very little yardage and almost no points in the first half, while Union's spread offense was gashing our defense. I spent the whole first half writing down my postgame speech to the team because I knew with our lack of focus we were going to get drilled in front of half of the state of Oklahoma.

My mother always told me, "Son, if you don't have anything good to say, don't say anything at all." So on the long walk to the locker room at halftime, I decided to challenge my team to fight back and play like they had been taught. I was tempted to scold the team and chalk up the loss to a lack of preparation on my part. Instead I told them that nothing the coaches could write on the ink board could change the outcome of the game unless they were willing to go out on the field and play with passion and execution. I told them how fortunate we were to be down only 17 to 7 with the way the first half had gone, and that if we played flawlessly in the second half, we could make a run. I had no feel for the squad except that I knew we had some veteran players with tremendous pride. I thought they would turn it up a little against the archrival.

We opened the second half by giving up an 80-yard drive for a touchdown and going down by 17 points. I was completely down. I wasn't going to show it to the players or fans, but I was really disappointed. As the game progressed, the offense began to play a lot better. We scored to stay within striking distance, but Union kept coming right back and stretching the lead. In fact, we were behind by 17 points twice in the fourth quarter, but our kids kept playing. We made a few big plays on defense and, with 1:34 to go in the game, scored the go-ahead touchdown, making the score 34 to 31. I told our defensive coordinator, "If they can go 80 yards in a minute, we deserve to lose." My attitude was still suffering from the mishaps of the game. Exactly 1:13 seconds later, Union scored and took the lead 38 to 31 with 21 seconds to go. My heart was completely shattered.

We got the ball on the 20-yard line with one time-out left. My offensive coordinator wanted to throw the ball across the middle to our great running back Kejuan Jones, but I said no because we had only one time-out left, and if they tackled us we would have to use our last time-out and risk not getting a field goal attempt. He sternly requested the play across the middle again, adding that he had been saving the play and thought it would be there. I finally backed off and let him call the play. Kejuan caught a perfect ball from Scott McCoy, picked up a great block downfield by Blaine Cooper, and ran 80 yards for the winning touchdown. I was in shock. One side of the field was completely silent and the other side of the field was in pandemonium. We had won the game in spite of my attitude and lack of faith. Since that night, I have never thought about doubting my coaches or players again. Never, never, never give up.

POSTGAME

After the final horn blows, it is important to display sportsmanship toward and respect for your opponent by shaking hands at midfield. Congratulating your opponent on a hard-fought battle is a sign of mutual respect and a tribute to the great sport of football.

After the handshake, we gather as a team at midfield. I say some departing words to the squad. Emotion is still thick, either in triumph from the victory or sorrow from the loss, and I consider this before I address the team. I also understand that coaches will learn a lot more about the game after viewing the film the next morning, so I usually don't try to evaluate the game until I watch the film myself. The setting at midfield is usually not very private, so my remarks are only important reminders and general statements about the game. If I feel the timing is right to have a private meeting with the team, I announce it at this meeting. A few members of the team enjoy leading our squad in prayer after the game, and we close the evening with "All the Trojans say . . . Amen!"

We expect players to finish the game with the same intensity and focus with which they started it. As long as time is left on the clock, every player must give great effort.

CHAPTER 16 EVALUATING PLAYERS AND THE PROGRAM

Evaluating staff, athletes, and the program itself is vital for ensuring that all systems are headed in the right direction. In staying consistent with our philosophy, we want the program to be goal oriented, so we carefully monitor the journey as we strive to achieve these goals.

Strong research and honest evaluation of accurate data are the keys to an effective evaluation. Assessment cannot be done often enough. Precisely monitoring personnel on the field, off the field, and in the classroom leads to accountability and improvement.

I always seek out managers, leaders, and coaches of successful organizations to see what they do to make their particular organization successful. In this chapter I discuss some of the elements to consider when evaluating players during the off-season, preseason, practices, and games as well as evaluating staff and the overall progress of the football program. I tell parents that evaluation of athletes takes place 24 hours a day, 7 days a week, and that's the same approach I take with myself, my staff, and the entire organization. Like the old saying goes, your reputation is how you are perceived by your peers, and your character is how you really are when no one is around to see your actions. Certainly, I want the entire organization to have a great reputation, but more important, I want everyone in it to demonstrate strong character at all times.

PLAYER EVALUATION

We, as coaches, want players to know that we are pulling on the same end of the rope that they are. We are all in the same boat, paddling for the same goals. Building relationships with players enhances a coach's ability to motivate and coach them. The more you know about a player's family life, character, personality, and other intangibles, the more you will be able to make an accurate evaluation of the athlete.

Preseason Evaluation

We begin each preseason staff meeting by evaluating every varsity player on the roster.

Each coach ranks every player with a number from 1 through 40. Ranking criteria are based on overall value to the team. The criteria include athletic ability, leadership, character, and special skills or traits that cannot be replaced. The player who receives a 1 is deemed to add the most value to the squad; 40 is assigned to the player who adds the least. Each coach casts his vote for each player and makes notes about his score for the athlete for discussion at the staff meeting.

After each coach assigns a number to each player, we add up the points to get every player's overall ranking. We talk about why we feel the way we feel about the athlete. This provides insight about each player and allows us as a staff to make educated decisions regarding personnel. Because our program is dedicated to helping young men achieve their fullest potential, it is hoped that these initial evaluations will change for the better as players are exposed to the program.

The more information you have about players, the more insight you have for putting players in position to be successful. I encourage frequent player evaluations early in the season to monitor individual improvements in leadership and attitude or for detrimental changes in attitude and performance.

I don't believe in cutting football players. No matter how limited the player may be in ability, if he has a great attitude and a great work ethic, he is welcome to stay in camp. Many times the players who have limited ability set the example for those who are talented. I will never deprive a young man of the benefits of being on a football team as long as he understands his role and keeps his priorities in order.

I have seen many players who were judged too small or too slow when they were young grow and mature into outstanding ball players in their final seasons. I have also found that players who have the perseverance and attitude to stick with it are hard to beat when they finally get their opportunity to play. It means too much to them for them to give up. Great programs have great-program kids who set the standard for work ethic, attitude, and perseverance. You never know if you are

hurting the team or the player when you cut a player because he's not good enough. I let players go only if their attitude is detrimental to the program or if they violate team rules and are not interested in improving.

Coach's Keys: Player Evaluation

1. Evaluation of players takes place 24 hours a day, seven days a week. Individual evaluation is critical for developing a plan to place players in position to better the team. The more information you can gather, the better the decisions you can make.

2. Don't let the scoreboard be your guide when evaluating the team. Consider effort, execution, and talent level when evaluating team performance.

3. Use off-season evaluations to build relationships with players. Help them align their priorities and build their faith, family, and their grades. Football comes easy to those who have their priorities in order.

4. Practice evaluation is critical for ensuring that the team improves daily. Evaluate daily. Make sure you don't repeat mistakes and that you are progressing toward game day.

5. Game evaluation helps the coach make the right adjustments during the game. Develop methods of evaluation and communication to expedite game adjustments.

6. Wait until you have studied game film to make specific remarks about postgame evaluation. Be general and cautious right after the game because emotions are still flowing and the media might be hovering around.

7. Use video to evaluate each player as well as offensive, defensive, and special teams units. Video evaluations hold players and coaches accountable.

Team Evaluation

Evaluating a team can be a little more complex than evaluating individual players. Individual relationships and evaluations are important, but team performance is the number one priority.

Some coaches are guilty of judging team performance and success by simply looking at the scoreboard after the game. Remember, winning and losing do not define you or your team—performance does. An accurate team evaluation should involve the following components:

- Did your team play with great effort? If your team didn't play hard, they probably did not play very well.

- What kind of talent did your opponent have? Did you play against a superior, talented team or an average team?

- Did your team execute offense, defense, and special teams at a high level with few mental mistakes? Mental mistakes are a sign of poor performance.

Never be satisfied with mediocrity. If you are, you will always be mediocre. Never allow victories to make you believe that you played your best. If you do, you may go through many games without improving as a team because you believe victory is a sign of quality. Don't wait until you get beat to evaluate your team carefully and make improvements.

I strongly suggest grading every player's performance on every play of the game. Compile an offensive, defensive, and special teams performance index and monitor it weekly (figure 16.1). Are players improving in required areas, or are they staying the same? Grading players and units allows you to track progress and make the adjustments necessary to continue to grow as a team.

Some coaches are big stats guys—hold the opponent to less than 100 yards rushing, score 35 points a game, and other things like that. However, focusing on stats may take a coach away from the truly important perspective of team performance. Some opponents will be great running teams; holding them to less than 100 yards would be virtually impossible. I suggest focusing on the two main indicators of team performance: team execution and effort.

Off-Season Evaluation

After the football season ends, we organize off-season workouts and complete our inventory. This is a great time to sit down with each player to discuss the past season and lay the groundwork for off-season goals in the weight room and in the player's priorities of faith, family, academics, and football. The ability to align and maintain your priorities makes the game of football a lot easier. The off-season is a great time to build relationships with players and assist them with their personal life at home and in the classroom. Letting players know how much you care about them as people leads to enhanced trust and loyalty on the playing field.

The off-season is also a great time to move players to different positions to fill vacancies left by graduating players or to take advantage of a player's new-found potential. We let players know exactly what we are thinking and why we are making the change, keeping the best interest of the team in mind. If the player flinches, we let him know that we believe the position move will help the team and allow the player to get on the field sooner. This approach usually comforts and excites the player heading into off-season.

We remind our kids that we will play the players who earn their playing status through hard work and dedication in the off-season. Seniors know that they have their positions until someone takes them, which makes for a very competitive off-season in the weight room and in training sessions. Normally, we don't establish depth charts in the off-season unless it involves a returning starter. We like to leave the door open to everyone. We establish the depth chart early in the season after a few practices. This method keeps more kids interested and striving to get on the field during the off-season.

Figure 16.1   Trojan Defense Grade Sheet

Game _____ Date _____

	Player				
Tackle +3					
Assist +1					
Big play +3					
Caused fumble +9					
Oskie +9					
Broke up pass +2					
Forced pass +2					
Blocked kick (team) +6					
Touchdown (team) +6					
Sack +4					
Caused oskie +8					
Tackle for loss +3					
QB hit +3					
Extra effort +2					
Total positive points					

	Player			
Mental error –5				
Missed tackle –5				
Caught loafing –5				
Missed oskie –5				
Missed fumble recovery –3				
Foolish penalty –6				
Total negative points				

	Player			
Total positive points				
Total zeros (no points)				
Total negative points				
Number of positive plays				
Total number of plays				
Percentage				

Practice Evaluation

Practice is the lifeline of team performance. A team will play exactly like it practices. For this reason, we film every practice session and evaluate it daily with players and coaches. I never want to wait until after the game to know whether we had prepared well enough or not.

Evaluating practice allows almost instant adjustments and improvement for a squad.

You should see a progression of improvement as the week of planning and preparation transpires. Is your team making the adjustments fluidly, or are they confused? Is your offensive line picking up blitzes on Wednesday that they missed on Tuesday? If you don't see day-to-day improvement, you probably are not planning and organizing practice sessions effectively. By evaluating practice sessions, players and coaches understand that they are accountable for their performance and will strive to improve daily.

Game Evaluation

Having been a head coach for quite a while, I can normally get a sense of how the team will perform by watching them during pregame warm-ups. Are they focused and excited, or are they flat and tight? Are warm-up drills and sessions crisp and up-tempo, or are they sluggish? You can feel the intensity from the sideline when your team is playing with great effort and enthusiasm. You can see the special teams busting their tails down the field and making gang tackles and the defense making plays, but you can't view every player until the postgame film session.

Game evaluation is critical when making adjustments on the sideline and at halftime. The ability to gather and translate information during a game and communicate the information to players can make the difference in the outcome of the game. With a great communication system, each coach knows the offense, defense, or special teams play that is called. Watching individual players at the point of attack is also a big help in evaluating performance and making adjustments on the run during the game. NFL coaches use still photography to help them learn about the alignments and position of their opponents, but until you can actually sit down and watch the game video you really don't get the full perspective of the team's performance.

Postgame Evaluation

Usually, emotions are still at a fevered pitch immediately after a game. I try to make general comments about team performance. Until I can study the video, I can't get too specific about team performance. I am usually aware of the type of effort the squad gave and whether we executed well or not, but I am cautiously optimistic after the game until I have all the facts from the videotapes. Players usually know if they played a good game and gave great effort, so I keep postgame comments general.

We videotape every game from three angles to ensure accurate evaluation of each player and position. The wide angle encompasses wide receivers and defensive backs as well as special teams. The tight angle works well for interior linemen and all the players in the box. The end-zone angle is a great teaching tool for both offense and defense because they can see their actual alignments and approach angles and correct them. Video is a tremendous game evaluation tool because you can grade each player and correct his mistakes, and you can grade offensive, defensive, and special teams units as well. Just because a defensive tackle gets a tackle for loss doesn't mean the defensive squad played the play correctly. Make sure to grade the whole squad's responsibility and effort as well as each player's responsibility and effort. Keep in mind that the opponent is studying the same video. Understanding your squad's strengths and weaknesses will make you a better ball team.

Generally speaking, we evaluate players on alignment, assignment, effort, and execution. Did they line up correctly? Did they do the right thing? Did they play hard and get the job done? They are simple questions, but the answers help to paint the whole picture of football evaluation.

PROGRAM EVALUATION

The more accurate information you have about your football program, the better the evaluation you can make. I use different methods to gather information from assistant coaches, school administrators, support staff, and players. As the head coach, you need to be fully aware of the program's current condition and the direction the program is heading. Gathering honest and accurate data is vital for making decisions and adjustments that will improve the program and for developing a mental picture of where your program is and which direction you need to go.

Coach's Keys: Program Evaluation

1. Research the structure of the dynasty programs and use the information that will help you build your program.

2. Gather precise, honest information from fellow coaches, administrators, and players and study it thoroughly. Accurate data is vital for making an appropriate evaluation.

3. Be honest and open minded when evaluating your program. Don't make excuses and don't be negative. Work hard each day to find solutions and improvements for your program.

4. Begin with the end in mind. Make your decisions and adjustments with the future of your program in mind. Be proud of your program's accomplishments, but never be satisfied. Remember your purpose—the constant pursuit of excellence in the sport of football.

5. Remember all the good things your program accomplishes. Constantly focusing on the problems can be overwhelming and get you down. Focus on the positive.

Evaluating Championship Programs

I am a huge John Wooden fan. I have read many of his books about leadership and team building. For UCLA to have won so many championships at the highest collegiate level is not just amazing, it's also a sign that Coach Wooden and his basketball program were doing a lot of things right. Great coaches are creative, but they are also smart enough to learn and borrow from others in their profession who are successful.

I encourage everyone to take a look at the great athletic dynasties and learn something from each of them. The Green Bay Packers under Vince Lombardi; the Oklahoma Sooners under Bud Wilkinson, Barry Switzer, and Bob Stoops; the UCLA basketball program under

John Wooden; and the New York Yankees all won consistently over an extended period during their championship runs. Each of these programs and others I have not listed can be helpful in building your football program if you are willing to study and learn the methods that have proven successful.

One thing all the great dynasties have in common is great leadership. All the men were different and led in their own way, but there is no doubt about who was in charge of their respective programs. All made program-based decisions. They always did what was best for the team, even if it meant letting go very talented players who were not interested in team success before their own. Their ability to make team-oriented decisions brought their programs to great levels because of the trust and belief in each member of the program.

Programs that maintain a high level of excellence and consistency play by the rules and emphasize ethical and moral conduct at all times. There are few shortcuts to success. Teams that try to take shortcuts may realize success at times but normally will not maintain it. Discipline in all phases of life is essential for consistency.

Teamwork forms the cogs on the wheel of all the successful programs. The ability for players to work and play well together is the key to consistent program development. Often the most talented team does not win against a team whose members play with and believe in each other. Team members that execute together and believe in each other will usually triumph. Dynasty programs develop unity and teamwork through sound methods and understand how vital camaraderie is to their success.

Evaluating Your Football Program

The head coach must take a long, honest look at his overall football program and understand the strengths and weaknesses within his system. Being fully aware of the areas of greatness and the areas that need improvement is invaluable to the leader of the football program. Honesty is the key.

Don't hide flaws; bring them out and work on them or fix them. Emphasize what your program does well and strive to improve those areas as well. Lay all your cards on the table and take a long, honest look at your program to ensure that your program's journey is a successful one.

I'll be the first to tell you that my assistant coaches are the foundation of our football program. For the most part, I have hand picked them from hundreds of men who would like to be a part of our program at Jenks. They are the ones I trust with everything. I want every member of my staff to take ownership in the program and make decisions as if they were the head coach. Their honesty in discussing problems and solutions is crucial for evaluating the program. I surround myself with wise counsel and get as much feedback as possible. Everyone's ideas and concerns can lead to program improvement. That's what building a football program is all about.

At the end of each season, I have a meeting with each assistant to gather information in several areas. I ask for the assistant coach's assessment of the season in general—what he did well and what he can improve on. We discuss his personal goals as an assistant as well as his responsibilities and whether he wants more or less responsibility.

We also discuss staff unity. It is important to get each staff member's feedback and perspective in this area to ensure growth and unity within the staff. It is important to sort through personal issues and selfish ideas when discussing staff unity. Be prepared to deal with each assistant's ideas and perspectives. Each will be unique, which requires you to think about what is best for the team and what is best for individual coaches. Base your decisions on what is best for the program and make the adjustments that you feel are necessary to continue the positive journey of your program, even if it means dismissing a coach or removing and adjusting his responsibilities.

The players in a program are the best way to evaluate whether or not you are coaching and developing in a positive way. If there are problems anywhere—coaching staff, player–coach relations, leadership, or any of a variety of issues—players will be the first to know and the first to respond. It's up to you, as the coach, to get them to respond in the right direction.

Communicate with players when making course adjustments to keep your program moving in the right direction. During the season we elect a council of players to keep the lines of communication open so that I can make adjustments if needed. This also reminds players that we are all in the same boat and their ideas are respected. At the end of the season I schedule interviews with each player to get his honest ideas and opinions about how the team performed and how the coaches performed and get his ideas for improving the team. I encourage all my coaches to watch and listen not only to the player's words but also his actions. These indicators are probably the most important feedback you can get as a head coach. It's our responsibility to act on them and put the players in the best possible position to succeed.

Understanding your program's weaknesses doesn't give you the right to make excuses for not succeeding. When evaluating your program, if you determine that the weight room is too small, the overall team speed is average, the lineman are a little light in the pants, or the administration is not supportive enough, these are reasons to be concerned, but they cannot be used as excuses for lack of program success. Work hard to find solutions. Surround yourself with people who can make a difference and who care enough about the program to invest their time and money to make it better. If we have a picture of the program and have done the proper research, we are fully aware of our program's strengths and weaknesses. It's our job as coaches to find ways to overcome adversity. Take the cards you are dealt and play them in the most skillful and advantageous way you can. If you have areas of concern in your program, find creative ways to overcome them. Use the improvements as a positive message to everyone involved.

Focus on the positive. I have many faults, and one of them is being critical of myself

Championship football teams display more than just trophies. They exemplify leadership, excellence, and teamwork.

and the program to the extent of sometimes forgetting to look at the positive things the football program has accomplished. I place high expectations on myself and everyone involved in the program, and at times I forget that we are doing a lot of things well. Take your own strengths and your program's strengths and build on them. Highlight them for all to see. Growth and success breed more growth and success, especially when it comes to building a program for the future. Veteran players have a sense of pride in being a part of the success, and younger players feel a responsibility to not only maintain the level of excellence but also to take it to the next level. Search for the good in what you do. It's a great building block for a program.

Be open minded in your perspective. In the eyes of the media, the public, and sometimes the school administration, wins and losses are the only evaluation. They seldom consider important factors about a program and simply look to see if the team won or lost last week. Keep in mind the talent of your squad, the talent of your opponents, and the league you play in. Some of the best coaching jobs ever done were on teams that didn't win championships or didn't even win their divisions. Evaluate your program with an open mind. Remember that your program is either getting better or getting worse; there is no middle ground.

Keeping Accurate Data

I am not big into stats. I'm big into execution and playing well. Still, keeping accurate stats from season to season is a big help when evaluating program improvement. I had my assistant coaches assess each of our seven championship seasons and compare their information to the stats during the season we didn't win the championship. We learned some staggering facts. In each of the championship seasons, the team met or exceeded all of the offensive and defensive goals we established at the beginning of the year. We used this information to develop a standard of excellence to compare each season to (figure 16.2). We also learned that our championship teams achieved a minimum of plus 11 in turnover margin. The season we didn't win the championship, the team reached only plus 2. Statistics and records are valuable tools when used properly in the evaluation process. Do a great job compiling and recording team statistics.

Another important area in which to keep accurate records is injuries to athletes. Many injuries are purely accidental. No matter how much planning and hard work you put into the season, nothing you can do will prevent these injuries. One year we had a rash of hip-flexor strains, some severe enough that athletes missed practices and games. We did the research and found that our off-season training regimen had included an imbalance between hip and quad exercises and hamstring exercises. Players had developed their quad and hip-flexor strength faster than they had developed their hamstring strength. This imbalance led to the nagging and sometimes severe hip-flexor problems. The problem was easily corrected with subtle changes in in-season and off-season lifting schedules. Make sure your training staff monitors and records all injuries and treatments so that you and your staff can conduct research and make adjustments as necessary.

Building for the Future

Keep in mind that building a football program is a journey, and the path and terrain are constantly changing. A football program constantly evolves through the players and the plays they run. Gather meaningful information from postseason evaluations and apply what you learn to develop a plan of action for the next season using the information you have about the upcoming year. No one cares what your program did last season. Fans have very

---

Trojan Football Landmarks for Success

Offense

1. Rush for 200 yards per game.
2. Rush the ball at least 60 percent of the time.
3. Average 36 points per game.
4. Average at least 65 plays per game.
5. Complete at least 55 percent of passes.
6. I-back averages at least 6.8 yards per carry.
7. Average fewer than 1 turnover per game.

Defense

1. Allow opponent fewer than 2.4 yards per rush.
2. Create three turnovers per ball game.
3. Allow no touchdowns after a sudden change.
4. Allow no bombs for touchdowns (35 yards).
5. Force five three-and-out series per ball game.
6. Have no foolish penalties called on defense due to lack of discipline or effort.

Special Teams

1. Hold opponents to fewer than 20 yards per kickoff return.
2. Hold opponents to fewer than 10 yards per punt return.
3. Average at least 35 yards per kickoff return.
4. Average at least 15 yards per punt return.
5. Allow no blocked kicks or punts.
6. Block at least three punts or kicks.
7. Have no foolish penalties called due to lack of discipline or effort.

Figure 16.2 Standards of excellence.

short memories. Develop an action plan with accurate data. Make program-improving decisions while there is enough time to adjust and improve.

Be where you are. Many coaches are so busy looking for the perfect coaching job that they forget to put their best effort into the job they have. I remind my young aspiring coaches to be where they are. In other words, do your very best work at your current job and great opportunities will come. Encourage coaches to seek extra responsibilities and broaden their coaching knowledge by coaching different positions and accepting different staff duties. The more areas they become familiar with, the more career doors they open. Our program has developed several young coaches into outstanding head coaches because these assistants worked diligently to excel at the jobs they had.

Coaching football is coaching football at any level. The ability to develop and lead young men for a common cause is the same at any level. I have always been interested in coaching at the Division I level for many reasons, but the opportunity has yet to arrive. I strive each day to work as hard as I can to improve as a person and as a coach in order to place myself in position to take advantage of college coaching opportunities when they come.

No matter what your career objectives may be, focus on your priorities and strive daily to keep them in the correct order. Coach from the heart and give it all you've got, and great things will come. It's better to shoot for the moon and miss than to shoot for crap and hit. If your career goal is to coach in the NFL or at a top-10 college program, go for it with all your might; run your race to win, no matter what arena you are competing in. Winning and losing don't define you as a person— your character, attitude, and effort do. We are in the greatest profession in the world no matter what level we coach at. Never take it for granted and make sure that you are a positive influence on your players, coaches, and profession.

INDEX

Note: Information contained in tables or figures are indicated by an italicized *t* or *f.*

ABOUT THE AUTHOR

© Ervin's Photography

Allan Trimble has been the head coach of the Jenks High School football team in Oklahoma since 1996, boasting a 111-9 record and six consecutive Class 6A state championship titles, which is a class record. Over the course of nine seasons, his teams have amassed a total of seven state championships with a 32-2 career playoff record. Trimble's teams have also set records for overall winning streaks (38) and consecutive playoff victories (25).

Throughout his 15-year coaching career, Trimble has produced more than 25 Division I football players and has been recognized with Coach of the Year honors from *Sporting News* and *American Football Monthly* as well as *USA Today's* Most Caring Coach award. In 2001 he was named Russell Athletic National Coach of the Year. Trimble is a member of the American Football Coaches Association, Oklahoma Coaches Association, and Oklahoma Football Coaches Association.

In his spare time, Trimble enjoys fishing and spending time with his daughters and wife, Courtney. The Trimbles reside in Jenks, Oklahoma.

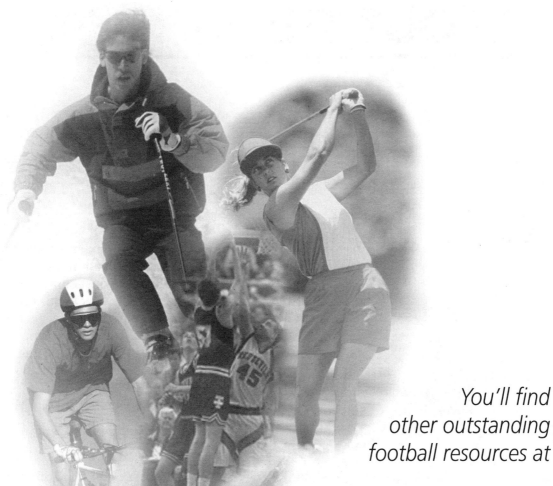